More Than Things

More Than Things

Margaret Randall

University of Nebraska Press
Lincoln and London

Library of Congress Cataloging-in-Publication Data
Randall, Margaret, 1936–
[Essays. Selections]
More than things / Margaret Randall.
pages cm
ISBN 978-0-8032-4590-7 (pbk.: alk. paper)—ISBN 978-0-8032-4697-3 (pdf)—
ISBN 978-0-8032-4933-2 (epub)—ISBN 978-0-8032-4934-9 (mobi)
I. Title.
PS3535.A56277M67 2013
814'.54—dc23
2013008683

Set in Adobe Garamond Pro by Laura Wellington.
Designed by Jesse Vadnais.

This book is for Robert Schweitzer, wise friend

Contents

Illustrations

Acknowledgments

"Cuban Postcards" first appeared in a slightly different form in the online publication *Doony's Café*. "Coyote Grin" first appeared in the online publication *The Persimmon Tree*. "Roque Dalton: Myth, Man, Martyr, and Poet Who Defined an Era" first appeared in *The Malpais Review* 2, no. 2 (Autumn 2011): 78–106. "Closing the Gap" was published in *Sin Fronteras / Writers Without Borders* 16 (2012): 54–59.

Introduction

The Magical Seam

Just about anything gets me started: thinking back over a lifetime of politics, writing, or even sex; connection with a child or grandchild; my great good fortune in having found the perfect life companion; a conversation with a friend; a myth or fairy tale; a journey to some part of the world I had no idea exists in the particular sociocultural configuration I find when I get there; an ancient ruin; one of the many criminal acts—large and small—that our government and corporations try to pass off as necessary to our national security and the well-being of our communities; or the magical seam where water and rock come together on the Colorado River.

These pieces range from personal narratives to more traditional essays, passing through a few dreamlike prosodies. They move from mentors and a contemplation of the issue of suicide, through social mores and governmental criminality, to travel and my writing life. Meridel LeSueur's last poem is like a gift from the beyond, and I riffed on it with immense gratitude. All these texts were written over a three-year period between 2009 and 2012. They are not presented in the order in which they were written but rather arranged so that a concern in one is sometimes continued in the next.

I think of these pieces as my end of an ongoing conversation. I hope they will spark response.

More Than Things

Shaping My Words

for Silvia Gil

One balmy Havana night, toward the end of 1980, the man with whom I was apprenticing as a novice photographer, a couple of others who shared my make-shift darkroom, and I were spreading an evening's worth of prints across our large dining room table to dry. I was looking critically at my images when the phone rang. I no longer remember who called, but the expression on the face of my friend who answered remains with me after all these years: profound sorrow tinged with horror and the hesitant shadow of some other emotion that seemed caught midair between nervous apprehension and an understanding that defied immediate release.

Haydée Santamaría—revolutionary heroine, member of the Cuban Communist Party's Central Committee, visionary president of the country's important cultural institution Casa de las Américas, and beloved friend to all creative artists who had ever met or found themselves in her presence—was dead. Dead. It took a few moments of stunned silence for the reality to sink in.

The caller said Haydée's body was lying in state at a nearby funeral parlor. There was no question we would walk the few blocks and join what we knew would be an enormous crowd of grievers. No reach of imagination could predict how large or how intense. As I mechanically positioned the last of my prints on the table and hurriedly dried my hands, I looked to my friend who had answered the phone. I wanted to know what he hadn't been able to bring himself to say in that first shocking outburst. Macías couldn't meet my eyes as he responded to my silent question: "She shot herself."

Suicide is always problematic for those left behind, who cannot approach the emotional state of the person ending her or his life. *Radio bembá*, or gossip, travels hurricane fast throughout Cuba's popular culture. Before daybreak, this sort of news would invade every home on the island. It was an event that would elicit a far deeper response than some unexpected change to our food ration book, an attack from the ever-aggressive enemy to the north, or the loss of almost any other beloved public figure—with the exception of Fidel. As far as any of us knew, Haydée was in good health and vibrant with ongoing projects. Her decision to end her life shook us profoundly. It felt personal, and also deeply troubling in a larger, more overarching sense.

This was a woman who embodied all that was promising about the revolution: its uniquely Cuban roots and risk, its brilliance, creativity, and passion, a genuine appreciation of difference, and the authority to journey where others didn't know enough or didn't have the courage to go. One of only two women among 135 combatants who participated in the 1953 attack on Moncada Barracks, she had been imprisoned following that failed attempt. Most of her comrades died in the brief battle or were tortured to death in its aftermath. She lost her brother and her lover, along with dozens of close friends. Her narrative of the debacle, *Haydée habla del Moncada*, is one of the Cuban Revolution's most moving and iconic texts.[1]

Many of the surviving Moncada veterans died during subsequent decades; fewer and fewer remained. But each year, as July 26 approached, those few would dutifully make the rounds of schools, workplaces, and military units, telling their collective story, trying to keep the history alive, and providing some continuity for younger generations engaged in a stage of social change that was less dramatic but much more difficult to achieve. It was Che who said winning the war was the easy part. Only a few weeks before her death, Haydée had spoken at the office where one of my friends worked. Later, in the restroom, that friend overheard her murmuring: "I just can't do this again . . . I can't."

Over the ensuing weeks and months, two popular explanations for Haydée's decision became common currency on the streets of Havana. The first was the emotional strain of having lived through so many years of terror and loss, what today we call posttraumatic stress disorder (PTSD). Maybe she had finally reached her limit. It was also rumored that her recent marital separation and the fact that her husband had remarried a younger woman were to blame. People wondered and came up with these and other possible reasons to try to satisfy their need for answers.

I bought none of them.

I knew Haydée only slightly, although I loved and admired her beyond our casual friendship. We had met on my very first visit to Cuba in 1967, and from that moment on she personified to me not what the Cuban Revolution was but what it could be—free of competing power struggles, inevitable errors, occasional repressive periods, greed, and pockets of corruption. On Haydée's lips revolution seemed simple and exuberantly creative. It meant justice and a better life for every person. Her goodness and imagination refused to recognize the limits imposed by underdevelopment, a corrosively tropical climate, small minds, petty jealousies, or even the U.S. blockade.

We exchanged letters, and I sent her snapshots of my children. After I moved to Cuba in 1969, she once impulsively took me to see those pictures tacked up inside her bedroom closet door. I interviewed her at length for my first book about Cuban women.[2] That interview is as cutting-edge in 2011 as it was in 1970. She coerced me into being a judge for the country's biggest beauty contest, and when I complained that she had forced me into something she must have known I detested, she smiled and admitted she'd done it because she knew I would use the occasion to find a way to help bring such contests to an end. We both suffered sudden and devastating asthma attacks, which she patiently taught me to manage so they would rob me of as little daily energy as possible.

At her wake, among hundreds of other mourners pressed together in the heat of that keening Havana night, someone asked if I would like to stand guard at the head of her open coffin. Family, public figures, and friends were taking two-minute shifts. At a certain point, I lowered my eyes to Haydée's reconstructed face. It may have been at that moment that the seed of this essay was born. Since then I have known other suicides, of course—some slow, some fast, some of very close friends—but something about Haydée's choice and what I believe may have been behind it has stayed with me to this day.

As the funeral parlor filled and crowds overflowed into the street, an unsettled sentiment surfaced in many conversations. Why was this wake being held at a commercial establishment rather than where other heroes and heroines were mourned in Revolution Square? It was a rhetorical question. We knew the answer: the Communist Party, like the Catholic Church, disapproved of suicide; in the former, one's life belonged to the people—in the latter, to God.

Haydée was being punished for her act. But popular disagreement with the decision became more and more evident. By morning, in an obvious gesture of atonement, she was carried with full honors to the section of Colón Cemetery designated for the nation's beloved sons and daughters.

It's not that I want to dwell on suicide. I don't feel that it solves any but the most personal of dilemmas. It is an individual choice though, and one I respect even as it often makes me rage and weep.

What I want to write about today is this time in which we find ourselves: a time of such perverted values, sanctioned violence, greed, and corruption perpetrated by governments, armies, corporations, and individuals—a social distortion so powerful it seems it cannot be stopped. It is a time that has certainly made me contemplate the possibility of leaving and enabled me to understand why some make that choice.

I confess there are moments when I am glad my generous and justice-loving father didn't live to witness this world he would have found so hard to accept, and times as well when I myself can imagine the peace of oblivion.

Then I think of my grandchildren.

We have reached a moment in human evolution that foretells an uncertain future at best, and a future that in palpable ways is already here. It is a future that shows its voracious fangs and seems to mock our attempts to pursue a course that favors a culture of life over one of death.

When it comes to climate change, those in power have all but brought our earth to a point of no return. When it comes to war, there are always new ones to wage, and old ones we must continue fighting because our country's skewed sense of patriotism goes where reason no longer resides. When it comes to economic survival, everyone but the rich and entitled are expendable. Workers are replaced by machines or by their counterparts in other countries who will labor for less and in worse conditions. Then they are simply downsized en masse because, well, the country is suffering an "economic downturn" (read: recession, depression, what you will). It can't be helped. Despite periodic exposés, I know those responsible will never be held accountable.

When it comes to shelter, the United States is showing the world how corporate interests get away with luring people into buying houses they cannot afford and then punishing them with eviction when they are unable to pay their mortgages. When it comes to health and public education and caring for the elderly, there's no money for any of that, because we're spending it all on war. And so it goes, in a disintegrating and out-of-control downward spiral.

What can we do to break the cycle? Where can we sink our teeth into viable forms of resistance?

Many in the United States believe that in our democratic system we can vote our way out of the morass and that our democracy should be eagerly embraced by peoples everywhere. But to even get on a ballot in our country today one must first be able to raise billions of campaign dollars and then feel comfortable telling obscene lies about others and making promises impossible to keep. Political interests are such that it is irrelevant to ask if politicians are breaking promises because they are forced to or out of unadulterated deceit.

I am almost seventy-seven and have only once had the opportunity to vote for, rather than against, a presidential candidate. My exercise of suffrage started with a 1960 vote against Nixon. I am ashamed to say I thought it would be different with Obama; for a very short time, it felt good to have finally voted for a candidate about whom I could get excited.

Al Qaeda chalked up a victory on September 11, 2001, far beyond taking the lives of three thousand men and women and devastating treasure in its three coordinated attacks. The element of surprise caught the United States off guard, and there are arguments that claim there was no way we could have avoided that aspect of the tragedy.

The other part—ongoing, ruthless, and threatening to destroy everything our nation is supposed to stand for—we brought and bring on ourselves. I am talking about the Bush administration's refusal to look at why a crazed fundamentalist faction of Islam would attack us as it did and that administration's preemptive declaration of war against a country that had nothing to do with the assault. I am talking about a government's rash decision to limit personal freedoms. And I am talking about Obama's continuation of his predecessor's racist and national security-centered policies, which only deepen the divide between "them" and "us."[3]

You may be wondering why I begin with a suicide and then offer my hopeless reading of what I perceive as power politics gone mad.

My question is, what can we do? Realistically, what can those of us in the United States who despise U.S. exceptionalism, war, and the arrogance of nation building do to end our military's presence in Iraq, Afghanistan, Pakistan, Libya, and so many other places where lack of trustworthy news keeps a naïve public unaware of our belligerent involvement?

What can we do to save Medicare, Medicaid, education, arts, and other social services already compromised and pitifully meager when compared with those provided as rights in most of the industrially advanced countries? What can we do to preserve what's left of our public education system and work toward universal health care? What can we do to keep gains such as freedom of dissent and women's reproductive rights—won through such intense and costly struggles—when they are being eroded each day by legions of Bible-thumping, Tea Partying crazies? What can we do so our nation may truly become a place where all its citizens—of all races, genders, and ideas—can feel at home?

I link suicide and our government's grotesquely lopsided value system and set of priorities because, for as long as I can remember, this is the first time I feel a sense of utter defeat about the future. Is "checking out" a real alternative, be it quite literally as Haydée did or figuratively by ceasing to struggle for a better world and simply contenting oneself with "getting by"?

On the thirtieth anniversary of Daniel Ellsberg's release of the Pentagon Papers, I was struck by his public reference to the fact that every one of the crimes committed against him by Richard Nixon, crimes that cost Nixon the presidency, are legal today. The Patriot Act has legitimized those crimes and given tacit permission to the justifications behind them, once anathema to American ideals. When this sort of criminality is permitted, indeed encouraged and applauded, where does that leave those of us who have struggled all our lives for justice, peace, and tolerance? Where does it leave our world?

It may leave some of us heading for the exit.

Without claiming any sort of inside track, my poet's intuition has always told me that Haydée Santamaría chose death rather than continuing to live in a society she may, even then, have understood was not living up to the ideals for which her brother and lover gave their lives. PTSD may have played a role. Perhaps her husband's abandonment did as well. But exceptional people are privy to huge hope and generally give up only under exceptional conditions. The PTSD Haydée had lived with for more than twenty years doesn't seem to me to have constituted an exceptional condition; midlife divorce, even less.

No, I believe something weightier and more terrifying than those issues—either or both of which may well have helped tip the balance—pushed Haydée to make her fatal decision. We will never know. Certainly I will never know. I am not aware if she left a note; and if she did, even radio bembá could not have made it public.

By virtue of her history, Haydée belonged to the revolution's inner circle. She knew all the dirty secrets. By virtue of her gender, and perhaps also her visionary quirkiness, she probably had little real power. Did she feel helpless and alone? When I think of the situation facing us today—the many small and larger obstacles to choosing life over death—Haydée invariably comes to mind. Even taking into account the important differences, I wonder if Cuba back then may have seemed to her like the United States seems to me today: quite simply a disappointment overwhelming enough to cause despair.

Contrary to what you may be thinking, I am not saying that suicide is the answer to profound and reasonable discouragement. I believe in an individual's right to end his or her life, whatever the reason; but I do not confuse that right with a solution to our sociopolitical problems. What I am asking is, what do we do, what can we do, when faced with such weighty evidence that those who would destroy life as we know it are winning on every side?

What we face feels enormous and can seem insurmountable to some. Distraught as I may feel, however, I keep one last card close to my breast. It's not suicide. Neither is it the card that can win the game, but it is one that keeps me playing another hand.

That card is my unique, very loud, and irreplaceable voice.

There is one thing such a voracious enemy cannot take from us, and that is our knowledge of where we come from, our attention to the multiple struggles and what they have cost, and our voices, which, together, weave the image of the harmonious future we may not live to experience. In a scenario such as the one we face, these voices—our voices—become precious beyond description. I remain convinced their combined energy makes a difference.

Lines scrawled on the walls of a Turkish prison. Diaries smuggled out of the Warsaw ghetto or a Nazi concentration camp. A song written in Chile's National Stadium, in the horrific days following that country's 1973 coup. Poems and protest songs from Vietnam, Nicaragua, Guatemala. A Native American drum circle, beating the rhythm of hearts that refuse to give up. Spirituals sung by slaves dreaming of freedom. Stories from our own civil rights and women's movements. The child who speaks out against her abuser. The soldier who turns his back on war. Words whispered from mouth to ear, through our long human history of atrocity and resistance.

I am a poet, so when I say voice, I mean that quite literally. But I do not believe poets, or even artists working in other mediums, are the only ones capable of giving voice to a culture of hope and possibility. Scientists who search honestly for answers to the questions that concern us contribute to such a culture. Teachers who help their students discover how to think, health professionals devoted to curing the ill and accompanying the dying, cleaning personnel who take pride in their work, and that rare public servant more interested in improving the sustainability of life than in his own narrow status—all these and many others sing in the chorus that still, just possibly, may be able to drown out the death dirge that deafens us today.

When I am tired beyond my ability to protest the lies we are told and the lies we absorb, I do not think of ending my life—to become one less among those who fight the good fight or at least try to preserve the memory of so many good fights, intimate as well as public. I think of how I may whisper or shout, shaping my words into ever-new configurations of a dignity that documents and empowers.

Things

No ideas but in things
—William Carlos Williams

The Wooden Apple

If I cup my palm around this wooden apple, my flesh knows a heft just a bit too light, a texture not moist or juicy enough. Not the life of living fruit but the history of art, of making things. Who recognized the raw possibility, held the chunk of local pine, whittled the navel of its stem, the indentation of seeds, and marks along the edges of the cut?

Imagined teeth bit desire along those edges, going all the way back to the Garden. One side is sliced and faintly browned, the absence of skin welcoming the tarnish of air. The outer, rounded side is stained deep red and shows small blemishes, the fate of all picked fruit.

I can still feel Elaine de Kooning's exuberant fingers placing this object in my hand and my own fingers curving around it, how it felt that day more than half a century ago. "Isn't it perfect" was never a question but recognition of another woman's skill, the Appalachian artist from whom she'd purchased an entire bowl: orange, lemon, banana, plum. The watermelon was a wedge of course, all the better to display its range of color, succulence of pulp and seed.

"Pick one," Elaine urged. I followed the pull of instinct, straight to the apple.

I knew there was something special about that sculptured fruit, and something special in my friend's generosity. Each its own voice.

A working artist was telling a young woman still trying to find her space and rhythm that she too could choose a life of creativity. It would be easier and harder than I knew. The wooden apple quickly took up residence everywhere I lived. It would stay with me through rejections, early publications, and the eventual discovery of my own voice, along my long journey into art.

Last night I dreamed of Cape Cod houses standing proud on broken granite cliffs, wooden shingles against a battering wind. Second-floor windowpanes set in small frames gleamed flushed blue and pale green, like those contact lenses fabricated to change the color of a person's eyes. Elaine looks at me from wherever it is she now wields a paintbrush. She laughs.

Each time I hold this apple, I am holding artistic flight dismissed as craft— what that has meant and means everywhere, for women in particular. *Anonymous Was a Woman* is still a bitter truth. Women's diaries and recipes versus men's philosophical treatises. Personal versus public; the body versus a world stage; tireless implication that what she does is lesser—what he does, always more.

When I hold the wooden apple, I am holding Elaine's encouragement of my own life in art, my memory of her in me. I am holding a tangible object that speaks to me of creativity.

The air I breathe. A need that grows on the inside of my skin.

The Tool

It is a dark stone, heavy for its size, a slightly flattened inch–by–half-inch round mass whose weight suggests a piece of meteor from outer space rather than material shaped from rock here on earth. Only because I saw it first sitting among hundreds of others, all similar in size and shape, did I know it was a tool. At that moment, eons of human progression filled me: the grip of an opposable thumb, the angle of an elbow.

I was visiting family at their cottage in the small Uruguayan community of Kiyú, a strip of humble summer dwellings on a cliff above the broad Río de la Plata. Just at this spot, seasons of weather have worn the riverbank away; and from time to time, deposits of glyptodont bones are found in the exposed mud. In recent decades, interest in the zone has moved beyond the locals, many of whom keep skeletal treasure troves in closets or as conversation pieces.

Someone mentioned a couple across the street. They had retrieved hundreds of pieces from a single dig. Not prehistoric bones but human-made objects of everyday use: hammerheads, grinding stones, sharp points for hunting, and edges that may have scraped animal skins. Among them were many of these slightly flattened balls, probably used for pounding or otherwise shaping softer stone.

A powerful pull told me I must see for myself. My son said, "Let's go," and we ambled across the way: casual beginning to a journey so far into the past. The couple was gracious, invited us to sit awhile. They talked about their discovery and their difficulty trying to interest academic specialists in the find. As I exclaimed over one piece or another, they were encouraged to bring out more, unwrapping and revealing objects ever more interesting and evocative than those I had seen so far.

I held a heavy round in one hand, closed protective fingers about it. I sat there asking questions and listening to answers. My lips moved, and I heard my voice as if from very far away. I was unwilling to return the stone to the table where it so recently sat among its companions. When it was time to go, the man of the house told me, "Keep it."

"Oh no . . . She couldn't!" said my son, uncharacteristically answering for me. I looked at him in astonishment and said nothing. It was clear to me and to our hosts that I could and would.

The stone had become mine.

Over the following days, I continued to hold that stone in my hand. It fit perfectly. I clutched it through family gatherings, shared meals, walks with grandchildren. I fingered it in the depth of a pocket. I even took it to bed at night. In the morning my fingers were still bent around a tool made by people perhaps a thousand years before my time, the energy of their daily comings and goings imprinted on my body.

Its weight speaks a language I have always known.

Small Clay Head

Broken off at the neck, this small clay head has been with me since the early 1960s. If its existence were to be represented by the twenty-four hours in a day, this half-century would be in the final minutes of its clock. There is so much we can only guess. Was this a figurine created for ritual or a child's toy? Was it serious or playful? Prototype or portrait?

I like to imagine a master potter scooping up the clay left over from making a cooking vessel or *tinaja* (a "jar" or "vase"), pausing for a moment before deciding how to use the dregs, then fashioning a small doll for a child playing at her feet. Perhaps the doll, in turn, inspired its owner to become one of a next generation of potters.

Laurette Séjourné emigrated from her native France with Victor Serge, her husband at the time. They came to Mexico to escape Stalin's murderous reach and the anti-Semitism that was exploding across Europe as World War II got underway. History is filled with peoples forced to flee home for elsewhere; migration continues to define our times, the repeated tragedy.

Laurette forged her migration into discovery. In her adopted country she found love and vocation. The love was Arnaldo Orfila, Argentine intellectual and activist who recognized and nurtured her genius. The vocation was archeology. But Laurette was never the archeologist who settled comfortably within Mexico's establishment. Her ideas were brilliant and radically her own. A woman whose opinions did not conform to those put forth by her colleagues. Despite her great dignity and eventual prestige, I can still remember the relegation and hurt she suffered almost daily.

Every Wednesday, I accompanied Laurette to her dig at Teotihuácan. She picked us up in her gray Peugeot. She would bring an old-fashioned, two-sided cane picnic basket filled with delicacies: fresh bread, pâté, magical vegetables like chayote and *flor de calabaza*, and exotic fruits. I would bring my young son, Gregory. As she drove and we talked, I gazed at her small gloved hands firmly planted on the steering wheel. Laurette's demeanor was always upright, almost stern, although it masked a deep sensibility, intense passion, and bottomless tenderness.

A group of workmen waited at our destination, quiet, ready for instructions from this woman who directed their careful labor. Their foreman had readied the objects unearthed the previous week, and Laurette would examine each, deciding which to take back with her to the city. It was on one of these trips that she placed the small clay head in my hands. She told me it was four thousand years old.

We never talked about the issue of such a relic's ownership. I knew Laurette considered what emerged from her Palace of the Butterflies to be a nation's patrimony; every important object was classified and eventually turned over to the proper authorities. I supposed in that context this little clay head was insignificant, just one of thousands the local children played with and made their own. To me its significance was immediate and remains: something I frequently look at and touch, tracing the power of human continuity.

The features of this face are both crude and spectacular. Crude because they are little more than rough clay pinched into eyes, eyebrows, a slightly more ornate though broken nose, and expressive mouth: lips pressed together in a gesture that haunts time. What might have been said or withheld? The back of the head is strangely flattened, and there is a suggestion of headdress or coil of hair spread outward like small wings above each temple. Spectacular because they stare back at me millennia beyond having been fashioned by hands whose intention I can only guess.

Teotihuácan, just outside Mexico City, is one of the country's principal tourist attractions. Its pyramids of sun and moon are known throughout the world. All who are able climb those two pyramids. More-inquisitive visitors may also walk among the ruins of Laurette's Palace of the Butterflies, although her name is mostly absent from all but the most specialized literature. Although she left a visionary interpretation that will surely be honored when the world catches up, it was too easy to discredit, as obsessed or mad, a foreign woman who challenged the official storyline. We have her detailed assessment, but she herself has been gone for many years.

The small clay head speaks to me of my friend and of the culture she so thoroughly understood. It also reminds me that even now, two decades past her death, women who think or disagree are considered dangerous.

Kahao Rongorongo

After spending time on Easter Island, Rapa Nui to the inhabitants of the ten-by-fifteen-mile speck of land in the middle of the central South Pacific, I needed an object. Something tangible I could hold in my hand and take with me when I left. Something solid. I had walked in awe among the giant stone *maoi*, fallen to earth or reerected as they once stood, in rows facing the sea. I had taken photographs, made notes for poems. And I had interacted with the people who populate the island today, those who live in the small village of Hanga Roa.

The village has the usual souvenir shops, with items made from what one would expect in a place surrounded by sea: shell jewelry, miniature moai, crudely carved wooden art, a few pamphlets and books. I was attracted to the *kohao rongorongo*, oblong wooden tablets covered with rows of mysterious characters, but lost interest in acquiring one when I saw that each had "Rapa Nui Souvenir" or something similarly disappointing on its reverse. I almost expected to read: "Made in Taiwan." The thing would be to seek a more authentic example, I thought, but how?

Exploring distant reaches of our world is important to me; as is coming to know the variety of peoples who weave its diverse histories. Particular objects keep these experiences close, feeding me with constant streams of memory. Obviously, I was in no position to covet an original kahao rongorongo; those few known to exist reside in museums, most of them far from the island itself. But perhaps there were copies less banal than these souvenirs. I asked an island authority who had become a friend. He said he would find one for me, and did.

My kohao rongorongo is about nine inches long and three wide, with rounded corners and a thickness of a couple of centimeters. I do not know the type of wood. Trees are extremely scarce on Rapa Nui, and people often use pieces of driftwood or other sea-worn materials that wash ashore. The board is inscribed on both sides, four lines to a side, with a repetition of symbols or signs. To my mind one of these tablets' great attractions is that its "writing" does not constitute a language in the conventional sense.

These are neither hieroglyphs nor letters nor words. Their lineal repetition removes them from the petroglyphic tradition. Rather, the incised symbols—many of them simulating plants or human or animal figures—are thought to spark the imagination of the "reader," nudge memory into story. Is that a joyous dancing woman? Are these arrows or fish spines? Research has shown that the lines start in the lower left-hand corner, snaking to the right and then back to the left in the line above. The four lines on my board zigzag or switchback this way, from lower to upper left.

When outsiders observed the tablets being "read" in rituals of one kind or another, the same story was never told twice. They considered this proof of deception. Natives contend the symbols remind them of what they must say, trigger their imaginations. Sadly, the last generation to have been able to read the kohao rongorongo is long gone. Some of the boards represent family genealogies.

And so my kohao rongorongo means nothing and everything. I raise it to my nostrils and smell the air of an island once covered with 200,000 palms that now has none. Resistance in the face of every obstacle. I run my fingers over the incised figures and remember a landscape, a culture, a people who sailed into the unknown to find a home and then carved immense statues, raised them from their quarries of origin, and moved them—no one is yet entirely sure how—to their sentinel spots along the coast.

Endurance enters my body to stay.

Replacement Metronome

My father's metronome could be heard ticking through his cello practice, the private lessons he gave after coming home from teaching music in the public schools, and his Friday night string quartets. Its regular pulse calmed me. I'm talking about the original-style, nineteenth-century mahogany box, not the electronic or software versions popular today. There's no app for what I remember. The soft sheen of beautifully polished wood beckoned to my fingers, much like the rosewood bowls of Dad's favorite pipes.

His metronome sat atop the baby grand in our living room, that moody presence that only saw use from the fingers of visitors. First, my father would place his sheet music on a foldout metal stand, opening it to a chosen page and smoothing the paper to insure it lay just so. Then he would turn toward the magic box. With his thick forefinger and thumb, he would slide the little metal weight up or down the inverted pendulum and free the end of the rod, which would then begin swinging back and forth, producing a clicking sound. Faster or slower, depending on the required tempo.

I was fascinated by the box and its pyramidal face. My childhood home, like many, broadcast one story line while juggling or running away from others. Mother yearned for more of everything: love, intellect, adventure. Dad did his best. Ours was a household where unfulfilled need and a seething underbelly of erratic emotion always threatened to slice through our parents' genuine love for their children. Among the chaos and volatility, a steady beat was welcome.

As a teenager, I would try to drown out those Friday quartets with my country and western 45 RPM singles: "There were tears in my ears / as I lay in my bed / crying through the night / over you." I was awkward and unpopular, and those tears mirrored my own. But I loved my father and eventually learned to seek solace, as he did, in his music.

According to recent neurological inquiry, which bases some of its assumptions on string theory, music is at the root of everything. It was at the heart of primitive communication, predating speech, which is located in a different part of the brain. Babies in the uterus are privy to all sound and are born with innate musicality. These theories will be transformed and refined over the coming decades.

In a musical family, I was the black sheep, the one who couldn't carry a tune, the daughter proclaimed tone-deaf by my parents.

In the wake of my first, sad marriage, for a while I tried to take cello lessons from my father. It may have been my way of staying close. I couldn't master the instrument; and after about a year, he suggested I might want to try something with a clearly defined keyboard. Despite my failure in a musical family, I kept my eye on the metronome. Little did I know that most musicians disdained its use as favoring device over musicality. To me it spoke the magic of the expected.

Many years later, when Dad and then Mother died, the contents of their house had been reduced to an apartment and finally a single room in assisted living. My brother, sister, and I talked about what meant something to each of us: a particular painting or piece of furniture, copper kettle or worn Navajo rug. We were kind to one another, considerate of each other's attachments. No death quarrels for us.

But when I looked for Dad's metronome, it was nowhere to be found. I mourned the loss of that little mechanical timekeeper as if it were a missing link in my ongoing search for self.

That was when you, my darling, bought me a stand-in, visually identical although the mahogany was simulated wood-grain plastic. The face was just as I remembered it, its little cross lines closer and closer to one another as they climbed its narrowing stalk. The same little brass handle protruded from the right side of the case. The same rhythmic click transported me to childhood, assuring me everything would be alright.

You alone understood the metronome's historic power against the evil of secrets.

Roque Dalton

Myth, Man, Martyr, and Poet Who Defined an Era

One of the many sad byproducts of a culture that shuns other languages is our ignorance of their literatures. We may read the acknowledged classics in translation, but our contemporaries are often less familiar to us. Roque Dalton García was one of the great Latin American poets of my generation. In his tragically brief thirty-nine years of life, he left an astonishing eighteen books and a legend that still clothes him in mystery and myth.

Dalton (San Salvador, El Salvador, 1935–Quezaltepeque, El Salvador, 1975) came from a tiny Central American country, yet he engaged with other Latin American intellectuals in debating some of the pressing issues of the 1960s and '70s, producing brilliant treatises that are still being referenced today. He wrote innovative essays and novels and interviewed Miguel Mármol, a revolutionary who survived the 1932 massacre of thirty thousand Salvadorans, giving us the exceptionally relevant and compelling oral history novel of the same name. But his poetry, the genre in which he excelled and made his greatest impact, initiated a whole new direction in twentieth-century literature in Spanish.

Roque didn't just talk the talk; he walked the walk: leading to his commitment—ideologically, poetically, and finally fatally—to his country's armed struggle for revolutionary change. The stakes were high, and it was in this context that on May 10, 1975, he was murdered by a member of the People's Rev-

43	44	45
DR. ROGELIO ALFREDO CHAVEZ. Origen: San Salvador. Padre: Eugenio Salvador Chávez. Madre: Leonor Barillas. Viajó a Cuba: 1963.	Ob.FRANCISCO RENE DURAN CARCAMO. Origen: Cojutepeque. Padre: Aquilino Durán. Madre: Jesús Ramírez. Viajó a Cuba: Sepbre/62.	Br.ROQUE DALTON GARCIA Origen: San Salvador. Padre: Winnall Dalton. Madre: María García. Viajó a Cuba: 1960.
46	47	48
Empl. VICTOR MANUEL DUARTE SANDOVAL. Origen: Texistepeque. Padre: desconocido. Madre: Francisca Duarte Sandoval. Viajó a Cuba: Julio 62.	Br. RAFAEL DIAZ BARRIOS Origen: Chirilagua Padre: Santos Díaz Madre: Timotea Barrios Viajó a Cuba: Julio 1962	Br. MANUEL DE PAZ VILLA Origen: San Salvador. Padre: Manuel de Paz Madre: Mercedes Villalta Viajó a Cuba: Julio 62.

1. Salvadoran police document from around 1964. Roque is at top right. All these men were persecuted for having traveled to Cuba. Courtesy of Museo de la palabra y la imágen, San Salvador.

olutionary Army (ERP), an opposing faction within his own organization. Even in an era characterized by enormous risk and almost superhuman courage, it was a crime that shocked a generation.

Much about Roque's life is shrouded in a series of myths the poet himself invented, product of his fanciful imagination as well as one of the ways he seems to have worked through some of the contradictions inherent in his origins and ideas about class. Any odd or fortuitous incident might become the kernel of a great story.

One of these myths concerns his father, Winnall Dalton, a man the poet often claimed descended from the Dalton brothers of Kansas-outlaw fame. Roger Atwood, who has been researching the poet's life for a number of years, has published an article about Roque's relationship with his father.[1] Atwood discovered that Winnall Dalton, who had no connection at all with the infamous outlaw band, was from a Tucson, Arizona, family that emigrated to Mexico and eventually El Salvador in the early part of the twentieth century. The Daltons and Linda Ronstadt's family intermarried in at least three different configurations; had the poet chosen to mythologize this part of his history, he might have explored a tie with a more accurate basis in reality.

In El Salvador the elder Dalton married well, became a landowner, and achieved considerable wealth. Following an attempt on his life, he was coaxed back to health by a nurse named María García; and what appears to have been a single sexual encounter produced the child she had long wanted. Until he was seventeen, Roque used his mother's surname. He was Roque García, until his father agreed to legally recognize paternity.

María never married, but lived with another woman who was a close friend and helped raise the boy. Roque's mother demanded that Winnall support his son, and there is evidence that he not only dropped by with sums of money from time to time but also paid for the boy's education—an expensive Jesuit high school and later a Jesuit university. The poet's work is filled with allusions to his infrequent, emotionally important, albeit complicated, contacts with his mostly absent father.

Winnall may have hoped that the Jesuits, especially at the university in Santiago de Chile, would set his son on a conservative path. Instead, as Roque has written, his Jesuit education freed him from an early belief in God. At least one scholar has suggested that Roque's poetry can be read as religious. I don't believe this to be the case. In our many conversations, I never sensed that he believed in a "higher being." He returned to El Salvador with socialist leanings that would later develop into solidly Marxist positions. His knowledge of Hegel, Marx, Lenin, and other important theoreticians such as Gramsci was comprehensive and detailed.

After his undergraduate work in Chile, Roque was accepted into the University of El Salvador's law school but didn't end up pursuing that career. He joined the Salvadoran Communist Party and, although he later developed substantial differences with its line, remained a member for most of the rest of his life. In 1955 he and Guatemalan poet Otto-René Castillo founded Círculo Literario Universitario, which published some of Central America's best writers. That same year, Roque married Aida Cañas. They would have three sons: Roque Antonio (Roquito), Juan José, and Jorge Vladimiro.

From 1959 on, Roque's short life was marked by arrests, imprisonments, and exiles. As early as 1960, when he and his wife were hiding at a hacienda, the police raided the refuge, arresting the poet, Aida, and four semiliterate ranch

2. Police photo of Roque, his wife Aida, and four ranch hands
arrested with "subversive literature," 1960. Courtesy of Museo de
la palabra y la imágen, San Salvador.

hands they accused of reading Hegel, Marx, and Lenin. The police themselves
may have planted the books displayed in figure 2.

One of his prison escapes also figures prominently in the life story Roque
wrote and rewrote—perhaps true, perhaps invented, perhaps rooted in reality
but embroidered to enhance the developing legend. His version claimed an
earthquake destroyed a wall of the prison in which he was being held and at
which he was scheduled to be executed by firing squad the following morning.
According to the poet, he walked out, melted into a passing religious proces-
sion, and managed to flee the country, making his way to Mexico and eventually Cuba. This was early 1964.

But this was not Roque's first visit to Mexico, a nation that has given refuge
to so many poets fleeing war and repression. He first lived in that country in
1961, when he studied at its Escuela de antropología. This was when he became
familiar with the great Mesoamerican indigenous civilizations and rich tradi-

3. Rostock, GDR. Roque with Guatemalan Nobel Laureate Miguel
Angel Asturias, 1967. Courtesy of Wolfram Morales.

tion of Nahuatl poetry. He also sought out the venerable Spanish poet León
Felipe and Mexicans Efraín Huerta and Eraclio Zepeda—with whom he shared
the similar cultural stories of Chiapas and El Salvador. His friendship with
Zepeda would be important and lifelong.

Roque Dalton and I were friends, comrades, and coworkers. We met in
Mexico City in February of 1964 at El encuentro internacional de poesía (the
International Gathering of Poets) hosted by *El Corno Emplumado* and several
other literary magazines.[2] Roque appeared one day with his earthquake story
and a backpack of marvelous poems. From then to the end of his life, he
remained a powerful presence and influence in mine.

I saw Roque again in Cuba three years later, when we both attended El
encuentro con Rubén Darío (the Meeting on Rubén Darío) in January of 1967.
This was an invitational of poets from a number of different countries who
came together on Varadero Beach to honor the great Nicaraguan modernist's
hundredth anniversary, to experience the revolution, and to share our own

work. At that time, Cuba represented possibility—vibrant political change and the "new man" about whom Che spoke so eloquently. Experiencing the reality for oneself was practically a requirement of the era.

Roque had been living in Prague, where he worked as a correspondent for *The International Review: Problems for Peace and Socialism* (an important Communist theoretical journal). There he wrote what is considered his major poetic work—the experimental, multigenre, and deeply lyrical *Taberna y otros lugares*, which would break new ground in Spanish-language poetry. This collection won the 1969 Casa de las Américas poetry prize. The distinguished Haitian René Depestre, who was one of that year's judges, remarked on its unique mix of nostalgia and irony, calling the achievement "a perfect integration of intimate and social circumstance."[3] In Prague, Roque also completed his yearlong interview with Salvadoran revolutionary Miguel Mármol.

But Roque would soon relocate his family to Cuba and there participate with other brilliant leftist writers of the era in some of the mid-twentieth century's most intense political polemics—tested in action as well as theory. The Cuban Revolution of 1959 signaled the possibility for social change throughout Latin America. But Che Guevara's defeat and death in Bolivia in 1967 caused many to question the *foco* theory, the idea promoted by the Cubans that a small group of guerilla fighters could become the nucleus of a successful fighting force. Roque's essay *Revolución en la revolución y la crítica de derecha* (Revolution in the Revolution and Critique from the Right) was an important contribution to the discussion. Cuba's Casa de las Américas was, and remains, a vital center of this cultural effervescence. Roque was a member of the institution's inner circle for a number of years.

Following the repression that resulted from the Mexican Student Movement of 1968, my family and I were forced into hiding and also moved to the Caribbean island. It was there, in 1969, that Roque and I became close. He would drop by our apartment on Avenida Línea, filling the place with his high level of energy, sharp sense of humor, and profound assessment of whatever might be in the news. We lived blocks apart in Havana's tree-shaded Vedado neighborhood, our children were friends, and we worked together in a number of cultural venues.

One of these was the 1970 Premio Casa de las Américas, the yearly literary contest that was then ten years old and already one of the Spanish language's most important prizes. Each of several genres—poetry, novel, short story, essay, theater, and eventually several additional categories—was judged by five writers:

4. Poetry jury, Casa de las Américas, Cuba, 1970: Washington Delgado (Peru), Roque Dalton (El Salvador), Margaret Randall (United States), Cintio Vitier (Cuba), and Ernesto Cardenal (Nicaragua). Courtesy of Dalton Family Archive.

one from Cuba and four from elsewhere. Along with Nicaragua's Ernesto Cardenal, Peru's Washington Delgado, and Cuba's Cintio Vitier, Roque and I judged the poetry that year. I was the first to spot the potential of the winning book, among the almost two hundred we read, and Roque quickly concurred with my response. His strategies for convincing the other judges drew on his considerable psychological and political savvy. We were excited to award the prize to *Diario del Cuartel* (Prison Diary) by Uruguayan Carlos María Gutiérrez.

In Roque, I felt a kindred spirit. Among foreigners at the time, his family and mine were the only ones I knew who opted for the ration book used by Cuban citizens rather than the special and more generous one offered to non-Cubans living in the country for one reason or another. I was attracted to his casual no-nonsense demeanor, incisive mind, and wild creativity. His use of language—in conversation as well as in his writing—fascinated me.

His poetry showed a profound knowledge of Brecht and Hikmet but was influenced as well by Spain's Golden Age and by that country's Civil War generation—notably Federico García Lorca and Miguel Hernández. One can also hear traces of Vallejo, Huidobro, Benedetti, and the popular vernacular of his native El Salvador. What do we mean when we speak of a poet's influences? Are we saying they write in so-and-so's style, approach craft in a way that is reminiscent of another, or seek similar solutions to expressive problems? Probably all of the above and more. I see a mutual give-and-take between Roque's work and that of his friend Otto-René Castillo. Although Roque was, even then, prolific in a range of genres, I always sensed that poetry was at the center of his creative drive, as it was for mine.

Roque was concerned with political theory and practice that provoked passionate discussion and influenced life and death situations. Cuba was a focal point of social change. At the time, many other countries on the continent had revolutionary movements of lesser or greater impact, and those ideas put forth in the country that had so far managed to wage a successful revolution carried enormous weight.

But Roque was also imaginative and highly creative. Poetry, as I say, was his medium. As a kind of brief introduction to *Taberna y otros lugares*, he included a note to his youngest son: "Dear Jorge, I came to the revolution by way of poetry. You will be able to come to poetry (if you wish, if you feel the need) by way of the revolution. This gives you an advantage. But remember, if there's ever a special reason for you to appreciate my comradeship in the struggle, you have poetry to thank as well."[4]

Roque was laugh-out-loud, roll-on-the-floor funny. He was quick-witted and often caustic, with a highly ingenious sense of humor. He loved devising and playing intelligent tricks on friends and acquaintances. And he was the first to laugh at himself. He could be self-deprecating but also knew how to stand up for what he believed. He was fiercely loyal and expected the same from others.

Although well educated by Jesuits, Roque was never merely a scholar. Although a member of the Communist Party of El Salvador from a very early age, he was anything but a dogmatic thinker. He never failed to speak his mind—often vociferously—and this would cause him problems in a number of venues. Like most Central American men of the time, he drank heavily. Sometimes a discussion would become a falling out, although meaningful relationships were usually mended. An innate discipline kept him working steadily. He always had several books going at once.

Roque's political ideas were enriched by his poetic vision, and his poetry was political in the deepest sense. But he never wrote tracts or incurred in clichés. He was far too artistically sophisticated to adopt a social realist style, except in

5. Roque visits Isle of Pines prison cell, Cuba, 1970.
Courtesy of Dalton Family Archive.

instances of well-placed irony. His poems were original, luminous, and they stand up to scrutiny. Read today, even in a time so chronologically and politically distant from the events that inspired most of them, they continue to be unique and moving. This is because the events were points of departure. The poet's concerns lay with larger truths and values.

As I've said, we shared many literary endeavors. When I wanted to translate the extremely difficult and absolutely transcendent poems of the great Peruvian César Vallejo, Roque spent hours explaining the history and nuance that I needed in order to understand the man's lexicon and style. I remember walking with him along Havana's sea-washed *malecón* (its sea wall); he brought Vallejo's difficult language as well as the time he inhabited to life. I felt as if there were three of us on those walks. When Roque was writing *Miguel Mármol*, I typed the text of more than a thousand pages—back when typewriters and carbon paper were our messy tools.

We also sustained raucous arguments. Roque had a huge personality, a larger-than-life sensibility. He loved women and had a well-earned reputation for enjoying many and overlapping relationships. Only his great capacity for seeing the whole person kept him from being a womanizer, although many may have considered him one. I didn't. Writing these pages, I have thought quite a bit about this aspect of Roque's character—how I saw him at the time, when "free love" was the norm and exuberant connection at every level the practice, and how I see him in retrospect. *Mujeriego* is a Spanish term that refers to a man who has multiple relationships and, because it does not necessarily denote use or abuse, is not really the equivalent of the English "womanizer." Many women of my generation who shared that time and place have our personal stories. Feminism was becoming important to me in the early 1970s, and I shared my incipient convictions with my friend.

I think those discussions made more of an impression than I knew at the time. When Roque left Cuba to return to his country and fight, he produced at least one last collection of poems, published posthumously. *Poemas clandestinos* was written in five invented voices, one of them a woman's. The poems "by Vilma Flores" reflect some of the ideas we'd discussed just before Roque's departure. I include one of them here.

For readers interested in an exceptional mind, as yet little known in the United States, I particularly recommend the panel discussion in which Roque spars with Carlos María Gutiérrez, Roberto Fernández Retamar, René Depestre, Ambrosio Fornet, and Edmundo Desnoes.[5] For those who want to read one of the great multigenre novels of the era, there is *Pobrecito poeta que era yo.*[6] And for those who want to explore the breadth and depth of the man's poetry, a complete three-volume edition is available in El Salvador.[7] Here in the United States, Curbstone Press of Willimantic, Connecticut, was the independent publisher that has made Roque's work most available: several volumes of his poetry as well as a couple of his political essays and *Miguel Mármol*. Ocean Press, in Australia, has plans to bring out a complete works in English.

Roque Dalton left his home and family in Havana in 1973. When he stopped calling or coming around, most of those close to him knew where he was headed. It was a journey traveled by many revolutionaries at the time. Friends suddenly dropped out of sight; the rest of us discreetly refrained from asking questions. I received a letter from Roque the following year. It was postmarked North Vietnam, but I later learned he had been receiving military training in Cuba itself.

For tens of thousands of "soldiers of the revolution" this transition to the front lines of battle was logical and considered a privilege. We all wanted a more just world, and many of us were convinced that legal efforts had played themselves out, that the only road to liberation was through armed struggle. But for intellectuals and poets, committed as they were, the decision could be complex. They didn't always have the physical stamina and military skill to withstand the rigors of war, and their intellectual contributions might be of more value. Still, many poets of my generation died on the front lines of battle: the aforementioned Otto-René Castillo; Nicaraguans Rigoberto López Pérez, Leonel Rugama, and Arlén Siu; Argentina's Francisco Urondo; Chile's Víctor Jara; and Colombian priest Jorge Camilo Torres among others.

In fact, Roque represented a new type of Latin American writer of the left: no longer the "official" Communist like Pablo Neruda or even someone such as Mario Benedetti, whose identification with the revolution clearly cost him international honors, but rather the rank and file political activist for whom the intricacies of underground struggle—passwords, safe houses, escape routes, physical makeovers, forged documents, and the constant threat of death—were as familiar as creative angst and café dialogue. It was a difficult and dangerous profession, in which the event that sealed a writer's reputation was often precocious martyrdom. In Roque's case, his impressive written legacy would have assured his place in literary history, whatever his destiny.

I have always believed that Roque intuited that his life would end prematurely. Mexican poet and close friend Eraclio Zepeda cites a 1966 interview with Radio Habana Cuba in which the poet, speaking of his writing methods, said, "the problem is, I work very fast. For a few years now I've tried to write as if I'll be dead the following day."[8]

Roque was slight of build. His talents clearly lay more in his intellect, theory, and poetic vision than in his physical qualities. But he was determined to test his beliefs and commitment in action. Years after his death, I learned that when he sought admission to the Fuerzas Populares de Liberación Nacional Farabundo Martí (Farabundo Martí Popular Liberation Forces, FMLN), the organization's leader, Salvador Cayetano Carpio, rejected his application, arguing that Roque's role in the revolution was as a poet and not as a foot soldier. As a result, Dalton joined another of the armed struggle movements then active in his country, the People's Revolutionary Army (ERP).[9]

From the time of his arrival, the poet's brilliant power of analysis, quick tongue, and perhaps also his known connection with Cuba led one faction to perceive him as a rival and a threat. In mid-May 1975 a mutual friend called me from Mexico. She asked what I knew about Roque Dalton having been killed in El Salvador. I called Roque's wife, Aida, who seemed shocked but said she would get back to me. A few days later, the terrible news was confirmed.

But Roque's death, like his life, would be anything but transparent. It seemed he and another comrade had been imprisoned, tortured for several months,

6. Berlin, 1965. Courtesy Wolfram Morales.

and then executed by the leaders of ERP's opposing faction. To justify their crime, they accused the poet of being a Cuban agent, then an agent of the CIA. These were the sorts of lies sometimes put forth back then to discredit or cast doubt on those whose brilliance and/or unaligned positions caused fear and jealousy in those of lesser stature. It took a while for the Latin American revolutionary community to investigate what had happened, retrieve Dalton's name, and fully defend it.

In Cuba we didn't hesitate. I was one of a group of young poets who met to read and discuss our work every Saturday morning on the grounds of the University of Havana; we soon renamed our weekly workshop *El taller Roque Dalton* (The Roque Dalton Workshop). We also held a memorial, attended by members of Roque's family and a couple of Latin American revolutionaries who were in the country at the time. I remember I contributed a scratchy tape I had of the poet reciting his poetry, to which we listened in silence and grief.

Joaquín Villalobos was the intellectual author of Dalton's murder, perhaps even the man who pulled the trigger. Many years later, Villalobos publicly confessed, saying the crime had been the worst mistake of his life. Roque's son Juan José, a noted journalist, interviewed his father's killer. It is one of the most courageous and poignant interviews I have read. Today Villalobos makes his home between England and Mexico, where he has worked as an advisor to repressive governments.

Perhaps even more troubling, according to Juan José and his brother Jorge, is the fact that Jorge Meléndez, the director of civil protection in El Salvador's Ministry of the Interior, was also involved in their father's death. They have demanded—so far unsuccessfully—that President Mauricio Funes fire Meléndez. El Salvador's brutal war finally ended, and the FMLN transformed itself into the political party now in power. But as with so many victories mitigated by circumstance and concession, peace can be more complex than war.

Roque Dalton was not the only member of his family to give his life for his country's liberation. His oldest son, Roquito, died in battle six years later. In a testimony of the time, Juan José writes, "My brother Roque and I went to war. Roque died in combat in the October 1981 offensive; we don't know how. His body was never recovered, but his dream of a more just country remains ongoing and urgent. I survived the war, my wounds, and imprisonment by the Salvadoran dictatorship, as well as our quasi-victory."[10]

Juan José's piece is only incidentally about his brother's death. It is a portrait of Cuba in the 1970s and '80s, the young people who grew up there—many of whose parents made the ultimate sacrifice for a future they believed was possible—and a hope shattered by successive historic events. The last paragraph reflects the double take many have experienced in recent years: "Cuba, my Cuba, you are everywhere. . . . Thrown to the winds and wounded . . . , and with a hope that refuses to die. . . . The Revolution and the Empire gave our generation everything it needed to live in a state of permanent contradiction, but they didn't prepare us for peace. So many lies turned out to be true and there are so many truths we never believed. How much laughter has turned to sadness? But . . . here we are: survivors of an uncertain future."[11]

This paragraph, more than many, defines an era and its actors great and small. Roque Dalton was one of its most brilliant minds and creative protagonists. Although he died much too young, and as the result of a decision both heroic and perhaps misguided, he left a vast *oeuvre* that remains as pertinent and exciting today as when it was written. I remember the revolutionary. I remember and miss the dear friend. But most of all, I remember the poet who wrote, "Poetry, like bread, is for everyone." It is to his poetry that I often turn in time of need.

The following is a very small sampling of Roque's poetic production. The translations are mine, either because no other English versions exist[12] or because

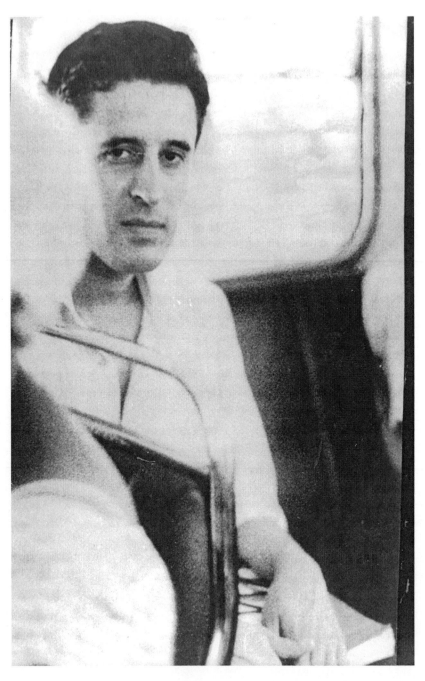

7. 1972. Roque Dalton on a Havana Bus. Photo by Chinolope.

I'm not satisfied with those that do. The first poem, written in 1961 or '62, was part of a series the poet called *Para elevar la ira* (*In Honor of Rage*). This and others from the same period were published in El Salvador, in a variety of clandestine magazines, during the severe persecution of the Lemus government and the military directory that followed. Dalton considered them a tribute to the brave men and women who showed such heroism during that time.

The next poem, almost certainly only a fragment, may be unpublished to date even in the original. Roger Atwood sent me the Spanish version, which he found at the *Museo de la Palabra y la Imagen* in San Salvador. Atwood says, "[It was] hand-written by Dalton and a few words were illegible, owing partly to the fact that it was a bad photocopy or carbon copy . . . A notation at the top of the document said the original was with the Dalton family."[13] I suspect these sparse verses may have been notations, ideas for a poem yet to be written. I offer all these translations in loving memory and with the hope that they may bring Roque's genius to a broader reading public.

Referencia de pasos

¡Se me murió el ayer de parto
y lo velo cantando!

Como a una guitarra sola
a quien se le quebrara la sonrisa circular y la música,
solo,
sin desbocados animales interiores,
hueso en actividad,
reciente hueso,
hacía como que caminaba entre los hombres casado con mi madre,
pueblerino feliz, poblado de olas.

¡Ah, estúpida frontera,
munincipal y en paz con los estómagos:
cómo tenía que morderme los retratos
para poder reírme hasta de mí
con todo y tus pesares, tus costosísimos harapos,
la franca suciedad que te conoces!

¡Cómo no tenía sola y atrozmente
que bajarme los pasos de los hombros
y caminar . . . !

Speaking of Steps

My yesterday died in childbirth
and I mourn it in song!

Like a lone guitar
whose circular smile and music are broken,
alone,
without the invasion of runaway animals,
bone acting up,
recent bone,
pretending to walk among men married to my mother,
provincial man, overflowing with waves.

Aye, dumb frontier,
municipal and without indigestion:
how I had to bite the portraits
in order to laugh at myself
with your remorse and all, your extremely expensive rags,
the honest filth you recognize!

How I had only to descend
those steps from my shoulders
and walk . . . !

(Poema inédito—fragmentos)

Las influencias
Mas grandes de mi vida:
los jesuitas, el Comité
Central,
Roma y La Habana . . .

Comulgar,
Soportar la tortura,
decir "culo"
doctorarse,
silbar,
¿no caben igualmente
en el mismo tonel de Hegel?

Luego
terminan
produciendo [illegible]
sueño.

(Unpublished Poem—Fragments)

The greatest influences
In my life:
the Jesuits, the Central
Committee,
Rome and Havana . . .

To take communion,
Bear up under torture,
Say "asshole"
earn a doctorate,
whistle,
don't they all fit
in the same barrel as Hegel?

They end up
making me [illegible]
tired.

Y sin Embargo, Amor

Y sin embargo, amor, a través de las lágrimas,
yo sabía que al fin iba a quedarme
desnudo en la ribera de la risa.

Aquí,
hoy,
digo:
siempre recordaré tu desnudez en mis manos,
tu olor a disfrutada madera de sandal
clavada junto al sol de la mañana;
tu risa de muchacha,
o de arroyo,
o de pájaro;
tus manos largas y amantes
como un lirio traidor a sus antiguos colores;
tu voz,
tus ojos,
lo de abarcable en ti que entre mis pasos
pensaba sostener con las palabras.

Pero ya no habrá tiempo de llorar.

Ha terminado
la hora de la ceniza para mi corazón.

Hace frío sin ti,
pero se vive.

(from *La ventana en el rostro*)

Nevertheless, My Love

Nevertheless, my love, through my tears
I knew in the end I'd stand
alone on laughter's shore.

Here,
today,
I say:
I will always remember you naked in my hands,
your delicious smell of sandalwood
strong in early sun;
your young girl's smile
or dry river smile
or birdlike smile;
your long loving hands
like a lily betraying its ancient colors;
your voice,
your eyes,
all I could hold of you and believed
I would sustain with words.

Now there is no time for tears.

The hour of embers
has left my heart.

It's cold without you,
but I survive.

Los Locos

A los locos no nos quedan bien los nombres.

Los demás seres
llevan sus nombres como vestidos nuevos,
los balbucean al fundar amigos,
los hacen imprimir en tarjetitas blancas
que luego van de mano en mano
con la alegría de las cosas simples.

Y qué alegría muestran los Alfredos, los Antonios,
los pobres Juanes y los taciturnos Sergios,
los Alejandros con olor a mar!

Todos extienden, desde la misma garganta con que cantan
sus nombres envidiables como banderas bélicas,
sus nombres que se quedan en la tierra sonando
aunque ellos con sus huesos se vayan a la sombra.

Pero los locos, ay señor, los locos
que de tanto olvidar nos asfixiamos,
los pobres locos que hasta la risa confundimos
y a quienes la alegría se nos llena de lágrimas,
cómo vamos a andar con los nombres a rastras,
cuidándolos,
puliéndolos como mínimos animales de plata,
viendo con estos ojos que ni el sueño somete
que no se pierdan entre el polvo que nos halaga y odia?
Los locos no podemos anhelar que nos nombren
pero también los olvidaremos?

(from *La ventana en el rostro*)

The Crazy Ones

Our names don't fit us crazy ones.

Other people
wear their names like new clothes,
murmur them when meeting friends,
print them on little white cards
that later pass from hand to hand
in ordinary exchange.

How happy the Alfredos and Antonios seem to be,
the poor Juans and shy Sergios,
the Alejandros smelling of sea!

All raise their enviable names like war flags
from their throats,
their names that dream beneath the sod
although they have gone with their bones to shadow.

But we crazy ones, oh lord, we crazy ones
who choke on memory loss,
we poor crazies who confuse even laughter
and who cry from joy,
how are we supposed to drag our names along,
caring for them,
polishing them like tiny silver animals,
watching with these eyes not even sleep can subdue
that they not lose themselves in the dust that praises and hates us?

We who are crazy cannot hope they will speak our names
but will we also forget them?

El Cínico

Claro es que no tengo en las manos
el derecho a morirme
ni siquiera en las abandonadas tardes de los domingos.

Por otra parte se debe comprender que la muerte
es una manufactura inoficiosa
y que los suicidas
siempre tuvieron una mortal pereza
de sufrir.

Además, debo
la cuenta de la luz?

(from *La ventana en el rostro*)

The Cynic

Of course I don't have the right
to kill myself
not even on a languid Sunday afternoon.

On the other hand one must understand
that death is an informal product
and that suicides
have always been mortally afraid
of suffering.

Do I still owe
my light bill?

El Descanso del guerrrero

Los muertos están cada día más indóciles.

Antes era fácil con ellos:
les dábamos un cuello duro una flor
loábamos sus nombres un una larga lista:
que los recintos de la patria
que las sombreas notables
que el mármol monstruoso.

El cadaver firmaba en pos de la memoria
iba de nuevo a filas
y marchaba al compás de nuestra vieja música.

Pero qué va
los muertos
son otros desde entonces.

Hoy se ponen irónicos
preguntan.

Me parece que caen en la cuenta
de ser cada vez más la mayoría!

(from *Taberna y otros lugares*)

The Warrior's Repose

The dead are more restless every day.

They used to be easy to manage:
we gave them a stiff collar a flower
we honored their names on a long list:
you know, every corner of the nation
you know, such notable shadows
you know, illustrious marble.

The corpse signed its name for memory's sake
and returned to the ranks
marching to the rhythm of old music.

But hey
the dead
are something else these days.

They indulge in sarcasm
ask questions.

I think they understand
they are becoming the majority!

Para un mejor amor

El sexo es una categoría política.
—Kate Millet

Nadie discute que el sexo
es una categoría en el mundo de la pareja:
de ahí la ternura y sus ramas salvajes.

Nadie discute que el sexo
es una categoría familiar:
de ahí los hijos,
las noches en común
y los días divididos
(él, buscándo el pan en la calle,
en las oficinas o en las fábricas;
ella, en la retaguardia de los oficios domésticos,
en la estrategia y la táctica de la cocina
que permitan sobrevivir en la batalla común
siquiera hasta el fin del mes).

Nadie discute que el sexo
es una categoría económica:
basta mencionar la prostitución,
las modas,
las secciones de los diarios que solo son para ella
o sólo son para él.

Donde empiezan los líos
es a partir de que una mujer dice
que el sexo es una categoría política.

Porque cuando una mujer dice
que el sexo es una categoría política
puede comenzar a dejar de ser mujer en sí
para convertirse en mujer para sí,
constituir a la mujer en mujer

(continued on p. 48)

Toward a Better Love

Sex is a political category.
—Kate Millet

No one would argue that sex
is a category in the world of the couple:
the tender root, its wild branches.

No one would argue that sex
has its place in the family:
leading to children,
nights in common
and days apart
(he out making a living in the street,
in offices or factories;
she in the rearguard of domesticity,
the strategy and tactics of the kitchen
allowing for that shared struggle of survival
at least to the end of the month).

No one would argue that sex
is an economic category:
think of prostitution,
fashion,
the sections in the dailies that are just for her
or just for him.

The problems begin
when a woman declares
that sex is a political category.

Because when a woman declares
that sex is a political category
she stops being womankind
and becomes a woman for herself,
putting the woman back in woman
(continued on p. 49)

Roque Dalton   47

a partir de su humanidad
y no de su sexo,
saber que el desodorante mágico con sabor a limón
y jabón que acaricia voluptuosamente su piel
son fábricados por la misma empresa que fabrica el napalm
saber que las labores propias del hogar
son las labores propias de la clase social a que pertenece ese hogar,
que la diferencia de sexos
brilla mucho major en la profunda noche amorosa
cuando se conocen todos esos secretos
que nos mantenían enmascarados y ajenos.

(from *Poemas clandestinos*, in the voice of Vilma Flores)

from her humanity
and not her sex.
She knows the magic deodorant with a hint of lemon
and the soap that softly caresses her skin
are made by the same company that manufactures napalm.
She knows housework itself
is shaped by the social class to which the house belongs,
and that the difference between the sexes
burns much brighter in love's deep night
when all those secrets keeping us masked and separate
are revealed.

Closing the Gap

The ground beneath my feet rises with determination against the soles of my shoes. Its firmness provides a reassurance against which I test each step. The energy of my forward motion climbs past knees, buzzes anticipating vulva, flows into shoulders and down through breasts, glides along gently swinging arms and flutters to a stop in curious fingertips. Above the easy rhythm of the body's pace, my head takes responsibility, eyes alert. Stanzas and breath lines, unexpected turns of phrase, strophes, and counter rhythms fall from the bulk of cloud piling up across a tropical sky and scatter at either side of such purposeful parting of air.

Nevertheless, perspective reveals a lengthening journey. The gentle curve of sidewalk bordering Havana's wave-battered seawall appears longer than it did minutes before. I walk as fast as I can, but my destination recedes more quickly than I am able to keep up. A lone fisherman on the rocks to my left, a couple of young men walking their cranky loose-jointed bicycles toward me, the woman whose body extends itself vulnerable yet knowledgeable just ahead atop the well-washed stone wall, those children with their impudent laughter and oblivious games—all present themselves in precise proportion. But at the far end of the promenade, the massive stone of the Spanish fort inches farther and farther away, until it is swallowed by perspective itself.

Should I be picking up these poetic fragments falling from the sky or just kick them to unseen corners where water pools between one wave and the next?

I hang onto each landmark, equal measure of discovery and relief. There's the blue building beside the yellow. Now the warning fence where street work is being done. If the avenue widens here or reveals that side street with tangle of expropriated electricity there, I count the markers, reassured I am headed in the right direction. Such sad facades, tired glimmer of yesterday.

I pretend not to notice those words with their fiery wings landing about me on the rutted walk. But what the hell? The scene and my progress through it seem powerfully predestined. I give in to curiosity and lean down to pick one up, turn it over in my palm, breathe its light, running my tongue between gap teeth where a syllable sticks. The word doesn't burn my flesh, as I feared, but feels strangely heavy, like a surprise fragment of meteor among small desert rocks.

Those are not bombs or even fireworks exploding in air but brilliant metaphors, similes recognizable in any tongue, intentionally broken rhythms, rain sheets of nouns and verbs, unusual poetic forms, gardens of quotes a writer in Hiroshima or reader in Helsinki may underline for future use.

Although I try to keep my eyes focused on such a stealthily diminishing destination, I cannot help but notice William Carlos Williams walking toward me, his mother on his arm.[1] She looks sideways at her son, gestures conspiratorially, then translates an overheard conversation or line of writing on the wall. She looks like Flossie, his wife, and for a moment I wonder if I am watching mother or wife. Then I remind myself that men often marry women who resemble their mothers.

Not at all unexpected or out of place, a red wheelbarrow appears in the poet's path. White chickens strut about. One dissolves in an explosion of feathers as it tries to escape a white-robed *santera* swooping in for the catch. Williams's mother nudges her son's arm so he won't trip over the barnyard scene. Could that pale movement of stroke-burdened lip have been a faint smile of gratitude?

César Vallejo sits on the seawall, a neatly folded umbrella/walking stick by his side.[2] He is wearing a dark suit, inappropriate in this tropical heat. I imagine him in a white guayabera, simple tucking, nothing lacey or overly ornate. Breathe, I shout at the great weaver of words. Then retract a brief gasp of moist air, astonished at my temerity. Imagine telling the poet whose every breath condensed a meaning still unwinding on our lips to breathe!

Is it Thursday? Does he feel the rain, soaking through his suit? From which direction does memory come, descend, settle, and embrace?

Nancy Morejón appears between the two dead poets, taking each by a willing elbow as she steers them east.[3] I stop and consider the evidence. I had assumed all my companions on this journey were long dead, visiting from some other world. Now I must reappraise revelation, reconsider vision, reconnect to my sources. This is getting complicated.

Nancy's step is light but energized. No question she's alive. Her body moves with animal grace, the beauty of a lioness or leopard. Her eyes are like pinpoints of sugared cinnamon nestled in a shawl of purest silk. I hear her talking to William and César, confiding passing neighborhoods with all their human stories, deciphering evidence that would have been impenetrable in their time, offering the poetry of recent history. I hear their responses, each from his culture and language. Oh, I think, she must be the bridge. And I hurry, not wanting to be left behind.

Violeta Parra sidles up to Vallejo, hoists her body and long skirt atop the wet stone beside him, and takes her guitar from its battered case.[4] She accommodates her awkward limbs and imposing posture, then looks at him beguilingly, though there is nothing coy in her demeanor. Is she waiting for him to give her words? But no: she has a river of her own. Maybe a duet, something about being grateful to life although it requires all the dead combatants rise and walk? César isn't smiling. His grave countenance seems etched in tired flesh. Then their mouths begin to move in unison. The song they sing between roar and hiss of sea holds a harmony like none I've heard.

Across the broad seaside drive, far to my right Roque hops and skips along, unwilling to be left out of the picture. Despite all news to the contrary, death favors his small elf-like body. He still has a few surprises and is playing one last trick on betrayal, turning all predictions upside down, again and yet again enjoying the last laugh. Roque, I shout, as loud as I can, just in case he doesn't recognize his aspirin the size of the sun! And then Roque, Roque, Roque, Roque, until my throat dries and the name empties of sound. My lungs are raw from trying to compete with the waves, traffic, all these simultaneous conversations and their cross-dressed meanings. The repeated call remains locked in millennial silence. Only then does he turn his head and smile.

When I notice Haydée Santamaría seated with impeccable grace inside the curve of a *coco-taxi* parked a few feet ahead and on my side of the drive, I know this magical scene is about to fade. Even in the ridiculous contraption, she is elegant, proud, beyond any earthly attempt at imitation. Like Miguel Hernández's onion, each delicate layer of skin peels to reveal another.[5] This will be the final act; I welcome and fear it at one and the same time.

The effort to hold onto what I am dreaming to life provokes the start of an asthma attack. The single death as large as the life it ends warns me to slow, wait in my tracks, give in completely to the display around me. That which has turned an unexpected corner, the surprises that loomed along the way. I no longer wonder if I am part of this scene or outside looking in. Nancy's presence reassures, tells me it makes no difference at all.

The metaphors are ankle deep now, breath lines catching them in webs of exquisite pronunciation. The music of language is everywhere. I am amused that I perfectly understand the most obtuse poetic forms in tongue after tongue I have never heard. Clicks and tonalities, guttural *j*'s and silent *h*'s, ellipses of memory and the picture poems of glyph.

I laugh out loud.

No one notices.

Then, as sudden as the renewed jolt of confidence, a man in a white T-shirt comes around a far corner, firing an automatic rifle at shoulder height into the heavy evening air. This may create a problem, I think, arrest the steady ticking of clocks or murder the dead where they freeze. In the dusky corners of deepening shadow details begin to flatten and fade. Are all the stores closing? Will I make it through the heavy doors before they lock for the night? Will the raised threshold let me cross before it interrupts my stumbling step?

I conjure an invisible phone to ears and lips, listen for instructions, speak words uttered in their primal state before they cut through this sad curtain of polluted air. The phone is an early upright model, its mouthpiece like a dull black flower atop a somber stand, its earpiece at the end of a black wire. Each anxious breath shapes a syllable; each lurch is a stand-in for the truth my dream monitor captures but I refuse to claim as fully mine.

Acknowledgment and acceptance are identical twins, an egg split in prehistoric mud, two sides of a mirror where the mercury trickles south. For the moment, I have dodged the bullet, but danger still threatens these streets, drapes itself serpentine about the steel-cored barriers positioned to keep future rental-truck explosives from bringing all the buildings to their knees.

Inches from my face the hologram phone rings again, insistently. When I answer at Golden Proportion's precise calculation, I hear a young poet ask where I am, why I'm late, if I'm still coming as promised. I search for words to explain my lengthening journey. Streets unfold before me like winter's bitterest cold. I read a prepared speech about why night may test my strength beyond its ability to cast the perfect stone. We are never closer than in these last instants of inconsolable fingertips.

Then the man in the white T-shirt explodes and disappears into the staccato beat of his own weapon. Not even a trace of anger stains the air that holds his soiled image. Buildings and vehicles change places with lightning speed. Memory pulses like a giant heartbeat; swallows street, malecón, and all its inhabitants; then disappears with neither explanation nor remorse. Heat traces a breath line from my insistent forward motion to the young poet's velvet string of questions.

What's in a Name?

What's in a name? Some think everything. Others simply inhabit theirs with an easy amiability, putting less stock in complicated theories about labels. I constantly walk the map of naming. Although not convinced by the theories, my poet's conviction tells me names are powerful.

In Shakespeare's *Romeo and Juliet*, the Montague and Capulet families are longtime enemies. When Romeo Montague and Juliet Capulet fall in love, their family histories would seem to doom the romance. But Juliet tells Romeo that a name is an artificial and meaningless convention and that she loves the person who is called Montague, not the Montague name or family. Romeo, out of his passion for Juliet, rejects his family surname and vows to be "new baptized" as Juliet's lover. As we know, however, the dramatic unfolding ends with the impossibility of this love. Both young people die before they can be united. In the end, their names could not be overcome.

Curious about the history of naming, I went to the Internet. Prominent among sites promising information about the importance of names are several posted by the Kalabarians. Never having heard of the group, I allowed myself to be seduced.

Like so many other self-advertising quasi-mystical societies or institutions, "The Kalabarian philosophy offers a complete guide to life . . . a blueprint to human existence." It claims to be the culmination of thousands of years of intellectual thought, offering a broad perspective . . . through a harmonious blending of Eastern philosophy and Western science and practicality. It proclaims that it has developed, through the use of mathematical concepts, nothing less than a complete understanding of mind, health, and the cycles of time.

On a whim, I decided to enter my name, Margaret, in the blank, check the "female" square, and see what comes up. In seconds, I discovered that my name makes me "a sociable person who appreciates the beauties of nature and refinements of life, that I am moved by music and the arts, am very idealistic and romantic, and may have tried to express my beautiful thoughts through poetry or writing." So far so good, although entering other names brought almost identical responses, and checking the male rather than female box didn't produce much gender variation either. The Kalabarians also said that I "suffer greatly with a lack of confidence and self-consciousness, crave affection and understanding, and always wonder if I am doing the right thing, desiring to express myself but afraid to do so."

Not so much.

Enough pseudophilosophy. Let's get serious.

As a poet, I know how important words are, how powerful. The sounds of letters and syllables produce a particular energy, unlike any other. A word, designated as an individual's name, occupies a central place in that person's life. Baptisms and other naming ceremonies are special moments. Although I don't subscribe to any system claiming this or that way of deciphering who we are, I do know that names are words that define and accompany us throughout our lives.

Given or chosen? Today few remember that Marilyn Monroe was born Norma Jeane Mortenson or baptized Norma Jeane Baker, or that for a brief period she also went by the last name of Doherty, or that she took Di Maggio as her surname when married to the baseball great. All the glamour and tragedy of her life live on in her screen name, Marilyn Monroe.

Jolan Kovacs, Joanne Carter, and Joanne Siegel—known most famously as Lois Lane—all died the same day: February 12, 2011. It was no coincidence. The ninety-three-year-old was born Jolan in 1917. When she entered primary school, neither classmates nor teachers could pronounce the Hungarian yo-lan. More probably, the cultural insularity of Cleveland, like that prevalent throughout the country at the time, led those at her school to invent a thoroughly American stand-in rather than respect or even try to say the one they so cheerfully discarded.

From then on, Jolan was Joanne.

Little did those who so flippantly renamed her know she would become the most quintessentially American of them all.

Jolan, or Joanne, was of that generation of U.S. American women who grew up at the time of the Great Depression. During and after World War II, they entered the workforce en masse. Joanne sold new and used Chevys from a lot in Santa Monica, supported the war effort at a job for a California shipbuilder, and was an artist's model in Boston. It was probably in 1935 that she tried out for and got the job that would forever inscribe her in our popular culture.

She placed an ad in the classified section of the *Cleveland Plain Dealer*, declaring herself available for modeling work. She confessed she had no experience. Most of those who responded to the ad wanted to date her. But one response seemed serious and led her to present herself to the team of Joe Shuster and Jerry Siegel, who were just then developing the cartoon hero Superman.

Shuster and Siegel knew they wanted Superman's love interest to be a female journalist. Glenda Farrell was playing a clever reporter named Torchy Blane around that time. In a B movie, *Torchy Blane in Panama*, the title character was acted by a singer and actress named Lola Lane. People later said that name influenced the artists' choice for Superman's leading lady. Names have a mysterious way of threading their way through everyday history, and different historic moments bestow unique popularity on names given to both girls and boys.

Alliteration is always seductive: Marilyn Monroe. Sylvester Stallone. Donald Duck. Mickey Mouse. Lois Lane.

Joanne Siegel died on February 12, 2011, at the age of ninety-three, but Lois Lane lives on. Joanne's New York Times obituary says that during that initial modeling session she "struck various poses—draping herself over the arms of a chair, for example, to show how she might look being carried by Superman in flight." She and the two men, who were barely in their twenties at the time, became good friends.

Joanne had the fresh, girl-next-door Debbie Reynolds look so popular in the United States throughout the 1940s and '50s, with full bangs piled high above her broad forehead and long curls brushed back behind her ears. Shuster's drawings made Lois Lane quite a bit more voluptuous than his model. After failed first marriages, Joanne and Siegel eventually fell in love, married, and made a life together. As Joanne aged, other women played Lane in film and television.

Powerful as the original Lois Lane name was, making billions first for Detective Comics and then for its successor DC, for years neither Shuster nor Siegel nor Joanne herself made any money from the wildly successful brand. They began the legal fight for compensation in 1947, but it wasn't until 2008 that a federal judge restored Siegel's coauthorship share of the original Superman copyrights. Shuster was long dead. At the time of Joanne's death, the amount of money to which the Siegel family was entitled was still being adjudicated.

In the Christian West some names honor Old Testament tradition (Jonah, Elijah, Abraham, Rachel, Sarah). Others replicate New Testament figures (Mary, Peter, Paul, and John). How many Jewish parents still name their offspring Noah, Joel, Ebenezer, or Leah? How many millions of instances of Jesús and María are there in the Spanish-speaking world? Among Muslims, how many little boys are called Mohammed or Suleiman? Clearly this represents more than parents wishing to honor their religion's holiest figures. There is a sense, as well, that the namesake will develop some of the qualities ascribed to prophet, Christ, or disciple, and, perhaps most important of all, that with a name so indigenous to his or her community, the child will gain a solid sense of belonging.

Powerful cultural or literary works have been responsible for naming whole generations. The longtime popularity of Louisa May Alcott's *Little Women* produced tens of thousands of girls named Meg, Jo, Amy, and Beth, although this last name fared less well than the first three because Beth died so young. As Margaret Jo, I was the recipient of two of the March sisters' names. I don't know why girls' names especially seem to gain popularity in waves, but I remember a time when I had so many young women students named Brittany, Tiffany, or Ashley in a particular university class I was teaching that I had a hard time keeping them apart.

Marketing experts certainly understand the commercial value of a name. Beginning in the 1950s, almost any time you placed a call to a major service or sales company, the female voice responding to your call would answer with a cheerful "Hello, my name is Judy." Identifying herself in this way was a job requirement. The name Judy, it was believed, was sufficiently plain and pleasing to inspire trust, put people at ease, possibly even disarm them. The choice undoubtedly responded to some expensive demographic study about name acceptance on the part of the U.S. American public.

Today, when a real human answering such a call is rare, you're more likely to reach a bit of digital technology simulating the inflections of conversational speech. Machine-intoned phrases like "type or speak the last four digits of your Social Security number" may be followed by lilting recordings of "okay, thank you, let's move on now." It's hard to know whether the company hopes you may believe you are conversing with a live human being. The most astonishing and frequently irritating introduction is the one made by the male operator with an almost impenetrable foreign accent who tells you his name is Sally. Times have changed, and with them technological possibility. What hasn't changed is the importance we place on names.

Single names project whole personalities. Barbie, she of the impossible body measurements and thousands of identities, is still the doll favored by little girls on every continent. I have heard her iconic name pronounced with a variety of accents. Her male counterpart, Ken, is also popular within the acceptable heterosexual romantic model, but there's never been anyone quite like Barbie.

Some people dislike their names; some even hate them. Some legally change them or just tell their friends to call them something else. Some use nicknames that gradually take the place of those they were given at birth. Some people love their names, identifying with the culture they embody or family from which they come. In many cultures, women change their names at marriage; in Latin America it is still customary in the more traditional circles for a woman to assume her husband's surname accompanied by *de* or "belonging to" (e.g. Gloria García de Chávez).

Some names forever carry a racist overtone, like Sambo or Aunt Jemima. Some, like Carnegie and Rockefeller, instantly conjure immense wealth. Michelangelo and Picasso are synonymous with great art; Marian Anderson, Miriam Makeba, and Caruso, with a privileged singing voice. By shear strength of meaning and two-way exchange of memory, these names and what they signify have fused in an unbreakable embrace.

Although my analysis of naming has developed over many years, I took very seriously the names I chose for my children. Gregory was the first. And he was mine alone. I was neither married nor in a relationship with his father, and the full responsibility for what he would be called fell to me. I remember those hours after his birth, in the impersonal cold of a New York City public hospital ward. A woman appeared at the foot of my bed with an efficient manner, pad and pencil in her hand. Some of her indifference was surely in response to my unwed status, abjectly suspect at the time.

My visitor informed me I must name my son then and there. Apparently she was on some sort of schedule she was unwilling to discuss with the likes of me. After a thirty-six-hour labor, I was exhausted and more than willing to comply. In fact, I had already decided that if he were a boy, he would be Gregory. People assumed everything from Gregory Peck to Gregory Corso, but the truth was I just liked the name. And deep in the recesses of my unconscious there was also some vague connection to the Gregorian calendar, the instrument by way of which my culture keeps track of time. Even then, perhaps long before, time and its attributes were important to my understanding of the world.

I had my three daughters in Mexico, in a sweet little family-friendly clinic in every way the opposite of Manhattan General's grim confines. For their births there were also fathers in the picture. I wasn't alone, which on the one hand was welcome but on the other meant that another adult shared in choosing their names. Since I was a young girl I had fixated on the name Sarah. Many years earlier, in a Sunday school class, I'd learned about the Old Testament Sarah at the well and had decided my first girl child would bear her name. Sarah's father also had his preferences, so my oldest daughter became Sarah Dhyana.

Just before Ximena's birth I read *El Cantar del Mío Cid*, the almost four thousand–line anonymous Spanish poem that is thought to be the oldest and is certainly a classic of the language. Doña Ximena was the main female figure in that poem. I loved the name and also loved spelling it with an *X*, as opposed to its more conventional *J*. In Mexico the *X* evoked a connection to Nahuatl, language of those early Mexicans who tried to resist the conquest. Although I don't think I was conscious of this at the time, insisting on the *X* may have provided a healthy counterpoint to the use of such an old-country name.

Of my four children, only Ximena seemed uncomfortable with her name when she was young. From time to time she preferred to be called Lindsay or Andrea or some other popular U.S. American name she discovered in youthful glamour magazines. Today, though, I believe she identifies with the name I gave her. Ximena's love of all things Mexican is profound and knowledgeable.

My youngest daughter, Ana, originally had an extra *n* in her name: Anna. I named her Anna Laurette, because I loved the name Anna and because the French Mexican archeologist Laurette Séjourné was my closest friend at the time. Ana herself dropped the second *n* before she reached adolescence. I think she disdained its slightly foreign cast. I of course followed her lead. Around the time Ana was born and shortly after her birth, a number of people close to me gave their daughters the same name.

Names often continue through family lines, producing juniors, seconds, and thirds among their male members and sentimental namesakes among the females. Several of my children have created names for their children that have moved me deeply. Gregory and his wife Laura naturally named their firstborn

Lía, after Laura's mother, who died when she was very young. The name Lía is popular among the family's girls, just as there are a number of boys named Pablo, after Laura's father. But my first grandchild is not simply Lía; it is Lía Margarita, in honor of me.

Sarah's youngest son is Juan, after my father John. Reinthal is the middle name of Ana's youngest: Tolo Reinthal Bickford. Tolo is short for Bartolome, and Reinthal honors my original surname, before my parents changed it to Randall as a way of trying to deny their Jewish identity. That name change had been a sore point between my parents and me from the moment I understood what it meant, and Ana found a moving way of returning that part of our original identity back into the family tree.

So, what's in a name? Everything. Its syllables flash their colors and sound their energies. It is up to the person and also his or her society to imbue those syllables with a content that causes the listener to recoil (Genghis Khan, Adolf Hitler, George W. Bush), feel devotion (Jesus, Buddha, Mohammed), be inspired (Joan of Arc, Martin Luther King), laugh out loud (Chaplin, Borat, Kate Clinton), or experience familiarity and comfort, depending on what may be in style at the time.

Between people and their names an invisible synapse flashes in unbroken pulse. The importance of the individuation a name conveys is evident from the way names are replaced by numbers tattooed on the arms of concentration camp inmates or dealt out to prisoners throughout the world. The surest way to take a person's identity is to remove his or her name. The daily tragedy of Alzheimer's is often manifest in the person afflicted forgetting the names of those closest to them and, as the condition advances, forgetting their own.

Memory of identity itself may be the last to go.

New Map of Wonder to Explore

I'm not going to make you wait like I did for the word that eluded me yesterday morning. I'll tell you right now—it was *sectarian*.

For at least a decade, words frequently have been wandering off. I'll be speaking and my voice trails, then goes silent. There is only emptiness, like a weakness in the knees, where the word I want should be standing. I usually grab another—not quite as good a fit but similar enough—and keep on going. Sometimes the interruption is pronounced enough that I must acknowledge this problem that has come with age. I try to keep apologies out of it, the explanation brief and straightforward.

It's much more irritating when I am writing. I'll be sitting at the computer, my customary workstation, and as I sidle up to the word I need, it simply moves out of range. Where the word was supposed to be waiting for my lightning-fast fingers on the keyboard, there is nothing. Its absence is like a hole cut from a piece of cloth or from the earth itself.

My synesthesia generally leaves me with a *sense* of the missing word, its color and, more vaguely, its shape.[1] But this too can be problematic, because *C* and *S* often present themselves in the same hue and with a similar contour. *M* and *N* also bear an amorphous relationship. *T* and *G* as well. *Y* may be all over the map. All of which is to say that synesthesia may mislead as often as it defines.

Until yesterday, this hadn't been a real problem. I simply left a space or a couple of dashes and continued writing. I knew that if I stopped to try to recall the missing word, I would break my flow of thought and feeling. And the harder I tried to remember, the less likely I would be able to do so. Frustration would pile on initial surprise. My anxiety would intensify. Better just continue. Then, when I was relaxed and not straining for memory, the word was likely to present itself in a matter of minutes—sometimes shyly, sometimes flaunting a trickster sneer.

This act of loss and retrieval possesses a definite rhythm, and I often incorporate that rhythm into my writing practice. This is a way of "turning setback into victory," as the old Cuban revolutionary adage goes, of finding something useful in a situation that otherwise causes discomfort or concern. I might be upset for a few seconds, but when I've made my way through the impasse, I find I have an additional layer of meaning. An added ingredient in my ever-evolving exploration of my own creative process to this point in my life.

Until yesterday.

Yesterday, as I reached out to grasp the word I sought, I saw a splash of watery gray blue whose curled edges showed glimpses of metallic silver gray. I sensed *C*, or possibly *S*. But nothing surfaced. I was writing e-mails to a few friends and so—why not?—asked if they could provide the elusive word. Some responded, one even with a list of possibilities. None were the one I was looking for. I asked Barbara. She had no idea. I called my brother. He wasn't home.

My day unfolded. Hours passed. I tried to forget my need for the specific word but every once in a while found myself returning to that place where curiosity and anxiety do battle, the latter almost always getting in the winning jab. How could someone like myself, for whom words are palette and tool, solace and weaponry, lose one on such familiar ground? Lose one and not find it quickly—or at all?

Of course, it's not the loss of a single word that causes fear bordering on pain but imagining this as my future: a place emptied of language—what I love best, the tool kit I work with every day, what I need to keep expressing that which I still have to say.

Is this momentary or progressive? That's the troubling question.

"It's a stifling social quality," I insisted. "Counterproductive in the long run. And so many people on the left have it. It's the way so many political organizations treat those who don't think exactly as they do. And religions too . . . any sort of club, really." I was running circles around the lost syllables, still unable to gather them up and pin them down.

In response to my pleading, people came up with a few words that did indeed start with a *C*: coercion, (political) correctness. They weren't the one I sought. I decided to take a hot bath, immerse my body in its penetrating warmth, hoping the physical relaxation might help dislodge the nasty barrier from my brain. Nothing. Whatever it was that stood in my way, whatever pale membrane had stretched itself between me and the word I needed, seemed impossible to pierce.

And then, many hours later, talking to Barbara and calmer now, I revisited my dilemma, and she produced the missing word with the ease of someone conversing about the weather or a marketing list.

"Sectarian." It was a question, but the tone of her voice didn't rise at the end, no question mark at all. Even before I said, "Yes, that's it," and relaxed into gratitude, our shared familiarity with this game of hide-and-seek told her she'd solved the puzzle.

Like a film in which a giant jigsaw puzzle lays half-finished on the floor, in my psyche every piece fell quietly into place. No fanfare. No fuss. It all just came together as it should.

My body relaxed.

Okay, so the word didn't start with a *C* but with an *S*. I'm usually finally so relieved to be able to touch the contours of the straggler, I don't tend to think about what losing a particular word may mean. Rarely do I imagine its specific profile could have something to do with my misplacement of it.

Sectarian provoked additional questions.

I myself indulged in terrible sectarianism in my youth. As I've come to detest that attitude in all its forms, I've worked hard to banish it from my conduct and relationships. I may feel I am right, but who knows? I have learned to honor others' experiences and ideas, consider them fully instead of merely pretending to do so.

Was my forgetting the word *sectarian* a cover-up for some hidden milestone in my life? Could forgetting that word and not some other mean something I have yet to decipher? Up to now, I have only grappled with the rather prosaic phenomenon of forgetting itself. It might be any word or series of words. Moving past its absence, trying to forget there's been a problem, has almost always resulted in sooner rather than later being able to retrieve it from a mental database still fairly functional despite more and more frequent memory lapses.

Relax, oil the rusty cogs, think about something else, and the word will come.

But this time it wasn't just the anguished length of time between forgetting and finding that engaged my attention. It was also the word itself. Forgetting sectarian is different from forgetting the name of a long-ago acquaintance, a date, or a type of cheese rarely eaten. I wondered if my mind—still so full of the important connections even as it seems to disdain the trivia—was telling me something, something to which I should be paying attention.

As I grow older, and quite apart from those irritating alterations caused by the aging process, I find I am becoming more tolerant. It is not a tolerance with coddling room. My values, commitment, and sense of risk are as solid and rebellious as ever. But experience has taught me there are many ways of reaching a goal. These may depend on people's different histories, cultures, belief systems, and experiences, sometimes also on issues of class, gender, race, and age. Some may be more viable than those I have defended as the only way to go.

And sometimes elements of one approach and elements of another can build a sturdier bridge than the one I have crossed. Whatever the case, listening to another's ideas always has something to offer, even if it only reaffirms one's own convictions.

It may be the sectarianism of my youth that most shames me going forward. How many people did I humiliate, push away, or diminish in their dignity or creative potential? I remind myself that dogmatism is also a natural outgrowth of being young and passionate in a society wallowing in conformism and hypocrisy. A certain sort of sectarianism may have been necessary to structure my own commitment. It may have facilitated the energy and devotion that make twenty-hour workdays possible. Indeed, these are qualities that allow some to struggle, to give up all manner of comfort and security and die for causes that remain valid and rekindle my hope even today.

It is easy to disavow youthful excess or mistakes and important to acknowledge that it is often through them that one grows to embrace a more nuanced and compassionate attitude toward life—and self. As I have come to appreciate a gentler consciousness, I also want to be careful to honor the discovery and exuberance of my early years. If we pretend we came to our current positions without pitfalls or mistakes, we cannot be believable or viable role models for those coming along behind us.

At the same time, I want to honor what's happening to me now. On the one hand, I am coming to a place of greater depth and more comprehensive understanding of the complexities of human thought and experience. On the other, I am experiencing the alternating layers of distress and jubilation endemic to moving through the initial stages of memory loss, even as I recognize a place of greater connection.

I don't want to minimize the distress. My father died of Alzheimer's. Anyone who has lived with a loved one in the grip of that disease has seen it rip the skin of identity from a human being until it leaves only uncertainty and loss. Family members of the next generation cannot be immune to the fear they too may become afflicted. And inheritance isn't the only factor bringing the danger close. I believe that the many sorts of contamination to which modernity subjects us also take their toll: pollution of air, water, and food and the radiation emanating from our everyday use of so many commonplace electronic devices.

And then there is information overload. When we can Google anything instantly, thus making it unnecessary to keep the knowledge we once treasured in our minds, memory trembles on uneasy ground. When our Internet server reads and processes our mail, tells us to whom we must write, and tries to sell us products our own use of language tells it we may find enticing, information moves far beyond our capacity to keep up.

There are also those things that have been done to us, assaults that have erased whole pieces of our memories. These range from early childhood abuse to media misinformation and the system's refusal to teach us our real histories. All these things—from watching a loved one die of Alzheimer's and wondering when it may strike inherited genes to an awareness of the possible trade-off every time I lift a cell phone to my ear or walk through the radiation blast of airport security—are part of twenty-first-century living.

But perhaps forgetting the word sectarian points to a different kind of memory failure. Perhaps I should inscribe this experience on the positive side of my imaginary ledger. If I forgot the word, does it mean I may also be forgetting the conditioning that spawned it and can finally say sectarianism no longer comes so easily?

I hope so, for this would be a good thing, one of the many that hover at the edges of memory loss and, at least so far, give me a new map of wonder to explore.

Horizon

Most people think the world is round.

I'm sure it's flat, if not scientifically, at least incrementally or metaphorically. How else could we have horizons, those magical lines where everything converges, stops, and then (sometimes) is given a second chance? Advancing human thought doesn't always mean progress, at least not in the poetic sphere.

A horizon: that line at once so immediate and yet so inescapably out of reach. The two-headed serpent that draws our gaze even in nighttime darkness or with our eyes closed, keeping track of everything we say or do. Food without taste, song without melody, poem without words.

A silence darker than itself.

I remember when I used to work in the darkroom; I would transfer each roll of exposed film from its canister onto a stainless steel bobbin, a spindle with two end coils around which its width had to fit in perfect alignment. This had to be done in absolute darkness, and I learned to guide myself by touch.

No part of the film's surface could be allowed to rub up against any other. A narrow passage of air had to exist between each loop, so the developer bath could reach the entire length of the roll. If you finished and could feel that the film wasn't flush with the bobbin's outermost edge, you knew you had to unwind it and start again. Otherwise, an unknown number of frames would stick together in the developing process and be ruined. Sometimes, especially at the beginning, I wound and unwound and rewound several times before getting it right.

The transference of film to bobbin was accomplished in darkness, not even a safelight to illuminate my fingers along possible wayward edges. But I always shut my eyes as well. I knew squeezing my eyes shut didn't make it any darker than if I kept them open. It was instinct, a way of bringing the horizon of my task to skilled immediacy and also of bringing my own intimate horizon in line with the horizons I had photographed in my search for that moment that means everything.

Far-off happens on the horizon. It captures your attention, but you are never able to make it all the way there. It's always just at the edge of the field or top of the hill, a distance impossible to breach.

Weather is horizon's best friend and can also be a dangerous visitor.

A great dark funnel of swirling wind comes barreling from the horizon to where you stand, flattening everything in its path. When the tornado has passed (on its way to another horizon), no one could have predicted whether you would be the mother clutching young children while searching in vain for your neighbor's home, or the neighbor who is irretrievably somewhere else, perhaps in a place where horizons no longer matter.

Raging flames—their sight and sound and stench—fly to heights you cannot imagine, devouring life as they race you through the night, destroying your known horizon as they grow hotter and nearer and more menacing. Choking smoke closes in. Get out. Get out now. Make a run for a safer horizon, capable of knitting clean land to transparent sky.

Floodwaters rush down, then rise up. Your horizon disintegrates beneath your feet, climbs your legs. Those waters have your mouth and nose in their crosshairs. Perhaps they will soon congeal to the heaviness of mud, burying you before you know what hit. Or the dark silhouette of a volcano cone, clearing its throat in the night, spews dancing orange cinders meant to compete with any chorus of halos.

Like Pompeii's rage of lava, new spills imprison bodies in every daily activity. We will never know when or how the mind's horizon recedes in the moment that physical horizon melts and burns.

Avalanches wield a similar sword. Snow and ice travel down a mountainside, for all intents and purposes, faster than the speed of light. Little wands make a poor showing. Weight and cold bring numbness. Then they bring nothing.

I have often imagined a plane crash, the extinction of all horizons in a bursting ball of fire, or horizons tumbling every which way during the brief seconds of that last hurtle through space. This was how I pictured the horizons of plane crashes until I viewed a documentary about the Uruguayan plane that went down in the Chilean Andes in 1972. Amazingly, half the passengers lived. As they subsisted for more than two months, their horizon of absolute whiteness promised one thing and then another. Eventually, after a heroic trek by two of the survivors, a rescue was made, and a horizon of life reappeared. Horizons can change when we least expect them to.

When I am at the bottom of the Grand Canyon, more precisely at its deepest passage—in what they call the Inner Gorge—arms of polished schist in convoluted sculptural forms hold me close. They rock me back and forth. The canyon rim, rising a mile above, the visible blue of sky and its horizon in time, seems to belong only tangentially to the world I inhabit. There is a lip of rock I barely discern, head bent backward on straining neck. When the sun retreats, those last moments of light along its edge fade like disappearing gold: horizon as nature's last great gift, dazzling.

Horizon on the desert is always distant and sometimes broken by a line of enormous mountains appearing like gentle ripples from this place of my significant insignificance. Color guides that horizon to my eyes: pale oranges and tans and dusty purples, the gray green of sage and cactus, the ordinariness of sand and broken stone. Perhaps a dash of Indian paintbrush or the yellow or pink blossoms of a prickly pear. Long-armed chollas bloom fuchsia, claret cups deep cadmium. On Jordan's Wadi Rum, the dunes are a throbbing red and ancient rose. I watch my dissolving footprints behind me, struggling to keep up.

Another music sounds.

In cities, horizons hold overlapping strata of busyness between their sticky fingers. Depending on urban size and time of night or day, skyscrapers may blink grids adorned with a million lights. Concrete, steel, and glass blocks compete for my attention, take me by the hand, lead me into new stories with characters I meet for the first time. Raised highways loop into great arcs, with vehicles moving along them as if they are toys. Cityscapes hold me in their fists of steamy breath and competing colors. Language becomes cacophony. Under city streets, other horizons unfold along tracks disappearing through dark tunnels. Horizon beneath horizon beneath horizon.

Horizons are shape-shifters, morphing according to the cultures they shelter: minarets and domes rise along them in the Islamic countries, Gothic towers in Christian Europe, gilt gables in Buddhist Thailand or Vietnam, pontificating needles in Mormon Utah, simple steeples and weathervanes in the Protestant reaches of New England. Even landscape is different: how earth and weather respond to how we say their names.

And those cultures move backward and forward in time, no gesture of consideration for linear reason. China's Great Wall is a horizon that speaks its own language, just as England's Stonehenge, Cairo's Pyramids, Sidney's Opera House, or Paris's Eifel Tower. On Easter Island, horizon looms part seascape, part silhouette of great stone moai, sentinels in a place they have changed by virtue of continuing to stand guard in silent response to every unanswered question.

At Ollantaytambo, in Peru's Urubamba Valley, I climb slowly from the village to the much more ancient ridge of rock brought across river and plain to stand at the center of the world.[1] The stone steps are uneven and endless. Someone plays a reed flute, its minor key overflowing ears into anxious lungs. At the very top is the sectioned monolith with its faint stepped pattern, descending and ascending in equal measure. My Cicero tells me it means, "coming from nowhere, going nowhere," a horizon of mystical proportions.

In jungle canopies I sway and balance over narrow swinging bridges on cables that skim a leafy horizon, exploding density of different greens filled with birds and monkeys and all manner of living creatures. While on the Sahara or Mojave, the horizon can devour: endless treachery threatening plodding feet. In the Himalaya or Andes, towers of ice filter light through prisms of danger, and deep white chasms turn luminous blue a mile beneath your feet.

At sea the horizon often hides itself, water indistinguishable from sky, both coming together in a gray-blue envelope of calm demeanor, then without warning or excuse leaping in gigantic waves. Great bodies of water cover unimaginable depths of shipwreck and bone, wild gardens and free-for-alls, a world belonging to other species whose conversation carries thousands of miles.

Thunder may roll, rain may fall from the sky, glaciers may melt, waves may scream and mount and churn, but the ocean hardly notices her surface has changed until humans in their careless disregard decide a coastline is expendable or a tiny island nation too small to matter.

In moments of treachery we change horizons forever: Genghis Kahn on his rampage across Europe, slave ships sailing the Atlantic, the billowing smokestacks of Auschwitz, fire-bombings of Dresden and Tokyo, atomic leveling of Hiroshima, slash and burn in Vietnam and then Guatemala, or sea of machetes tearing at Rwanda's once-sultry air. Sudan's Lost Boys make their exhausted way to a horizon that never comes. Arrivals stumble and fall. And so, humans, in greed and criminality, continue to weave horizons according to whim. Like the crazed uncle, knitting an afghan of horror beneath his frozen smile.

We change horizons by erecting walls, cutting landscape open, breaking it apart. Commanding you to stay on that side, us on this. Berlin. Palestine. Mexico and the United States. Walls made of rusting bedsprings, recycled war materiel, concrete, or virtual espionage. Walls that separate people and animal habitats twist lives, tear life from life, death from death.

Artists, with a passion to change such horizons, plant and cultivate and, where the earth itself has died, paint trees and flowers on cement born in barren disregard. Activists offer water where there is thirst and solace where law, with its voracious fangs, lies in deadly wait.

When a person is exiled from the place where friends passing on the street elicit the nod of a head or tender smile, where greetings are easily understood and every gesture familiar and kind, horizon bends to accommodate new sounds and smells. When war or natural disaster uproots a person and he or she must embrace another language, other images and customs, horizons try hard to keep up and almost always fail.

Imposed migrations drag horizons behind them, holding tight but in constant terror of losing their grip. When evil descends on people, forcing them into ghettos, concentration camps, solitary cells, or torture chambers, within those last moments before death's relief, victims become survivors on the indelible horizons of their own voices, a fragmented scream, even one sad breath.

At the bottom of the world, horizon knits into an icy nipple. In all directions: the fish-eye perspective. Horizon is everywhere and nowhere, then, in that circle that has become a dot, figures walking forever, no one at all.

When the world "out there" becomes unbearable, horizon reduces to a point of imagination, deep within the still resisting self.

Sex

Not love. Not intimacy. Unadorned sex.

In most western societies it's the biggest marquee item, bar none. In the more sexually repressive societies, with their own codes and permissions, its culture is also as unhealthy and unfair as in ours. Only the mirror's surface shows a different face. How do we approach sex in social configurations so skewed by patriarchal values, with their hypocrisy and pressures, especially on women, to appear chaste and diffident while struggling with the same needs and passions most of us share?

Sex goes back to the beginning of time, fills myth and legend, and is pictured in ancient rock art and other imagery throughout the world. It is featured in religious texts, sometimes with beautiful illustrations. There was a time when it existed free of the distortions and misconceptions with which it is burdened today. But its seduction, hijacking, bribery, and blackmail potentials were always irresistible to those in power.

Prostitution, linked to sex in popular perception, has been called the oldest profession, although what prostitution is and how it fits into our social fabric is more often than not misconstrued. The buying and selling of sex is a business transaction, not a sexual encounter. Certainly it has little to do with pleasure for the woman.

Contrary to most modern-day business transactions, in prostitution it is the seller who is most often taken advantage of. In the United States she (most prostitutes are women) is punished, while pimps and johns enjoy the male privilege of impunity. In some places, over the past several decades, sex workers (what many prefer to call themselves) have organized; their demands range from better working and health oversight conditions to a more realistic way of judging the occupation within the overall framework of society.

Whether for occasional sale or practiced within the context of the longer-term business contract called marriage, sex in all our societies is overwhelmingly defined as a man inserting his penis into a woman's vagina and reaching orgasm. Anything else doesn't quite fit the definition, as Bill Clinton wanted us to believe when he tried to talk his way out of his affair with Monica Lewinsky.[1] Modernity has given women the hope that we too have a right to experience orgasm, but this is secondary. And many women, because perception is still so much more important than reality, have found ways of faking their pleasure.

Further, if women don't reach orgasm, it is generally assumed to be our fault. And since the main act is all-important and male pride is to be protected at all costs, asking for what we need or challenging the man often opens the door to embarrassment, derision, or abuse.

Mutual trust, comfort, foreplay, and other subtleties are less often discussed. Many acts of physical intimacy may be enjoyed by men and women, same-sex couples, and girls and boys who have learned to stop short of "going all the way," for fear of pregnancy or contracting a sexually transmitted disease. But these are not really seen as sex. Today many couples as young as eleven or twelve, ignorant of how disease is spread, practice oral sex in the mistaken belief that they can thus avoid all danger. The phrase "going all the way" says it all.

That accomplishing the sex act in this primary male-to-female way is essential to living a successful life can be seen in the inundation of advertisements for Viagra and other drugs that combat erectile dysfunction, the ill that seems to be the malaise of our age. To judge from the percentage of all pharmaceutical advertising that is given over to sexual malfunction, one would think it a more serious threat than cancer or heart disease. In the United States, health insurance also almost always covers male inability to perform, while it may not cover serious women's health issues. Physical problems and/or insecurities of all sorts may prevent men from achieving erections, and these performance-enhancing drugs are guaranteed to fix the problem, although most ads warn that if a man experiences an erection lasting longer than four hours, he should see his doctor. One has to wonder about the time frame.

This type of male-female penetrative sex is almost always meant, then, when the word sex is used, and a number of religions also stipulate that procreation should be its only or primary goal. But other acts between consenting adults also garner some degree of notice. Some of these are considered natural—others not so much. Position is important; the man being on top mimics his importance in patriarchal society. Tops and bottoms also insinuate power relations among homosexuals. In many societies, as long as men assume the top position, they can convince themselves and others that they are not gay.

It's not hard to understand, in the puritanical value system we have devised, that anal sex performed by two men may repulse traditional sensibilities. Lesbians still fly below the radar to the extent that most dyed-in-the-wool heterosexuals cannot even imagine how we can achieve sexual pleasure without a man. Although we now know that human sexual desire occurs along a long curve and that there are as many manifestations of desire as subjects on that curve, the seal of social approval is still only given to the most obstinately heterosexual.

In recent years, certain social groups also feel freer to speak about sexual practices that have been around for millennia but generally hidden from view. Bondage and sadomasochism (S&M) have been rather publicly reclaimed by some men and women and by a small sector within the lesbian movement as a practice allowing women to control the degree of pain they want to endure. (I say lesbian movement rather than lesbian population, because movements advocate for attitudes while populations may prefer their habits and preferences to remain private.)

I want to talk for a moment about sexual practices that involve the infliction and reception of physical pain. Particularly in an era in which torture is widespread and its legitimacy considered a subject for debate, I find it horrifying that some would advocate for the infliction of pain in sexual relationships.[2] Note that I say infliction. Consenting adults, in my opinion, should be able to indulge in whatever makes them happy, as long as it harms no one else. But the loud claim that S&M has feminist overtones seems to me to be specious at best. In an era in which war, illegal imprisonment, and even the presumed safety of the family subject so many human beings to the brutality of torture, what sort of physical and/or psychological damage causes some people to believe freedom from that damage may be found in situations of controlled pain? Has our need for trust through tenderness been dismantled beyond repair?

One thing that has changed in a positive direction since I was an adolescent is the double standard between young males and females. For one thing, we acknowledge that they experiment at ever-younger ages. How could they not in a society in which sexual images and messages are everywhere? Just Say No, purity rings, and other campaigns stressing abstinence have been tried, almost always unsuccessfully. More realistic parents and teachers advocate for good sex education and provide safety devices for young people who they know will engage in sexual activity whether or not they may be emotionally ready. In many Western societies today, young women initiate relationships almost as easily as men, and are much more able to end them when they no longer work.

No longer is heterosexuality assumed to be the norm, at least not in the more sophisticated enclaves here in the United States; and no longer do men enjoy the privilege of infidelity, while women are expected to be faithful. Many cultural communities still forgive all manner of male transgression because "boys will be boys," but young women who are abused can often find a safe place where equality is valued. And thoughtful individuals of all genders are creating communities where their needs and practices are honored.

One might not notice this change from the messages we are given. In films, books, songs, what passes for news, toys, commercial advertising, and so much else, images of women are still overwhelmingly heterosexual, subservient, and reactive—all those Barbie bodies and batting eyelashes. The fashion and cosmetic industries still dress us up as dolls. But some degree of rebellion and change is evident.

One instigator of this change is buying power. When groups such as gay men or women, young people, vegetarians, or even social-change activists become an important voting bloc or spend large amounts of money on marriage or domestic partnership, household goods, or vacation destinations, the establishment is willing to tolerate the sex they are perceived as having. In sexuality, just as in every other arena, there's always a group at the bottom of the ladder. And without a real understanding of difference, there is almost always fear. In this regard, transsexuals, transgender, and gender-neutral people are still hated, feared, threatened, and attacked, often with impunity.

It's taken a while for the most repressive attitudes to begin to wane, most of my lifetime in fact. I was born into a white, middle-class, assimilated Jewish family in 1936, right between the Great Depression and World War II. My parents experienced the flapper era of New York City speakeasies, the years of jazz, blues, and illegal but freely available alcohol. Mother used to tell stories of wild nights at Harlem's Cotton Club. But they had their children during the period leading up to the war, an era of greater uncertainty, austerity, and inhibition.

Soon the McCarthy fifties came along, and fear was a subtle companion. The big lie began eating away at every facet of U.S. American life. Appearance took center stage. What something looked like became more important than what it was.

I clearly remember the moment I learned the "facts of life," as they were called back then. I was ten. Our family was traveling cross-country, and we'd stopped for the night at a little midwestern motel. Dad turned on the clock radio in our room, and we found ourselves listening to a program on which the newly discovered importance of the Rh factor was being discussed. I asked my parents what difference the father's blood made. The Look passed between my mother and father, and Mother announced I would be sleeping with her that night; Dad would be sharing a room with my younger siblings. My parents subscribed to the modern idea that when a child asked a question, it showed he or she was ready to understand the answer.

That night my mother explained human sexuality. She began slowly, with the birds and the bees. I knew there had to be more to this important conversation and begged her to get to the point. But when she did, and despite her efforts at making the explanation acceptable, I felt confused and repulsed. Ever attracted to extremes, I decided then and there I would either give myself to science by mating with a large gorilla or join a convent. Looking back, I realize Mother's description must have focused on the mechanics more than on the emotions and feelings that should, in the best of cases, surround the sexual act. How could it have been otherwise? Hard as she tried, she had only her own experience to draw on.

Would it have been better or worse if I had found out about sex from neighborhood kids or school friends? Probably not better. Mother at least had the anatomical details down. In any case, my immediate reaction only lasted a short time. Like most other young girls of my time, class, and culture, I eagerly fell in line behind the messages and images fabricated to seduce me. For several years I was your absolutely typical teenager. It would take a while for me to question the accepted premises about sex or anything else.

My parents talked openly about sexuality—to a point. That is, they encouraged us to ask questions and were forthcoming with answers, insofar as they were able to provide them. In so many ways they were well ahead of their time. Nudity was common in our home; the human body was not something about which we were taught to be ashamed. Looking back, there may even have been a slight degree of voyeurism. But the main problem was that Mother and Dad's own sexual and love relationship was not a happy one, and this created a deficient model, rife with tense undercurrents and silences. Basically, we were taught to settle.

Mother eventually told us she had never really been in love with our father but had married him when the man she adored preferred someone else. Dad, for his part, never stopped loving our mother. Their sixty-two-year marriage unfolded around his commitment and patience, only occasionally punctuated by frustrated verbal explosions and her on-again, off-again affairs with other men. Ours was an atypical family, in which the wife sought pleasure elsewhere while the husband remained stoic, and neither of them knew how to approach their problem differently.

I would eventually come to believe that my mother suffered from undiagnosed depression, but she would have been the last person to acknowledge that or to seek help. So much less was known about the disease in her time; and for the uninformed, seeking psychotherapy was evidence of mental illness. I'm talking about a time when even mention of the word cancer was unthinkable. In an era in which appearances were everything, it was better to suffer in silence and without solidarity than to admit you were "defective."

Those affairs didn't ultimately afford Mother much joy. Once, toward the end of her life, I asked why she had gone with so many men. She responded without hesitation that she'd simply wanted to be wanted. Dad wanted her, desperately. But his wasn't the want she wanted. What Mother's pattern of infidelity did to me, I now believe, was give me the sense that sex was secret and somehow illicit and that there was no real connection between what one did in that area of one's life and what one said one did.

As a young girl, coming into my own sexuality, I simply assumed I would fall in love with the perfect man, marry, and have children. Heterosexuality and the nuclear family structure were the norms. We had an aunt who lived with her lifelong female partner, but the word lesbian wasn't yet part of our lexicon. My parents liked Janet, and we socialized with her and Phyllis fairly often. But even many years later, long after both were gone, when I referred to them as lesbians, Mother would say, "Well, we don't really know that, do we? They never used that word." I also had an uncle who said he was gay but "had never given into it." Presumably, he considered this to be a strength. He was depressed his entire life, his misery and resulting discomfort sad to behold.

And so, although homosexuals numbered among my parents' friends and family, it was still a heterosexual world. Antigay jokes and disparaging remarks were frequent and went unchallenged. Neither in my childhood home nor, more importantly, in the community at large did I get the message that it would be acceptable if I loved a woman. It just wasn't on the list of appropriate choices.

So I didn't think about it, but I did experience certain feelings. As I didn't come out as a lesbian until I was in my late forties, I can only revisit those youthful memories in retrospect: the way it felt to touch my childhood friend Meave's soft cheek when we played doctor in the back yard; the shortness of breath that surprised me each time I was in the presence of my high school gym teacher; and the recognizable longing, years later, during an encounter with a British theater director I knew for a few brief hours.

Some people clearly know their sexual identity from their earliest sense of self. Others must wade through layers of trying and failing to fit in. I would not say I was always a lesbian, rather that I was a sexual being who early on followed the social path of least resistance and later, when I was able to make a real choice, was able to find my life companion. Today I identify as a lesbian at least as much because of its political implications as because of the fact that I live with and love another woman.

But I want to return to sexual desire in and of itself. The strongest body memory I have of sexuality, as I began to notice boys and date, was a persistent sense of something not being right. It was always as if I just missed the bus or train. I would yearn for a particular boy to ask me out. There was no possibility of my asking him, and so right then and there I was forced into coy flirtation, that manipulative stance through which young girls were taught to make our desires known without alluding to them openly. From then on, it was more about power and powerlessness than about sex.

While working undercover to get a boy to notice me seemed normal at the time, I now understand that it fostered a way of being rooted in playacting and deception. It also fit with the way my mother related to others, not just Dad or her various lovers, but everyone. She rarely asked directly for what she wanted, preferring to steer a situation in the direction she wished until someone else suggested her preferred solution, to which she would then delightedly agree.

I was always a pretty good actor and became quite adept at getting what I wanted, whether or not I was able to ask outright. When I had my eye on a boy, he usually came around. But then another much more serious conflict arose, that between what he expected and what I was willing or able to give.

In my class and culture, in 1950s Albuquerque, New Mexico, being perceived as a Good Girl was paramount. Our high school had its smattering of Bad

Girls, and no one wanted that disdain heaped on them. A few had "easy" reputations, evidenced by their popularity among the school's studs. One or two, it was rumored, had even had to go off somewhere to a home for unwed mothers, to give birth to a child they would never see again. That tragedy, of course, went utterly unexamined. Rules were rules, and becoming pregnant was a "fate worse than death." And so I did my best to make acceptable choices and, I am deeply ashamed to say, also did my share of shunning those girls who didn't.

But it wasn't so easy to determine which of these choices was acceptable or whether it really mattered if others knew, because there was perception and reality, and the two didn't often coincide. Some of the more popular girls at my high school began dating boys with whom they would remain for years, sometimes even marrying them. For those of us who couldn't attain that early state of grace, there was a succession of superficial partners: some as timid and uncertain as we were, some schooled by their fathers in how to treat a Good Girl (there were always some Bad Girls available to take the pressure off), and some who felt entitled to take what they wanted no matter what. With all of these, there was the terrible contradiction between acting as we were taught to act and avoiding the "fate worse than death."

Despite my sexual insecurities, I was becoming enough of my own person to be able to protect myself against the latter. I owed this self-confidence to my father, who early on taught me to fight back against overeager men and other dangers. When I dated a dropout who roughed me up—I remember him thrusting his tongue into my mouth hard, as if it were a bayonet, something that felt more like basic training than pleasure—I broke loose and rejected his further advances.

When, much to my surprise and delight, the captain of the downtown high school's football team asked me out, and then tried to rape me, I brought my knee into his groin as my father had taught me, leapt from his car, and ran for miles until I made it home. At first I feared he would follow me, but of course he didn't. It wasn't me in particular he wanted, but the conquest.

My mother's response to that night of trauma was to get up when she heard my key in the lock and my near-hysterical crying and to ask what had happened. When I explained, her only question was whether or not penetration had taken place. I said no, and that put an end to our conversation. "Go to sleep," she said, "you'll feel better in the morning." In her mind, only penetration constituted sex. She didn't know how to grapple with my victimization or survival, believing if we just concentrated on the "positive," everything would work out.

So it wasn't about acknowledging trauma or keeping myself safe, at least not back then, but about keeping up appearances. I might have saved myself years of despair had I been able to identify my own feelings and act on them with a sense of entitlement rather than shame. For when it comes to sexuality throughout those early years, shame is the strongest memory I hold. Shame because my desires and the desires of the boys I dated never seemed to match, and I'd been conditioned to believe my desires were wrong. Shame around my mother's affairs, badly kept secrets always threatening our family's acceptance in the community. And shame at every hypocritical difference between what I felt and what I was being taught I was supposed to feel.

The vast majority of my friends must have been suffering as I was. The shame itself kept us from speaking honestly about what we were experiencing. How we talked to one another, or even if we confided in one another at all, followed rules as stringent as those determining how we acted.

And there were other problems, as well, that kept our emotional lives in turmoil. In my sophomore year in high school I found myself attracted to a tall handsome senior who also noticed me. He asked me out and we dated awhile. But it took him a while to kiss me for the first time; and when he did, his lips were pressed shut in a thin, hard line that exuded obligation.

Of course, I thought there must be something wrong with me. I wasn't beautiful enough or seductive enough. I wore the wrong clothes or came from the wrong family. Dave couldn't talk about what was going on with him, nor could I ask. One night, when he and I were at my house, my mother came into the room, grabbed him, planted a big wet one on his startled lips, and said, "See, that's how it's done!" Could she have thought she was helping? My shame was complete. Yet Dave, to his credit, didn't stop calling. I never knew whether his problem was shyness, inexperience, or something else and can only guess that the terrible standard of the day affected him as deeply as it did me.

Later, I had another boyfriend. He came from a welcoming Italian family. His parents liked me and clearly hoped our romance would prosper. But Larry was reluctant to kiss me as well. Had I not had several other boyfriends by then who seemed to enjoy the practice, I might have ended up with a painful complex. I eventually discovered Larry's reticence was because he was gay. He knew this, but in his family and in that era, he could hardly expect to relax into his identity. Despite his parents' eagerness for him to find a nice girl, settle down, and give them grandchildren, it wasn't to be.

After Larry and I stopped dating, we both moved east. We somehow reconnected and, freed from the pretense of high school romance, became real friends, the kind who can talk about the hard things. That was when he revealed his sexual identity, relieving me of the concerns I had harbored about myself. In the 1960s, even in New York, he had a tougher road to walk than I did. I remember a friend of his, also gay, who married a naïve young woman. They were sure, at the time, their love would "cure" him. Years later I ran into the friend, now comfortably living with his longtime male partner.

Male homosexuality was more visible back then, and at least in certain contexts easier to deal with, than its female counterpart. Patriarchy rendered lesbians largely invisible. By this time, the art world was my chosen community. Allen Ginsberg had published his first explicitly gay poems, and some of us began to realize that other great poets and artists throughout history had also been gay.[3] There were a number of painters among the abstract expressionists who were known to be homosexual. Although their identities were accepted, it was still not something most of us outside their most intimate circles discussed.

But again, it wasn't sexual identity as much as sexual desire that I needed to understand, in myself and others. Had I been able to claim the desire, fully and without shame, I'm sure my own identity would have become apparent to me much earlier. As it was, more and more as the years passed I heard myself uttering the strange phrase "I wish I were a lesbian."

In New York City, during the late 1950s and early '60s, "free love" was the order of the day. But it was still really free only for the men. With few exceptions, women in the art world and among the new poets either were groupies or quietly stayed at home with the kids, promoting their male partners' work whenever possible and respecting their demands for creative space. I thought of myself as an incipient poet and acted on the prerogative. I was insatiable enough to also want love, a family. What I most remember in terms of intimacy was that I almost never asked for what I wanted. Not in the sex and not in the relationship itself. The sophisticated stance was that it didn't matter.

I wasn't supposed to care.

I didn't perceive that I was being used by the men I slept with, because free association was the unspoken agreement and I thought it would have been annoying to them had I made demands. My perception didn't always reflect reality. I still remember a man I saw for a while, although I cannot remember his name. Uncharacteristically, I complained about something he had done or failed to do. Rather than take offense, he looked at me with real caring in his eyes and said he was glad I had finally told him what I wanted. I was stunned. Neither he nor any other man had ever given me to understand that was acceptable.

Loneliness was a big part of my life, of course. Loneliness, despite the fact that I had many friends and many lovers and definitely felt myself part of a community, indeed a movement.

Perhaps we women artists relegated the need to be loved to the work itself. And perhaps that made the work stronger. All I know is that when it came to sexual need, there was always some attractive friend or stranger available for an affair of a night or ten or twenty. This was the time before AIDS. We took minimal precautions against pregnancy and disease and managed to think of those sexual encounters as totally disconnected from love or even companionship. I probably had sexual relations of one sort or another with more than a hundred men. Never once did I feel loved—or even understood.

Recently, talking with a group of women friends, all between the ages of fifty and seventy-five, I heard myself referring to that younger version of myself as a slut. Everyone laughed. A great swell of recognition swept the room. We'd all yearned, experimented, stumbled, fallen, and picked ourselves up again and again throughout the initial years of our womanhood.

Later, though, reconsidering the evening, I realized the word didn't fit, not at all. None of us had had casual sex for the sake of the act itself. All of us were looking for something, something that would allow us to share our lives with another human being. We just hadn't been taught—either verbally or by example—where or how to look.

Soon I recognized the overwhelming need to have another human being in my life. There was one way I could achieve that. And so, without thought to marriage or even a stable relationship, I decided to get pregnant. I chose a poet whom I slept with on and off and didn't tell him of my plans for fear he would be taken aback. Which would surely have been the case. Joel Oppenheimer was a good man and a very good poet. He already had four sons from a failed marriage and was suffering from not being able to be a full-time father to them. Of course, I didn't know this, because we never talked about anything of importance, certainly not anything that intimate or difficult.

And so I had my son, Gregory, at a time when having a child without being married wasn't done, at least not in my family's social class and culture, and certainly not intentionally. My father thought my pregnancy had been an accident and offered to pay for an abortion (still illegal at the time). After I gave birth, in a bleak charity hospital on Manhattan's Lower East Side, Mother came to New York to spend some time with her first grandchild. Once this new member of our family existed in flesh and blood, both my parents were supportive—in spite of the shame they were made to feel by friends and other family members.

My maternal grandparents, who lived in New York City, were horrified. They went so far as to tell my parents they thought I should be institutionalized. Their own sexuality was truly sick (more about that later) but safely hidden beyond the stage on which we all operated. Only an uncle, one of my father's brothers, showed a loving attitude toward his grandnephew: he and his wife traveled from their uptown apartment down to the slums where we lived to visit and even babysit.

My artist and writer friends were jubilant at Gregory's birth. They welcomed him wholeheartedly. About three weeks after he was born, Joel came to see his baby boy. He was with a friend. They had been drinking and didn't stay long. Again, we didn't talk. He must have felt I should have considered his situation. I was simply radiant as a new mother, incapable of thinking about anyone other than my child and myself.

Thus began a period of almost twelve years during which Joel, unknown to me, kept track of Gregory through mutual friends and across borders. They eventually got to know one another, and their friendship, until Joel's death, was a joy for them both. Their ability to speak openly about their lives made it possible for Joel and me, as well, to become friends. The sort of friends we never could have been all those years before, when skewed values made real communication so hard. The times had changed.

I took Gregory to Mexico when he was ten months old. By then, I had gotten what I felt I needed from New York. I had learned one could be a writer anywhere. I was also tired of the difficulties inherent to my impoverished lifestyle in the city. In an era before childcare and other social systems, as a single mother working to support my son, I had very little time to enjoy him, and he was growing so fast. I finally understood, as well, that there must be more to an intimate relationship than casual sex, even when occasionally it might legitimately be called making love.

In Mexico I looked for what had been missing from my New York City liaisons, namely respect, commitment, and the desire to build a life together. I'm sure being a mother at least partially influenced my realization that I didn't want to continue as I had. Mexican poet Sergio Mondragón and I met, fell in love, founded a cutting-edge bilingual literary magazine, and eventually married. Sergio seemed to be everything the men in my life in New York weren't. He wanted to make a home, be a father to Gregory, have more children. All of which we did.

But as tends to happen in unexamined lives and would happen several more times in mine, in believing I was choosing someone radically different from my previous partners, I ended up with the same sort of men. Only their outward characteristics differed. In my effort to distance myself from casual sexual liaisons, I fell headlong into the red-hot crater of male jealousy. Latin male jealousy. Or maybe just the male jealousy this particular man exuded because of his own painful burden of social hypocrisy and shame.

Before we were even married, we were eating lunch in a small café one day, when my soon-to-be-husband suddenly fell silent, his face a dark mask of barely concealed rage. I asked him what was wrong, but he wouldn't say. When we left the restaurant, he exploded. Right there on the street, in front of dozens of amused passersby, he accused me of having stared at a group of men at a nearby table, of having "played him for a fool."

I hadn't even noticed those men. I was probably spaced out, immersed in my own thoughts. But no amount of frantic explanation on my part convinced Sergio he was acting irrationally. Eventually things between us calmed, and our relationship resumed its course. In later years, I often remembered that incident, though. I thought if I had recognized the warning signs, I might have avoided the marriage and saved myself years of grief. But then, I wouldn't have continued my process of maturation. And I wouldn't have had my two middle daughters, whom I adore.

Sex itself was no more the problem in Mexico than it had been in New York. It was what went along with sex that kept me frustrated and dismayed. And that was the thing: sex got all the attention, while other aspects of relationships needed so much tenderness and work. Giving birth to Sarah and Ximena, my two daughters with Sergio, as well as growing politically, founding and editing a literary magazine, and developing my own writing filled the ensuing years in ways that relegated thinking about sexuality to a distant sphere.

But answers were on the horizon, breathtaking and ferocious. In Mexico I discovered feminism. It wasn't yet Mexican feminism but that which was coming into its own at the time in the United States and Western Europe.[4] Documents, philosophical essays, and articles from the new feminist movement arrived in books and magazines, and friends brought tales of collective actions that shook me to the core.

My encounter with feminist thought marked an important before and after in my life, and the after has never stopped shaping me. For the first time, I began to understand that all the sexual shame and uncertainty, all those failures with men, weren't my "fault" but reflected a social double standard, millennia of patriarchal law and attitudes that blame women for every act not aimed at cherishing men. I cannot overemphasize the power of that revelation.

Anyone who knows feminist history knows the stages its second wave went through: from theoretical treatises to consciousness raising groups, new analyses of patriarchy to mass actions and revolutionary pronouncements, attacks on traditional media messages to struggles to break through the glass ceiling and change discriminatory law. Some women separated from men temporarily or even permanently, and a number of women turned to other women for their intimate relationships. Some of us eventually came to understand that patriarchal values and attitudes rob men of their humanity just as they rob women of ours. Which is not to say the damage is the same.

Some women who came out as lesbians discovered that to be their true identity. Others eventually went back to men or opted to live alone. Some chose celibacy. Most came to understand that this is not about sex per se but about a whole new system of values. The important thing for most women touched by feminism was that we were able, as much as possible, to throw off the burden of unhealthy lifestyles, shame, false expectations, overly sexualized fantasy, twisted ideas of male-female interaction, and the social hypocrisy that had affected us all so deeply. In my particular case, I believe I began having honest friendships with men for the first time, friendships not eternally burdened by sexual expectations. Women of my generation, although never entirely free of the damage done, gained a new basis from which to think, feel, and act.

There's a distance, of course, between studying theory and internalizing ideas and feelings. It's a process, often a very long one. My process took me from personal discovery to wondering about women in other cultures, getting excited about their lives, and embarking on a long career of writing oral history with women. Gradually I was able to incorporate feminist attitudes and actions more fully into my own life. And with some pride I can say I was able to model those attitudes and actions for my children, grandchildren, students, and contemporaries. My children may feel I failed them in certain ways, but I think they are emotionally healthier for having had a feminist mother.

I still had years to go before I could easily spot the danger signals with regard to my intimate relationships. My next partner was a U.S. American who declared himself a feminist—why not? He'd lived in the States much more recently than I and knew the jargon well. He talked a very good line. But we confronted the same struggles many couples were experiencing at that time, around trust, monogamy, jealousy, shared housework and childcare, and the ability to support each other's work in equitable ways.

Sex in and of itself was never a problem. It was mostly pleasurable. But I was beginning to learn to separate sex from intimacy and how easily the two could be confused. Robert and I had the added privilege (or problem, depending on how one looked at it) that came from having gone to live in revolutionary Cuba a year and a half into our relationship. Cuba helped us grow in so many ways. It embraced our children and taught us what working for a better society could be like.

But despite the revolution's stated commitment to women's equality, the Cubans still harbored many unexamined ideas about male and female roles. The fact that those roles still existed in a revolutionary society was even more confusing. Sometimes they came into conflict with Robert's and my home-grown attempts to create an equitable relationship. Making revolution, or building a new society, also provides a poor context for paying attention to personal issues. We tended to push our intimate needs and questions aside as we worked for the greater good.

Sometimes when I look back on our life together, I think Robert and I worked so hard at trying to create something different, something better, that success was inevitably sacrificed to the frustrations of the struggle itself. After he and I separated, I had two more long-term relationships with men. Both had their problems as well as their beautiful moments. When hurrying full speed ahead down a path of no return, one can spin far from one's deepest needs. Age also influences decisions. Children grow up and build their own lives. Creative work claims a more central place. Other battles encroach. All of this and more happened in my life.

Early in 1984, when I returned to the United States, I was exhausted by years of revolutionary struggle, the demands of another language and other cultures, the tragic loss of many beloved comrades, and the beginnings of the collective identity crisis that would come for so many of us with the worldwide defeat of socialism. Even without the U.S. government ordering my deportation and the five-year battle to regain my citizenship, reentry would have been tough.[5] I had to learn how to live without my children, how to operate in a capitalist system, how to earn a living. And I was closing in on fifty.

Sex was probably one of the furthest things from my mind. And yet, looking back, I realize I continued to use it as I had for years: as momentary diversion and solace. Importantly, a strong women's community welcomed me home. And it was those strong women, individually and collectively, who helped me center myself and become who I was meant to be.

It was a woman's movement, not a lesbian movement, although many of the women were lesbians. And the lesbian identity was unremarkable in this place where I landed. That alone was noteworthy. I had known and been close to lesbians in Mexico, Cuba, and Nicaragua, but all of them lived hidden or semi-hidden lives. It wasn't safe for them to do otherwise. In this new time and place, women-loving women had paid their collective dues. They had fought their way from outsiders to quasi insiders. They were ready and willing to live their lives in the open and to model that willingness to a sister.

And so it was that about a year after my return, in a casual conversation with a friend, I suddenly heard her say, "When you come out . . . " I can't even remember the second part of that sentence. All I know is that my own woman-identified sexuality had never specifically occurred to me before that moment. Now it did. Simple as that. Not two weeks later, I was involved in my first relationship with a woman.

Can I say the sex was better than it had been with men? Not necessarily. And yes, of course. It was different, perhaps primarily because making love with someone like oneself allows for a physical knowledge not always available between the genders. But, of course, loving is about much more than physical knowledge. Same-sex relationships have problems just as mixed ones do. Lesbian love, privy to many of the problems of patriarchal society, isn't automatically better just because it is between two women.

One of the things that coming into my sexual self taught me was that the idea of sex as separate from intimacy is wrong. If the sex is satisfying, it is always because it is intimately related to wonder, trust, respect, relationship, and that thing we have such a difficult time learning about but finally come to call love. After a bit more experimentation, I was old enough and wise enough to discover the love I was meant to have, with the woman I've been with now for more than a quarter century.

Barbara and I sometimes say we wish we had found one another earlier. But both of us know we wouldn't have been ready then. She comes from a Christian fundamentalist family in which values and expectations were far more damaging than those in my own family of origin. Hers was a constant minefield compared with my performance space. I suffered incest at the hands of my maternal grandfather while my grandmother looked on, something that surely affected me sexually as well as in other ways. But I had loving parents who provided a buffer, even when they couldn't provide the best example.

Barbara survived criminality; there's no other way to describe what she lived through. Sexually and in many other ways we have had to learn to trust one another, nurture each other's creativity, and grow together. For some time it was a daily challenge. Now it's our life: healthy, mutually nurturing, and built around our art, the people we love, and our hope for social change.

Sex is not about gender or position, gay or straight or bi, young or old, fingers or penis, vagina or anus, this sort of kiss or that. Ultimately, sex is not really about sex—at least not about the sex we have learned to identify as such in societies warped by deceit and shame. Beautiful sex happens when the relationship is beautiful, when both participants or a single individual loving her or his own body, trusts enough to listen and give—two hundred percent.

Wheels

I've never been one of those people passionate about cars for their own sake. It's hit or miss with me when I see an old car on the highway and try to guess its make and year. Living with Barbara, I've gotten a bit more adept at recognizing certain Chevys from the 1950s, especially if they sport that streamlined two-tone aqua and white that sends her heart racing.

Left to my own devices, I appreciate a car that gets me reliably from point A to point B. Like shoes that still have soles or pants and shirts that continue to fit despite the fact they're not the latest fashion. In fact, I derive a certain pleasure from wearing clothes that aren't fashionable or driving a car that is not the latest model but still moves dependably. It's my personal response to industries constantly building in obsolescence so the consumer continues to spend.

Still, I've had my share of automobiles, and they've had their share of idiosyncrasies.

The first car I drove as if it were mine was a pale-blue, bullet-shaped Studebaker belonging to my parents. In underpopulated New Mexico, with its great distances and eager ranch hands, back in the early 1950s a young person could get a learner's permit at twelve and a regular license at fourteen. I did both on my respective birthdays.

My father taught me to drive, kindly and patient until he insisted I learn to change a tire as well. Tires tended to blow or otherwise go flat in those days, so he thought that was important. The driving process involved learning to signal with the left-hand window rolled down. An arm held straight out meant you intended to turn left. Held up, it meant you were turning right. And dropped casually from the elbow, it meant you were about to stop. Your palm faced the car behind you, warning its driver of your intention.

This is such ancient history now that I feel like I must spell it out. I also learned to turn my head for a quick look at what might be coming up on the left side when about to make a turn; Dad warned me of the blind spot not seen in the rearview mirror. Of course, there were no outside mirrors back then. Driving my practice vehicle—which was also my father's car—up onto a pile of pumice blocks was not my finest hour.

Another memory is of the day I backed out of my parents' driveway just as Dad started up from where he had been parked in front of their house. The mild crash wasn't pretty. At such times, Dad's gentleness went a long way. About halfway through high school I got nephritis and had to take it easy for a year or so. Instead of riding the city bus to school like my friends, I had the use of my parents' second car.

After I earned my license, I drove the blue Studebaker a lot. It must have been a late forties or early fifties model. I don't believe my parents ever bought a new car. It wasn't that they could not have afforded one but their Depression-era frugality on display.

One of my most indelible memories with that vehicle was leaving it by the side of some state road and setting out into the desert on foot, geological survey map in hand, to find the perfect spot in which to spend the night, alone and dreaming of prehistory. I did this often, always telling my parents I was spending the night with a girlfriend. My girlfriends were sure I was with a boy. Those secret teenage journeys set my spirit free.

The first car I owned was a dull-brown Austin. I bought it for five hundred dollars from a woman at the insurance office where I worked, then sold it for the same amount to someone else in that office just before I left New Mexico to make my way in the wider world. Two days later that car, which had served me well, imploded. I can still feel the tension in my body when the buyer called me with the news. Did she think I had intentionally unburdened myself just in time? Should I return her money? Apparently she was only letting me know, perhaps waiting for me to make a further move.

I got my first driver's license by looking over a small black-and-yellow booklet about local traffic regulations, answering a few questions, and driving around a small parking lot at the corner of what has since become the New Mexico

State Fairgrounds. I don't remember an eye test or even having to parallel park. Later I taught my friend Elaine de Kooning to drive and suffered with her through two or three failed tests. Her third police officer was Irish, and she beguilingly talked him into passing her just in time for her to hurtle drunk through a low adobe wall and into her living room.

I would spend the next years of my life in Spain. My first husband and I were headed to India. We turned in every wedding present for cash, bought a Lambretta motor scooter, and drove it until it bit the dust (more accurately, an oil slick) on a southern Spanish road. We never made it to India. That little scooter, heavily laden with army surplus knapsacks and sleeping bags, had taken us from Albuquerque to New York, accompanied us on a steamship to Rotterdam, and carried us from that port city down through central Europe and over the Pyrenees. Transportation of the two-wheeled variety would figure in my life from time to time, which is why I decided to title this piece "Wheels" instead of "Cars."

In New York, people didn't have cars, at least not in Manhattan. I once spent several weeks parking a friend's vehicle on alternate sides of Lower East Side streets while he was recovering from appendicitis. Sometimes I had to circle those blocks for an hour before I found an empty space. In the city the subway was by far the better way to go.

Then in Mexico I began once again to own cars. I had to take a test to get my Mexican driver's license and failed it twice. This stunned me, since I had earned previous licenses without any problem in Albuquerque and New York. Perhaps the Mexican transit authorities expected a bribe. They may have been giving me two chances to catch on, because their explanations of my deficiencies were pretty vague. When I didn't cough up any cash, they gave in and issued the required piece of paper. It was very official looking, studded with embossed stamps and encased in a little red plastic jacket.

Sergio and I owned an old Volkswagen Beetle for a while. We drove it north to the border, visited with my parents in Albuquerque, and then took it west to California, all in a suffocating August. Water stains on the upholstery and a strange discoloration of the body should have told us it had been in a pretty bad crash, but we were innocents. The car had no air conditioning, and for some reason its heat couldn't be turned off. I remember driving across the Mohave, every window open, literally panting in the hot desert air. Otherwise that car did okay. There was a space in the far back just big enough for my son, Gregory, and he played contentedly in it throughout the trip. Our daughter

Sarah's basket bed occupied the width of the backseat. Sergio and I alternated driving. I was pregnant with Ximena.

I think it was in Mexico City that I bought my first new vehicle: a Datsun station wagon. Sergio and I had a couple of those through the eight years we were together. My most vivid car memory from that period was the time I parked, illegally, on the Calzada de Tlalpan, the busy thoroughfare that ran by the local post office where we picked up our mail each day. We edited a bilingual literary magazine then, and our postal box was full of letters, poems, and short stories—occasionally even a subscription or two.[1]

This particular day, in a hurry as I often was, I opened the driver's side door just as a young boy on a bicycle was riding past. The lower corner of my door caught the boy in the calf, slashing through his skin and breaking both bones. He lay on the pavement crying, his bike a sad tangle of twisted metal. In moments, a crowd had gathered, and people were urging me to split. "Leave before the cops get here," they said, "or it won't go well for you."

But how could I leave an injured young boy on the street, abandoned, writhing in pain? I entered the post office and called an ambulance; and when I got back to my car, the police were already there. That incident ended with my spending one night in the local precinct cell and another in the Tombs. The boy's parents, humble and concerned, had showed up at the police station, begging the authorities to free me. Of course, they weren't going to do that until they received the appropriate bribe.

Eventually someone who knew someone who knew someone else engineered a rescue just before I would have been transferred to notorious Lecumberri Prison. I'll never forget my relief when I heard my name called, was taken from the cell where I'd been with several other women, and saw the reassuring figure of a poet I knew standing in a circle of dirty light at the end of a long hall.[2] One way or another, people had been paid off. I made sure the boy got the medical attention he needed, and I never parked illegally again. My experience at the precinct and in the Tombs produced one of my first successful short stories.

Soon after this, Sergio and I parted ways. I wasn't alone for long, though, and soon began living with a U.S. American poet named Robert Cohen.

Robert and I were driving my fairly new Datsun when the repression hit, and we had to go underground in 1969. When we finally found a way out of the country, we sold that car for one thousand U.S. dollars, an astonishing bargain for the buyer. We were in a hurry and needed as much immediate cash as possible. Robert was able to travel legally, but I didn't know what costs I would encounter along the way. My journey ended up taking me from Mexico to Cuba via Prague.

In Cuba my transportation history was almost Kafkaesque. For the first year or so, we managed to get around on public transportation. In those years, one had to maintain a constant store of humor to confront Havana's buses. They came irregularly, often with crowds of people hanging from the doors and windows, and careened around corners as if on their way to a four-alarm fire. Despite the crowded conditions, the Cuban people's exaggerated (I thought) penchant for cleanliness caused them to open wide circles around anyone on the bus with the slightest body odor. You boarded those buses at your own peril for more reasons than one.

Soon a friend who was leaving the country offered us his Datsun for five hundred U.S. dollars. It was a far cry from the models we'd owned in Mexico: older and much smaller, with several things that didn't quite function. But a neighbor, one of the revolution's brave and brilliant amateur mechanics, said he thought he could put it in working order. So for around eight hundred dollars total, we had a vehicle that worked—for a while.

That car was painted a bright cerulean blue, making it, like almost every other automobile that had survived the U.S. blockade, quite an interesting sight. High humidity and corrosive sea air soon rusted the floor out, and I remember driving along while looking at swatches of pavement rushing by beneath my feet. I also remember the car's brakes failing completely one day, causing me to come to an erratic stop inside the Mexican Embassy's garden. Still, that vehicle took us where we wanted to go for almost a decade, and we were grateful.

The final problem came not from the car itself but from the Cuban Revolution's rules regarding vehicle ownership. Robert had registered it in his name, and when we eventually separated and he returned to the United States, I assumed I would be able to transfer it to mine. But that was not to be. The revolution had a law stating that all vehicles belonging to people who left the country would automatically revert to the state. No amount of protest was successful. The day I innocently went to change that car's registration, I lost it. I rode home on the bus, telling myself the revolution had reasons for its laws; I was simply an individual who had been caught in the messy intricacies of one of them.

In Nicaragua I had to take another driver's test. My license, encased in yet another little red plastic cover, was easily secured. My first car there was a dirty-yellow, overly used Skoda, built in Czechoslovakia but not to last. It gave me problems from the day I bought it, and soon I had to think about getting something else. Spread-out Managua, with its broad cobblestoned *pistas* and unreliable public transportation, was a place where having your own wheels was practically a necessity.

My son, Gregory, came to visit during my brief ownership of that Skoda and wanted me to teach him to drive. I remembered those long-ago sessions with my father and hoped to be able to display the same skill and patience with my son that Dad had shown me. Almost the first time he got in the driver's seat, Gregory slammed his large foot down on the car's fragile clutch, and that was the end of both lessons and car.

I sold the Skoda for junk and bought my first Mazda from a friend. He swore it would serve me well, and it did. I drove that car until I left the country.

It was back in the United States that I first started naming my cars. My first was a brand new Volkswagen Jetta, and I called her Mónika after Mónika Ertl, the Bolivian woman who traveled all the way to Hamburg, Germany, to carry out the execution of Quintanilla, the man who a few years before had cut off Che Guervara's hands. Quintanilla thought he was safe, but Mónika tracked him down. Later, back in Bolivia, she was shot down by that country's repressive forces.[3]

I loved Mónika's story, the fact that her father, to whom she was close, had been a German Nazi and yet she came to a different consciousness and gave her life in the struggle for social change. She had also been a feminist, one of the first of her generation in Latin America. For a while she ran a women's clinic. Every time I drove that Jetta, I thought of her—of her sacrifice, but even more deeply of her life. Such that, even when we replaced that Jetta with another, it too answered to Mónika.

All my cars from then on had names. A lumbering, second-hand Volkswagen van that Barbara and I bought to haul some of our things across country the first year I taught at Trinity College, Hartford, was Hortensia. She was named after the woman who had cared for my infant daughter Ana when I was still in hiding in Mexico and the Cuban revolution generously took my children in.

When I met her, Barbara had a two-tone orange-and-white Volkswagen van, which she called Baby Cakes. Where that name came from, I don't know. That vehicle had the same sort of history as my old Austin; it ran well but broke down just days after we sold it. Its new owner was far less understanding than the buyer of my Austin had been; she called in the middle of the night and angrily accused Barbara of knowing it was on its way out. We vowed never again to sell a car to a friend.

There was a little Nissan truck, a metallic blue Toyota, and then a few more Toyotas. We bought our last Corolla because of its enormous trunk. My mother was still alive then. She used a walker, and we figured we could slide it right into that trunk. We joked that it was a Mafia trunk, imagining thugs driving to the bank of some nighttime river, removing a body encased in cement, and letting it slide into the water and sink.

We bought a Volkswagen diesel at one point, hoping to save on gas. The day after we purchased that car, the price of diesel went above regular gasoline for the first time. Then the car itself turned out to be the proverbial lemon. By the time we traded it in, almost everything that could go wrong with it had. Once, driving out of a garage where it had just been fixed, both front windows noisily collapsed into their sockets. We made a U-turn and drove right back in.

Back when we lived up in the foothills and needed two vehicles, one was a base model four-wheel drive Jeep. We named her Emma, after Emma Goldman, who didn't want a revolution where you couldn't dance.[4] In retrospect, that was one of our favorite cars. She was great on trips, especially up in the Four Corners area, where we loved to get off-road to head for out-of-the-way trailheads or to search for ancient rock art. She only got sixteen miles to the gallon, which was the reason we sold her instead of the Corolla when we moved into the city and were able to get down to a single car. We've both been sorry.

Our last few cars have all been named Bikko, after Bantu Stephen Bikko, who fought for South Africa's freedom and died in one of its jails several years before liberation.[5] Although named after a man, we've always referred to those cars as she. They all represent a hero who gave his life for a change we're not likely to see fully consolidated in our lifetimes. Gender doesn't seem that important after death.

Our current vehicle is a Prius. We were driving the Corolla with the large trunk, quite satisfied and not really in the market for anything different. Then a postcard from the Toyota dealership arrived, offering big bucks on trade-ins. We had been interested in hybrids, hoping to leave a lighter footprint; but as I say, we had no immediate plans. One morning, I put a lamb roast in the oven, one of those slow roasts I thought would give us time to make a quick run to the grocery store. While there, we thought about that postcard. Why not drop by the dealership, we said, and see what they'd offer us for the Corolla?

Wheels 95

We decided to take a new Prius out for a test run. Or rather Barbara decided to drive it; I have never been able to get behind the wheel of a car in the presence of the stranger hawking it. The Prius handled beautifully. She was comfortable, too. And she seemed pleased at the prospect of being called Bikko.

While they had our Corolla in the garage, checking it out to see what kind of an offer they could make us, Barbara was on her cell phone with our credit union getting an idea of its blue book price. That was when I remembered my roast. I frantically demanded the immediate return of our old car and shot out of there like someone on a mission: a mission to prevent the roast from burning, and perhaps the house as well. Barbara stayed behind to do the hassling.

By the time I got home, there was a message on our answering machine. "Bring the title back with you," she said, "we've just bought a Prius." After turning off the oven (the roast was edible, though a bit dry), I picked up the title and headed back to the dealership. Barbara had argued them down to an acceptable trade-in, and we drove off in our new hybrid.

Two weeks later we took that Bikko on a road trip to California: Joshua Tree and Death Valley. She got sixty miles to the gallon, and we loved her. That was the last time she would get that kind of mileage, but what the hell: she's still twice as economical as most other cars.

Lately Barbara is upset with the Prius. It turns out to be too low-slung for some of New Mexico's back roads and doesn't handle well in certain situations, losing power as the front wheels disengage on slippery terrain. A little yellow warning light goes on then, and Barbara fumes. She is used to being in control of the vehicle she drives and hates that sense of helplessness.

But we've agreed to keep the car, at least for now. Over the past couple of decades, every car we've bought we've said: "Well, this should be it. No need to buy another." I don't know if we thought we were telling each other the truth or just trying to convince ourselves. At some point—and perhaps this is it—that's what it's going to have to be.

The reason I call this piece "Wheels" instead of "Cars" is because four-wheelers haven't been the only vehicles in our transportation history. With my first husband, I had that Lambretta, the one that took us down through central Europe to Spain. And Barbara has had a series of motorcycles. When we were first together, she had a Honda 750 she called Virginia, after her mother. I rode on the back of it once, the wind blowing through my hair, my body stiff with anxiety. She sold it soon after that.

But it would be a while before two-wheelers would be entirely out of her blood. In her early fifties she bought a Honda Ruckus. We had just gotten down to one car, and the Ruckus took her to work and back. Soon it didn't feel powerful enough, and she traded it in for a Piaggio BV 150. It looked to me like a motorcycle, but it was really a scooter, she explained. And as such, it wasn't enough either. She sold it and bought a BMW 800: big and powerful, though not nearly as big as many on the road.

What can I say about that time in our lives? Mostly, that I was terrified every minute of every day. Each time Barbara would leave the house and the phone would ring, I was frightened it was going to be the call I dreaded, telling me there had been a head-on collision somewhere, no survivors. I understood this process was something she had to go through, and I wanted to be respectful of that. I vowed never to make her feel, either by something I said or did, that I didn't want her driving a machine with a roar like a lion's. And I'm proud to have been able to keep that promise to myself. But I suffered.

The process lasted less than six months. Finally, it was Barbara herself who decided she'd had enough. One day, she admitted she'd lost her balance at a stoplight and the BMW had fallen against her, knocking her to the ground. "I'm not as young or strong as I used to be," she said. She sold the motorcycle, then, and went back to the Honda Ruckus that had started the spiral into motor-cycle madness. Her first Ruckus was white, and this one's red. It's exactly what she needs to come and go when it's not bicycle weather and I'm using our car.

I've had a few two-wheelers as well, all bicycles. My first was the dark-red girl's Western Flyer I rode around age nine. I had a paper route with that bike for a while. Then years passed, and I never had a bike again, until Barbara and I got together. She loved to ride and thought it might be something we could do together. I'll never forget the first time we rode; I barely made it two full blocks. Instead of berating me for not going farther, she told me what a great job I'd done: an auspicious beginning.

For more than a decade we rode together. I quickly got so I could ride ten or twenty miles, several times finishing a forty-mile tour of Albuquerque with her. But although a part of me loved the sport, I was always just slightly uneasy, unsure of my ability to control the bike. In 1992 I suffered a bad accident, exploding my right ankle when I lost my balance and couldn't extract it from the toe clip. After the operation and period of recuperation, I got right back on the bike. I knew if I didn't I never would. But in retrospect that was the beginning of the end for me. About five years later I gave up biking altogether. It's still one of Barbara's favorite sports.

Barbara's Ruckus is named Cooper, in honor of the beautiful little Mini Coopers she loves spotting on the road or reading about online. One of Barbara's hobbies is researching cars, from those old aqua-and-white Chevys to any number of current models. It's a pastime much like my reading about faraway places that I may never see but that intrigue me nonetheless. Barbara has even made a wonderful series of small paintings of cars: all shapes and sizes, personalities and attitudes.

As I say, for me it's always been about getting from point A to point B. But my cars still have names. And I'm more relieved than I can say that we're back to one trustworthy automobile, Barbara's couple of bikes, and a little red Ruckus with a top speed of 35 MPH.

Our Table

Our dining table was cut from Honduran pine, highly polished with a rich dark stain that speaks of jungles and twisted roots insisting themselves through the stone of ancient ruins. Copán,[1] or perhaps some lesser site, still half hidden beneath centuries of overgrowth. I retrieve the color of sky and scent in the air as we lay on our backs in that courtyard surrounded by a pulse of Mayan energy, moving our heads ever so slightly so as to be able to take in another view of moss-covered walls.

The map of my life stretches and recoils, turns corners and disappears into places I do not remember visiting in linear time. When it reappears, I am walking along a narrow country road. Long rows of olive trees disappear over hills in a narrowing perspective. The scent of old stone mixes with the pungent odor of goats. Heavy summer air carries the minor key of a wooden flute, perhaps a shepherd playing to his flock or to himself. Places bring objects and put them in my hands, tastes that envelop my tongue. More than just things, as the title of this book invokes. Ghosts from many eras walk together, telling stories to each other and to me. A spiral of heartbeats rises to fill my line of sight.

I have served food on narrow counters dividing kitchen from living space in the efficiency apartments of my youth. I have pressed my knees together under a drape of heavy felt, trying to ward off chilblains through Seville's winter nights. I have prepared food on a wooden board covering the in-kitchen bathtub in my New York City walk-up and organized eating on camping trips and in kitchens that were not my own. My tables have been large and small, square and round, sometimes nothing more than a makeshift surface but always a place where magic is served up.

Guests have fallen in love at my meals, stared at each other instead of the food, extended a tentative knee or calf in the hope of touching the one they desire. From time to time, passionate argument has threatened digestion, while awkward silences struck taste buds numb. On such occasions, I have wanted my food to open minds, provoke real answers to real questions, break down the barriers of misunderstanding, or build a bridge. Why not?

I love my current table's rounded corners, its ability to expand or contract according to the number of friends seated around it, six strong chairs: steel and wood. I love that it brings memories of that Central American country where I once witnessed the residual horror of state brutality and recorded a woman's voice of resistance, while alluding as well to other places and peoples. I am grateful it is large enough to include that extra place setting, welcoming the unannounced guest who may arrive.

Although men are always welcome, ours is a woman's table. Peruvian women wove the broad strips of color; and my beloved, a woman of very different origin, joined those strips with tiny stitches to make a cloth that would cover its sheen of generous wood. Or members of a Zimbabwean women's collective sliced and carved potatoes in traditional designs, then stamped the fabric with their magical squares using vegetable dyes in a succession of repeated images.

We may dine on delicate threads pulled by Vietnamese heroines, white on white, leaving tiny places of absence that can never be filled. Or the creamy lace from the rhythm of a Croatian grandmother's hands as she sat working beneath the old clock in Trogir's uphill square. At more casual meals, bright red placemats from the Philippines throb beneath each setting, evoking the energy of shrill buying and selling on crowded city streets.

Rarely does a centerpiece of spring flowers or winter arrangement of gourds and corn anchor my table. The middle is celebrated by food alone, in ample serving platters accompanied by ladles or large spoons. Candles might bathe other tables in elegant light, but I will not risk their wax threatening the integrity of cloth. Nor am I willing to alter the light in my guests' eyes, the need or exuberance residing there. I strive for a quiet that is broken only by connection—and by food.

With a shudder, I remember my high school home economics course: The neatly finished plackets and curious buttonholes we held up to the teacher's demanding eye. Old gas range ovens from which perfect cakes were expected to emerge. The young girl's conditioning in the stifling misogyny of my youth. While our male counterparts were building interesting items in shop class, I was bored to tedium in that mid-twentieth-century prelude to womanhood.

Still, I confess to a few teenage moments when Emily Post seemed relevant. Along with millions of women and girls struggling to find our way through the stifling 1950s, I studied where knives and forks and spoons should go, which are expected to grace the left side of a table setting and which the right, even those lesser salad forks and dessert spoons destined to lay quietly above the plate. Moving from outermost implements toward the center was deemed the proper way to use such cutlery. Who invented rules whose only purpose had to be shaming those who did not know them? Even in my era of skewed priorities, I quickly lost interest in that pomp and began to find it macabre. Now I simply ask myself what implements will provide the easiest way to eat what I have cooked, and extend to my guests the courtesy of their availability.

In fact, the table my memory retains as most hospitable, most suited to true giving and sharing of sustenance, was a long plank laid across two sawhorses in a small Peruvian village high in the cold Andes. The village was called Tinta, and all the women wore black veils in mourning for Tupac Amaru, the Inca leader who was executed in 1572. An open-hearth fire warmed the room's dark interior, shielding it from the wind moaning outside. Steaming platters of roasted *cuy*—those guinea pigs raised in stone patios—and high altitude potatoes appeared with as many enameled metal spoons as there were mouths to feed. We all dug in, eating from a single dish. Conversation was sparse but meaningful, in the way of those tough mountain people. The word "share" took on the ease of everyday life.

My dinner plates have their own stories: Simple white, where nothing gets in the way of the food's palette. Mexican Talavera, with its raucous dance of color. Or the special settings Barbara and I collected on birthdays and anniversaries until we had a full complement of those replicas of the service Mary Elizabeth Jane Colter designed for the dining cars of the old Atchison, Topeka, and Santa Fe.[2] Through the early years of the twentieth century, that railway opened the U.S. American West, and Colter adorned the journey with art. She took designs from Mimbres petroglyphs, evidence of an ancient culture found on stone and ceramic vessels in the southwestern United States. Those big horned sheep and desert tortoises, horny toads and birds whisper to us as we eat.

Mary Colter's life and designs are symbolic of what I want our table to be:

a vibrant tribute to women's work, ordinary tasks mostly taken for granted through a long history of cooking and serving those who have depended on our nurture throughout time. At our table we serve women and men, children and strangers, family and friends. I honor the centuries of struggle through which we have finally come into ourselves. Mary Colter was challenged by a world still surprised by women's gifts. Her legacy is a reminder of what we have had to battle and how much we still must overcome.

A silver serving spoon and fork occasionally make their appearance. They are among the few remnants from my early home. Mother used to tell me the story of how she and Dad saved through the early years of their marriage so they could buy the beautiful Georg Jensen pattern, much like Barbara and I saved for our Colter set. Those two pieces of Jensen and a few old turquoise and green Mexican glasses are what I keep from a childhood where meals were also set out on a large, heavy, dark wooden table—now stretched to its magnificent length when family sits down to a holiday meal at my brother's house.

Food in our parents' home was odd to say the least, and I struggle to retrace the warm memories as well as those that continue to confound. We grew up with great fifty-pound drums of powdered milk, ground horsemeat, and bloody eggs: all efforts at saving money where none needed to be saved. Our parents' memories of the Great Depression may have been part of the equation. Or some quirk too complicated to explain. As a young person, discomfort and impatience were my companions. I lived in constant fear my teenage friends would be startled or, worse, repulsed at Mother's displays of ingenuity.

We wore hand-me-down clothes, drove used cars, and had none of the household aids beginning to be so popular in our social class during the 1950s, when women were lured into confinement by shiny new implements of domesticity. It was argued these new devices would save housewives time, but they actually added hours to their workday, as the appliances aided in the shift from middle-class women employing domestic help to doing the work themselves.

Although women have routinely fed, clothed, and nursed whole families, their unpaid labor rendered them worthless as generators of wealth. Even with many women already supporting their families, the myth of the man as head of household was unassailable back then. My mother made her own peculiar way through that maze where her creative spirit played hide-and-seek with the image of perfect wife. There must have been more than a few times when she didn't know which door to open, which territory to defend, or which bounty to trade for short-term gratification.

And my early home didn't quite fit the pattern of the times in other ways as well. Dad supported the family but also did much more of the housework than was typical. My parents advertised a fictional poverty. Yet summers found us in Europe or South America, exploring the world. Mother claimed that what she saved by buying that embarrassing food paid for those trips. By the time I was old enough to do the math, she was into a new money-saving scheme. Family myth dies hard. As war brought the economy back, I often had the task of beating a dark orange powder into one-pound chunks of white margarine: it was the patriotic thing to do, and I remember being proud to be given the task.

Mother wasn't the type who baked after-school cookies or shared favorite recipes with her children. Yet her influence was strong. I know my sister, brother, and I all inherit some of her idiosyncrasies, even if the inheritance causes us to fall one step back for every two or three we move forward. With Mother you had to thrill to her destinations without worrying too much about how she got us there.

The few dishes Mother made again and again were artificially flavored and predictably overcooked. Still, I hold some warm memories on my tongue, like "cheese dreams" and "toastites"—both involving packaged white bread and prodigious servings of Velveeta cheese, the "toastites" melted with canned tuna fish pressed between two halve s of a steel case at the end of a long handle. One held this apparatus over a gas burner, turning it to crisp both sides. Thanksgiving turkeys, baked in an old black-and-white cast-iron roaster, were delicious— if you overlooked the soggy stuffing and can-shaped tower of cranberry sauce. Dad favored baloney sandwiches and sauerkraut.

Offering food is often about surprise: what we choose to give, how we arrange it on the plate. As surprise ripples through my life, I no longer think primarily of feeding my children, that long process that began with the breast and made its journey through so many years of staples and favorite treats. As each child has grown into adulthood, there's been a moment—perhaps unacknowledged or unnoticed at the time—when the tables turned (so to speak).

With my son it was one cold morning in Paris when I watched him making scones from scratch for the half dozen of us who would soon sit down to breakfast. It wasn't that I had never seen him cook before. In Cuba we'd all done our part, and I remembered him searching our old refrigerator for scraps that he would fry up with a couple of eggs, producing a kind of brick he and the woman who would become his wife took to the university to get themselves through the day. But those scones were different: a culinary specialty. Much later, in

Uruguay, I have observed him preparing the morning coffee for each person in the house, lovingly remembering how each prefers his or her first drink of the day. Or dishing up a casserole of vegetables so his son who hasn't eaten meat for years feels included in the meal.

Sarah, on a recent visit, showed me how they clarify butter at her house, a practice that goes with her yoga discipline and other healthy habits she's acquired. This was the daughter I least imagined would find an interest in food preparation. Of my offspring, she was the one most on the go, grabbing a bite wherever and whenever possible. Having her own children changed that of course.

Of all mine, Ximena is the one most deeply interested in cooking. So much so, that she recently fulfilled her dream of graduating from chef's school, where all sorts of complex dishes were on the agenda. She is a specialist in Mexican cuisine. And she doesn't only make the food, but offers stories as well about the parts of her country from which they come: histories of popular culture that embrace geography, social relations, economics, and art.

My youngest daughter, Ana, is a television producer in New York, a job that leaves little time for the kitchen. As a young professional with two sons, she orders her staples from Fresh Direct, that New York resource that delivers at any hour of the day or night. But Ana too has developed her favorite meals and has learned to delight in their preparation when she has the time to do so. Her black beans are exquisite. We've shared special moments buying a good knife or exploring the pungent corners of a Middle Eastern spice shop.

Yes, it's their turn now.

Still, I continue to love to cook, even as I understand that a part of that love is a reaction against the food mediocrity of my childhood. I never taste a dish, until I bring it to table. I don't know if it's superstition or laziness that keeps me from dipping a spoon, bringing it to my lips, and adjusting as most cooks do. Maybe it's the synesthesia that keeps me dependent on color as my only guide. I want to be surprised along with my guests. That first savor on the tongue tells me, as it does them, if there is too much salt or not enough, if the seasonings are right and one offering highlights or compliments another as I'd hoped.

At seventy-six, I've had some experience with my signature offerings, having made each often enough so even a bit of experimentation isn't likely to ruin the balance. In fact, making the same dish twice is against my nature; small differences add variety and keep things interesting.

Paella learned during those long-ago years in southern Spain. Enchiladas or chiles rellenos from my life in Mexico. Improvisation left over from revolutionary Cuba—or maybe from some of the dishes we longed for but knew we couldn't have, as we carried our ration books, empty bottles, and little woven string bags to the neighborhood grocery store and savored that special satisfaction that comes from knowing no one in the country suffered hunger. It still astonishes me when a child of mine refers with longing to one of my Cuban concoctions: a strange processed sausage we called *butifara*, served over plain white rice. Pumpkin pudding—though where we got pumpkin in Cuba I can't imagine: I may be conflating a memory here. Or a burnt spread made from boiling one of the six cans of sweetened condensed milk our family received per month.

Today it's chicken with prunes and green olives, a special low-fat version of chicken marabella to go with our generation's healthier approach to eating. Pork roast with vegetables. For spring or summer, a large green salad with raisins, nuts, and grated cheese. Lately, lots of soups. We shun meat with hormones and antibiotics, produce sprayed with insecticides, or any food high in added chemicals. But I am also constantly reminded of how much money one must have in order to eat clean. When I am able to spend two dollars on a single sweet red pepper, I never fail to think of those who must stretch that amount to feed three or more for a day. A couple of fast-food hot dogs will assuage your hunger, where a sweet red pepper won't.

On cold nights, I may make posole laced with fresh green chili and simmered all the way through a long writing day. It brings delight from my guests, although I myself don't care for those large starchy kernels of corn. They remind me too much of a time in my life when important things were broken, and I didn't yet know how to fix them.

Many of my dishes these days benefit from a unique mix of dried herbs my friend Patricia sent me from France. Its bouquet brings her generous friendship to whatever I cook. I understand the moral and even some of the health benefits of vegetarianism and enjoy preparing vegetarian dishes for friends. My grandson who hasn't eaten meat or fish for several years has made a vow that reflects his belief that all creatures deserve our respect and care. My own body responds with gratitude to a diet that includes modest portions of all the food groups. Fortunately, Barbara's does too.

A recent addition to my repertoire is roasted chicken or turkey with cornbread stuffing. I learned this from my friend Sabra, who makes it every Thanksgiving at her home on a high bluff above the village of Abiquiu in northern New Mexico. O'Keefe country, we call it, in honor of the artist who lived there and painted its colored mesas and cloud-dotted skies.[3] I bake the cornbread and let it dry for a couple of days, before crumbling and mixing it with the sautéed onion and celery, eggs and seasonings. Basted frequently in the bird's juices, that dressing is so good you can't get away without an extra dish. Barbara, who doesn't care for turkey but loves chicken, has become an expert at grilling the latter. I marinate the pieces all day, and she handles their final preparation.

Homemade bread brings a millennial scent to any meal. I enjoy proofing the yeast, kneading the dough, and letting it rise as it fills the house with the wisdom of wheat, corn, or rye. I love taking perfectly rounded loaves from the oven and setting them on a rack to cool. I make dozens of different breads, but my favorites remain tomato with fresh basil, the golden Chanukah braid with its sesame and poppy seed crust, thinly-sliced pumpernickel, and velvety potato. Whichever the loaf, I serve it wrapped in a napkin nestled in a broad basket Barbara and I bought from a young girl sitting under an acacia tree in the Botswana countryside. I can still see her slim fingers holding that basket toward me.

Although I love cooking with wine, I no longer drink any sort of alcohol. I like the idea of a glass of wine perfectly matched to a dish I have made and encourage our guests to bring their own. It is not that we mind friends imbibing in our home, just that alcohol doesn't sit that well with either of us. And there's also some silent vow of abstinence in honor of several people we've known and loved who were destroyed by alcoholism.

I love to cook and consider it on a level with any other art. A genre not that different from writing poems or making photographs, my two other forms of creative expression. An important difference is that those other genres produce lasting works, while food disappears into the mouths of those I feed, its enduring qualities remaining only in memory.

Another difference resides in the public perception of ordinary cooking versus writing a poem or essay. I'm not talking about the well-known, highly paid, and prestigious chef, more often than not a man. The former is what women do, three times a day, most of the days of our lives. The second is special. Very few of those we feed appreciate the time and effort we put into writing, like they do when we darn a sock, sew on a button, or feed them their three squares.

I once wrote a book called *Hunger's Table*, in which every piece could be read as a poem or recipe—or both.[4] Right down to the list of ingredients and order of their use. Readers had the information they needed to prepare a main dish or soup, dessert or bread. Featured were baba ganouj and chocolate mousse, bouillabaisse and potato latkes. I honored the women who have fed me throughout my life and those who failed to do so, the hunger that persists when sustenance of any kind is withheld.

One short poem in that book is about a time I was miserably sick and called my mother, asking if she'd bring over some Jello—the only thing I thought I might be able to keep down. Her fear of germs caused her to set the unopened box on my front porch, ring the doorbell, and flee. By the time I struggled to the door, all I could see was her back retreating up the hill and that small box sitting forlornly on my stoop. That collection of poems speaks as well of need and desire, fear and satisfaction, the mundane and spectacular of which all poetry is made.

These days, the indignation of war drives my cooking, hard. Each time my country's bully government sends troops to invade and kill in some far-off part of the world, I think of the foods native to those terrorized nations, how scarcities follow guns, crops are sacrificed, and staples disappear from markets and tables. Traditional tastes may be forgotten. I think of the seeds that will never again germinate because of Monsanto's genetic modification and death-dealing fertilizers, the farmers forced to relinquish generations of planting and sewing. Some of them kill themselves because the sorrow of seeds that will not sprout is too heavy to bear. I remember, in 1974, looking out across Vietnam's barren demilitarized zone just south of the seventeenth parallel: dead earth, not a single blade of green. I wondered if that strip of abused land would ever be fertile again.

Today I search for recipes from Iraq, Afghanistan, and the occupied territories of the Palestinian West Bank. I hunt down their ingredients and teach myself to follow them with a prayer on my lips and pain eroding my flesh. The prayer is not to some higher power—Christian, Muslim, Jewish, or otherwise—for none I know of has ever interceded on behalf of justice. The pain is secondhand and paltry; I know it cannot simulate what the inhabitants of those countries suffer from our mad conceit.

Still, making these dishes is a personal tribute, a way of paying attention and forging connection, of bringing a consciousness of the harm we cause into my home and onto my table. Afghan-style yogurt served over vegetables and grain, or date bars like those made in Iraq, seem to imbue it with a particular grace.

A certain conversation may ensue. Perhaps my guests, even as they enjoy the food, will give thought to the hunger we cause. Is this some sort of passive-aggressive idiosyncrasy? I don't know.

When Barbara and I got together, I thought of myself as an enthusiastic cook. Through her long influence, I now think of myself as a subtle one. Her uncanny discernment of tastes has meant that we can savor something unusual at a restaurant somewhere, and she will know immediately every ingredient and even to some extent the quantity of each. Cooking to her taste can be a lovely duet.

I live with a woman who knows that each time I prepare a dish, I am writing a poem. For a quarter century now, she has approached my cooking as art, never ignoring or disdaining it as mere housewifely duty. The old adage "the way to a man's heart is through his stomach" has no resonance in our home, and not only because we are two women. It's not about wifely obligation, that tradition that has kept women enslaved for centuries, but about delighting in a skill one enjoys.

Sometimes we stand shoulder to shoulder in the kitchen, she helping me prep vegetables or arrange fruit on a plate. I call her my *pinche de cocina*, then, remembering the Mexican designation for one who helps in the preparation of food. One of the marks of our relationship is the deep respect we have for one another, in the kitchen and every other room in the house. She finds my serving the dishes of aggrieved lands as natural as my writing an essay on the military industrial complex.

What Am I Going to Wear?

Clothes have rarely meant to me what they mean to others. They've always been more than just a way to cover my body, but fashion as yearning or requirement has never been important. In fact, as I've grown older, the fashion industry—its yearly reinvention aimed at keeping designers and outlets assured of new profit—has become more and more abhorrent. I approach dressing as I would paint on canvas, paper cutouts in collage, clay built up over an armature, or the tones I used to be able to caress out of photographic paper in the developer tray.

As children, my sister and I—just three years apart—were often dressed in matching smocks with shirred bodices, gifts from doting grandparents. Their presumptions about class and how it should dress were something my parents eventually fled. There was a definite break between those two generations, some of it manifesting itself in clothes. For example, my paternal grandmother, who had money, gave me a fur coat when I was a teenager. It was an ostentatiously inappropriate gift, one my parents never allowed me to wear. To my credit, even in the midst of considerable adolescent confusion, I didn't really want to wear it.

My mother's attitude toward fashion was similar to her feelings about food; making do or economizing in a variety of ways had less to do with saving money than with shunning consumerism and displaying creative ingenuity. She liked to call attention to something different or odd or homemade. After we moved west, she traded an East Coast wardrobe for the layered skirts and simple blouses modeled by the Navajo women out there. And her fascination with Navajo jewelry—turquoise and silver—influenced my own love of some of the old cast pieces, beautiful squash blossom necklaces and conch belts.

Then there was the other aspect of dress in my family. We always wore hand-me-downs, and in my case they didn't even come from girls who were older than me but from women who were my mother's friends. I remember a flared black wool skirt weighted at the bottom by a hem folded over and over until it formed a bulky and uneven rim. I don't know why Mom couldn't have removed the excess fabric. Perhaps if she had been better at alterations, that clothing we got from others would have been less embarrassing.

At that time in my life—junior high and high school—I ached to look like my contemporaries. I wanted the hoop crinolines, wide belts, angora sweater sets with a single strand of fake pearls, and saddle shoes. I wanted hair curled just so, requiring sleeping with bobby pins piercing my scalp. And I didn't want the dark fuzz beginning to show up in places it wasn't welcome, starting me on years of electrolysis—until I finally gave up. Mother must have suffered, juggling her own distaste for what was fashionable, strange need to advertise her "deals," and genuine desire to give me what I wanted. She must have understood all too painfully my young need to fit in.

One of the things for which I've always been grateful to my parents was their insistence we learn to manage money. This extended to buying our own clothes. As I entered high school in 1950, I remember my clothing allowance being twelve dollars a month. That twelve dollars had to cover everything, including putting a little away each pay period for the new shoes and winter coat I would inevitably need at the beginning of the next year. At the time, I often complained, but Mom and Dad stuck to the arrangement. I've always been good at managing money, and I'm sure my skill in that area comes from that early training.

Of course I wanted my budget to provide me the "right" or "in" items the popular girls wore. I learned that if I saved for one angora sweater set, it would make me feel like four or five ordinary sweaters couldn't. Just before my senior high school prom, Mother and I went looking for a formal dress. I remember being scared she would suggest a second-hand store or, worse, some rental place. She didn't.

We made the rounds of several department stores, where I delighted in trying on gown after gown. I had imagined bridal white with lots of tulle. But

Mom was persuasive with her love of the unique. I ended up with a deep-red floor-length tulle skirt with a strapless velvet bodice. I was destined to be different, always, but didn't appreciate that quality then. Mother surprised me at the checkout by telling me I didn't need to buy that dress with the allowance I'd saved for the occasion. She smiled and said it was a gift from her and my father.

Despite the fact that I married several times, I never actually wore a wedding dress, at least not the proverbial white model with long veil. I played a bride in my high school play and wore the dress our drama coach said had been hers. She confided that her marriage had lasted only a few days. Miss Shannon's breath smelled strongly of alcohol—something no one commented on at the time. Years after her death, I would come to understand she had probably been a closeted lesbian, living at a time when happier options for women like her were almost nonexistent.

Intuiting my artist's identity soon after graduating high school helped me move away from the desire to dress as others did. After I moved to New York, much of my wardrobe came from the city's thrift shops or Salvation Army. This was great for my budget as well as for my creative sense. The city's second-hand clothing stores were fabulous in those days. My friend Valerie was better than anyone I knew at finding one-of-a-kind bargains, still is. But those shops wised up. Today they are Unique Boutiques, their relics as costly as those at any upscale Madison Avenue shop.

Through my last years in Albuquerque and those in New York, I reveled in makeup and used it in the most creative ways. I covered my eyelids with oil-based blue and green mascaras and drew thick black lines along the wet strip of skin just inside my lower lid and from the outer corners of my eyes toward my temples. Those dramatic black lines mirrored my black mesh stockings. No red lipstick, though. That would have been too much in the style of a 1950s Levittown wife. We were artists, dark-eyed and hungry. I learned this palette and its tricks from my friend Elaine de Kooning, who extended her painterly talents to the canvas of her dancer's body.

Then came Mexico, where I was drawn to those shifts embroidered by indigenous peoples and called *huipiles* (wee-PEELS). Their bright colors and artistic stitching, often on a background of handwoven cloth, made my heart sing. They also covered my broadening girth as I gave birth to my second and then third and fourth children. I also wore the rubber-tire-soled sandals popular among Mexico's Indians, and my hair in one long braid down my back. Dressing in this way was a statement of appreciation for the great indigenous artists who were paid pennies for their extraordinary works, as well as a reflection of my own aesthetic.

The most beautiful huipiles came from Mexico and Guatemala. Each village had its own style and design. Some were extraordinary, although as tourism made its inroad into those countries, many of the artists began producing machine-made imitations they could sell more cheaply and in greater quantity. It's been sad to see the old traditions disappear, especially in the great Guatemalan markets of Chichicastenango and Antigua or in Mexico's Oaxaca, where craftspeople have taken to dipping beautiful fabrics in gentian violet or a rust-colored dye to make it look aged.

I once asked a group of Quiche women in the Guatemalan highlands how they felt about foreigners wearing their huipiles, since I knew the motifs represented such information as where a woman comes from, her marital status, and much else. They told me it wasn't offensive to them to see women from other places wearing the shifts, but they would be taken aback to see us in their *cortes*, the wraparound lengths of cloth they use as skirts. I realized I had been dazzled by the embroidered blouses and hadn't looked closely enough at the skirts.

Gradually I acquired a fairly large collection of huiples. They were almost all I wore throughout my years in Mexico. So much so that when I had to change my appearance in order to leave the country clandestinely, it seemed a natural solution for me to change to more ordinary garb. I bought a wide-striped navy-blue and yellow knit dress with innocuous navy-blue pumps and bag. I had my hair dyed black with bangs and teased into a bouffant style. I've often said I don't believe my own mother would have recognized me on the street. I felt like I was in drag, but didn't catch a stare as I passed through Mexico City's huge airport and flew under an assumed name to a city close to the border.

In Cuba, clothing took on a whole different meaning. Like food and household cleaning products, it was severely rationed. The Cubans had a penchant for cleanliness, and smartly starched cottons were the order of the day. Style remained somewhat reminiscent of the 1950s. I realized I stood out a bit too much in my bright huipiles. Cuban women passed inauspiciously in army fatigues, satin party dresses, or skirts so tight and short they hardly qualified as such. But my huipiles drew disapproving stares. Little by little I did a better job of fitting in.

I remember during our first months in Cuba, Robert was hospitalized with a bad case of hepatitis. Visiting friends from the States came down and wanted to see him. But when we got to the hospital entrance, we were stopped by a young soldier. My friend, who was about seven months pregnant at the time, was wearing pants and a maternity smock. "No women in pants allowed in," the soldier explained, "it might upset the male patients." We argued, of course, but to no avail. Finally, my friend simply stepped out of her pants. The maternity smock barely covered her underpants. But now it had become a dress. The soldier ushered us in without another word.

Those of us living in Cuba during the 1960s and '70s who had family or friends who visited from outside the country thought nothing about asking them to leave some of their clothing behind when they went home. Levis were particularly sought after. I inherited many different denim weights and pant sizes over my decade there. Some were just a bit too short, causing my teenage daughters to call me *pescadora*, fisherwoman. Some were too large and I easily took them in, while others were too small, encouraging me to try to lose a few pounds.

Nicaragua had more contact with the outside world than Cuba did, and also a more sophisticated approach to individual dress. The Sandinista Revolution made a valiant attempt at class equality, at least during its early years, and most people dressed casually most of the time. Again, military fatigues were common. And the tropical heat made light cotton apparel as popular as it had been in Cuba. When men dressed up, they wore *guayaberas*, pleated shirts with tucks or embroidery in white or pastel colors. Women, as everywhere, were more creative. This seems to be one of the most obvious things that distinguish us from the animal world, where males usually display the most beautiful plumage or elegant coats.

In 1984, when I came back to the United States, I was forty-eight years old. Dressing this way or that no longer claimed my attention. I retained my preference for Levis, increasingly a sort of uniform. Levis and short huipiles, reverting back to my long-term love of indigenous art. And I am rarely without turquoise jewelry, particularly Navajo. If I don't have two slabs of turquoise hanging from my ears, I feel naked. It was as if coming home also freed me to indulge my deepest tastes.

But two things would soon interfere.

One was the immigration case I was forced to wage when the U.S. Immigration and Naturalization Service tried to deport me because of opinions expressed in some of my books. Appearing in court, or on television, required a demeanor somewhere between ladylike and confident. I had to dress the part.

I remember the plain blue dress I purchased specifically to wear to my El Paso, Texas, immigration hearing in March of 1986. The hem was long enough. The neckline was high enough. The cut was loose enough. If I ever looked like a dowdy housewife, it was in that dress. Several years later, after I'd won my case, someone said the blue dress should have been kept as a relic of that struggle. I have no idea what happened to it.

The other consideration that impacted how I would dress during my first decade home was having to earn a living. I decided my best shot was teaching at a university. The idea that "clothes make the woman" is one we embrace when we have nothing else to go on. Despite the fact that I had published some eighty books, I had no college degree, nor had I held a previous teaching job. So I was very conscious of how I thought I should look when going for an interview or even in the classroom itself.

You couldn't go wrong with a tailored suit or other conservative outfit. Much like women lawyers trying to compete with their male counterparts in court, I acquired some apparel I might otherwise have avoided. I definitely played down the flamboyance or an accessory that might draw attention to anything beyond those qualities I hoped would get me though.

As I became more comfortable teaching, though, I realized what the fashion industry tries so hard to prevent us all from realizing: that what we wear matters little if we know who we are. Once I understood, emotionally as well as intellectually, that the schools where I taught wanted my experience, expertise, and creativity, and not that I conform to any particular dress code, I was able to relax and wear what made me most comfortable.

That meant, again, clean Levis, a simple sweater or shirt, and occasionally those huipiles that continue to speak to me of women's artistry. And of course the turquoise earrings. What I won't wear, ever, is makeup of any kind. I feel about it as I feel about the changing whims of fashion: something that makes us look like what we aren't and exhausts our skin as it does so. Sometimes I look in the mirror and see a pale aging face, one that could use a bit of color here or there. My hair, what's left of the once thick mane, is thin and white. But I just can't bring myself to color and paint. It wouldn't have the same exuberant meaning it did back when Elaine and I delighted in using ourselves as palettes of experimentation. And I don't like false promises.

There's also the issue of looking one's age, of not falling into the trap of "younger is better." I've lived every one of my years attuned to their joy and pain. Each line and wrinkle tells a story. I don't want makeup or touched-up photographs or anything else to pretend that I am younger than I am. This goes along with always trying to make sure my promotional photos look like I look now, not what I looked like twenty or thirty years ago. I won't wear misleading photography either.

An important part of my attire, perhaps the most important part, is the ring that matches the one Barbara wears. Unable to legally marry, denied so many of the things heterosexual couples take for granted, we find very special meaning in our rings. They are simple silver bands with a light inset of gold bordered by three crosscuts at each end. It has taken us years to settle on these rings—we went through almost a dozen before coming to them—but we've worn them now for a very long time. Only one other woman we know wears one like them. She is our good friend Jane. They are inexpensive, unpretentious, and comfortable, like an extension of the body, and they are a tangible reminder of our connection.

As the world's poor grow poorer and there become more of them, dressing up seems more obscene to the values I hold dear. Wearing an expensive outfit, even if I could afford it, would be like eating at an expensive restaurant, even when invited by someone for whom the indulgence may be an everyday event. Good simple food and simple innovative clothing seem appropriate like never before.

Of course, I sometimes desire a particular piece of apparel. Then I remember the woman in the Peruvian Amazon whose meager hut I visited in 1974. I was traveling throughout the country, training teams of oral historians. We had left the jungle city of Iquitos on a small naval vessel and motored down the Amazon to the Río Napo, from the banks of which we had walked until we reached this woman's home.

The several hours I spent with her were memorable for a number of reasons, but none more than because of what she was wearing. You really couldn't call it a dress, since there was more fabric missing than covering her emaciated body. I could see one gaunt breast hanging flaccid beneath the mass of holes. Yet she didn't seem self-conscious, nor did she apologize. Indeed, what she wore that day may have been the only piece of clothing she owned. In her home, a single mesh bag hung from a nail sticking out from a beam. It contained what looked to be her family's few possessions. A couple of scrawny chickens strutted across the wooden platform that was her floor.

This woman and her family earned their living—such as it was—gathering and selling ornamental fish to a middleman who came down the Napo about once a week. Our conversation, the entire visit, was bathed in grace. Despite the immense differences in our lives, we connected on some visceral level. When I left, she handed me a single egg. It was a gift I hesitated to take, but the coworker I was with, much wiser in these matters than I, gave me to understand my refusal would have hurt her feelings irreparably.

The Amazonian woman's attire has been a reference for me ever since. It's not that I believe I should dress in rags to make some absurd statement about intentional poverty. In fact, I've never thought of intentional poverty as poverty. It's when it's not intentional that it carries so much pain. But when I point my remote to the TV and casually switch channels, trying to avoid the latest commercial for this season's fashions, followed by a commercial for a weight-loss program, followed by another for cheese-stuffed pizza, that woman clothed in rags stands before me: a hologram of rebuke.

My disgust at fashion is profound. If the industry says blue, I search my closet for red. If it says short, I wear long. If shoulder-length curls are in, I shave my head.

I'm not under any illusions that a single woman's dress constitutes useful protest. It doesn't constitute protest at all.

It just feels good on the inside.

Do You Really Believe All That?

I'm going to try to retrace the map that brought me to this place where I can say I hate religion and mean it. Not only hate it, but blame it for the intolerance, violence, and fabricated ignorance that keep us warring with one another. Because it wasn't always this way. As a child and young person, I remember being fascinated by religion, actually seeking it out.

I wanted to belong.

My earliest memories of any sort of religious instruction date to my early childhood in the suburbs of New York City. My parents, taking their cue from my maternal grandfather, who was a Christian Science practitioner, had a lukewarm relationship to that odd faith.[1] I retain a vague image of my father performing as an usher in the church, wearing gray suede gloves. Their involvement must have been short-lived, because I don't think I ever attended Christian Science Sunday school.

In those days, as today, the prevailing idea among middle-class U.S. Americans who weren't that religious was that they should at least give their children the opportunity to grow up with a faith. Not doing so was considered bad parenting. Having a belief system seemed the moral imperative. Why it wasn't deemed as laudable to allow children to grow up free of religious faith, I don't know.

As a child, my mother had gone for a while to a Quaker school and had great respect for the Society of Friends. They were short on ritual and long on silence, and their good works were legion. So for a brief period, my parents sent me to Quaker Sunday school. I remember large felt boards with brightly dressed biblical figures our teacher moved around to illustrate the comings and goings of the ancient peoples with whom she tried to acquaint us. An image of Sarah at the well stayed with me, and I vowed to name my firstborn girl Sarah, which I did.

Many years later, for a brief time, my partner and I attended Friends meetings in Albuquerque. It was one of those periods in our relationship when we were looking for a community, trying out different groups. Although we loved the silence, someone inevitably interrupted it with a comment we found less than interesting. We soon realized it was the silence that had lured us, and we preferred getting out on our bikes of a Sunday morning, or simply sleeping in. Eventually we studied the origins and tenets of Quakerism and found it too Christian for our philosophical worldview.

In my preteen years, it wasn't silence I sought, but ritual and a sense of belonging. When our family moved to New Mexico—I was ten—my first need was finding a group of new friends. I told my mother I wanted a church youth group where I felt comfortable. Why a church youth group, who knows? Perhaps because the Bordelon kids across the street spoke so glowingly of their activities at Our Lady of Fatima. Mom, always eager to help her children explore new venues and make new friends, said she would take me to a different church every Sunday until I found one that suited me.

And it was definitely Sunday, not Saturday: certainly not a Jewish youth group, which would have had some connection with our family heritage. Our parents moved us west at least partially to distance themselves from their Jewish roots, just as they changed our surname and, when asked, lied about the reason. They didn't like admitting to any connection with Judaism. Their eagerness to claim a Christian identity was undoubtedly part of that need.

I am reminded of the Crypto-Jews in northern New Mexico, whose ancestors had been expelled from Spain during the Inquisition. They converted to Christianity to save their lives and only practiced Jewish ritual in hidden back rooms. Their denial was born of fear. My parents' denial may have been provoked by revelations about the Holocaust or the anti-Semitism they were subjected to as children; Mother told us that she had been chased on her grade school playground and called "dirty Jew," something that hurt and clearly stayed with her throughout her life. Dad attended college at a time when there were quotas for Jewish students. But I grew up wishing they might have responded to anti-Semitism with pride rather than by hiding. Their Jewish self-hate was one more family secret and, as such, was like a quiet cancer.

And so Mother and I made the rounds. The Catholics seemed dark and laden with layers of icons, tradition, and rules. They demanded a blind allegiance I couldn't muster. Lutherans were too severe. Methodists and Congregationalists too boring. Baptists seemed to teeter on the edge of a slippery slope, at the bottom of which were Pentecostals and Holy Rollers: groups more cultlike and raucous than our white upper middle-class culture would have been able to handle. Although Mother was helping me make my own choice and had no thought of subscribing herself, in retrospect I'm sure her running commentary influenced how I perceived each group. Much later, with my first husband, I would visit a Holy Roller tent that appeared on our city's desert edge. But that was more from curiosity than religious attraction.

Eventually I was drawn to the congregation of St. Mark's on the Mesa, a friendly Episcopal church in our neighborhood. There was something about the pageantry that appealed to me. It seemed saner than Catholicism but with similar vestments, ritual, and music. I had long since become the young girl who wouldn't take anything on unless I took it on with a vengeance. Within a year, and much to my parents' chagrin, I had been baptized and confirmed in the Anglican faith.

What was it that attracted me to Episcopal pomp and ceremony? Probably not the belief system, which I wasn't old enough to have researched thoroughly, as much as those elements of ritual absent from my family home and which appealed to my theatrical nature.

I remember around that time riding in my parents' car and crossing myself each time we passed a church of any denomination. I wanted the adults to notice. Perhaps I wanted to annoy them, as the gesture certainly did. Was this something we were taught at St. Mark's? I don't think so. Rather, it was a way of defining myself in a manner that differentiated me from my parents. It provided me with a secret sign that helped solidify some sort of budding individuality.

As I say, I wasn't one to do things halfheartedly. Soon I was teaching Sunday school. And sure that I had found the one true system of belief, I began putting a not so subtle pressure on my mother, father, and siblings to join St. Mark's as well. My sister Ann followed my example and remained an Episcopalian long after I extricated myself. My brother, the youngest, mostly escaped the trap. For a while, I was successful at shaming my parents into tithing, that astute requirement that claims 10 percent of one's earnings for the church. And it was precisely that issue of tithing that brought me to my rather dramatic rupture with St. Mark's on the Mesa.

Each Sunday, we were expected to place our weekly offerings in little envelopes that had two sides, one printed in black, the other in red. The black side was for church maintenance, and the red for missions. I guessed most of the children split their twenty-five cents, or whatever they gave, as equitably as possible. But it was around this time that I began reading voraciously. One of my favorite books was one I found in my parents' library. It was called *I Married Adventure* and had been written by Osa Johnson, wife of the photographer Martin.

As I read this and other books about great white hunters going to other lands where one of their stated intentions was to convert the natives to their own more civilized way of life (religion included), I thrilled to the sense of adventure but realized something was wrong. I didn't like these writers' attitudes toward those they referred to, condescendingly, as childlike natives. And I didn't think their religion necessarily made more sense than those practiced by the peoples they invaded.

Conquest and proselytization began to seem criminal to me. I'm still not sure why. Maybe I was gleaning such ideas from other books, maybe from someone I met along the way. Although liberal, my family wasn't particularly politically conscious, and I doubt that I picked up that critique at home. On the other hand, I may have. My father, especially, had a deep sense of social justice. He may well have questioned the colonialist assumption.

As my own ideas about missionaries developed, I began to put my whole Sunday offering in the black side of the envelope, leaving the red side empty. One day, the minister's wife confronted me, asking why I never contributed to missions. I was thirteen by then and had been a faithful member of St. Mark's for almost three years. And I was outraged. One, because I believed those contributions were anonymous. Two, because I felt I had the right to divide mine any way I saw fit.

Pete LaBarre was St. Mark's minister at the time, a relaxed and forward-thinking man. I cannot remember his wife's name. But I can't forget the confrontation we had: the thirteen-year-old parishioner unexpectedly and vehemently sparring with the modern minister's wife. Apparently, the argument spiraled out of control, and I left the premises in a huff. I resigned from that church then and there: the end of my experience as an Episcopalian.

Over the next few years, I began to think seriously about what I believed. Informal debate seemed to exercise some invisible muscle in my brain, and I engaged in it whenever possible. I began to gravitate toward artists and free-thinkers and absorbed those ideas that seemed most rational to me, and also most alluringly creative. When I attended my high school senior prom with Sam Stone, whose ambition was to become a Baptist preacher, we ended up in our finery sitting on a rock in the Jémez Mountains, arguing through the early morning hours about the existence of God. It goes without saying, he was pro and I con. When I told my friends where we'd been and what we'd been doing, I don't think one of them believed me.

It must have been as I left my teens and entered my early twenties when I decided I was an atheist. Not an agnostic, as my mother always claimed she was (fence-sitting or trying to cover all the bases seemed cowardly to me), but an atheist. How could one believe in a higher power, when there was so much horror in the world? Surely an all-loving God would have prevented that. A wrathful or punishing God never even occurred to me. (It may be that my early brush with Christian Science steered me in the direction of a loving god; in that religion the phrase above all others was "God is Love.")

Although I defined myself as an atheist and fifty years later haven't strayed from that position, I didn't hate religion. Not back then. I was in a distinct minority among my high school friends. I felt everyone had the right to choose his or her system of belief, and tolerance was my guiding principle. I couldn't have imagined the holy wars that would be fought during my lifetime, but I could see that a live-and-let-live attitude was healthiest for all concerned.

The four most formative periods of my life were the years I spent among New York City's abstract expressionists and writers in the late 1950s, my decade in Mexico City in the 1960s, my life in revolutionary Cuba from 1969 through 1980, and my time in Sandinista Nicaragua during the early 1980s. Each of these periods provided a different take on religion and religiosity.

Certain New York writers and artists surely held religious beliefs—parapsychology and different forms of mysticism were popular at the time—but as a group they tended toward nonconformity, and that extended to their attitudes about organized religion.

My good friend Elaine de Kooning had a loft on Broadway across the street from Grace Church, also Episcopalian. She was raised in an Irish Catholic family, but one that bent the rules in line with a person's needs. And Elaine was never one to subscribe to anything that would have put an obstacle in the way of her freewheeling life. She may have been attracted by the same pomp and ceremony that had called out to me when I was young, although on second thought it was probably the young minister at Grace Church who caught her eye. She didn't attend services but related to the place as a neighborhood focal point and could often be seen wandering its beautiful gardens. Many of the artists were Jewish, but again, I knew none who were observant. My years in New York were characterized by, among much else, an absence of religiosity.

Dorothy Day's Catholic Worker organization was active in downtown New York, and one of its members, Ammon Hennacy, became a friend. But we never once discussed religion. The Workers were much more interested in alleviating hunger and homelessness than in proselytizing. They would have considered it a sin to require church attendance from the people they helped. My most enduring memories of Ammon were from the demonstrations against the government's urging people to build little atomic bomb shelters, at which he always carried a prominent sign that read: "I am Ammon Hennacy. Arrest me." When I gave birth to my son, he brought one large perfect peach to the hospital as a gift.[2]

The panorama was different in Mexico. None of my close friends defined themselves as believers, but the country's popular culture was almost bipolar in its devotion to the Catholic Virgin of Guadalupe on the one hand and its strong separation of church and state on the other. The Mexican Revolution of 1910 and subsequent Cristero Revolution a few years later had produced a nation of secular law. But how could one ignore the influence of the Catholic Church with its yearly pilgrimages of thousands making their way on bloody knees to the Guadalupe shrine?

Our Lady of Guadalupe was the people's Virgin, in contrast with the whiter, more austere *Virgin de los Remedios*, imported from Spain and worshipped by descendants of the conquest. Guadalupe was dark skinned, familiar, and had first appeared to an illiterate shepherd. It was a matter of independence, race, and class. You could be a devotee of Guadalupe without going to church or observing Catholic restrictions. Overwhelming numbers of Mexicans conversed with Guadalupe on a daily basis, telling her their most intimate problems and feeling comforted by her love. In Mexico ancient indigenous belief systems can be felt in the stones of every imposing ruin. And the overlay of Catholicism, even when it isn't officially recognized by the state, is just as strong.

Mexico's religiosity manifested itself in processions, pageants, saints' days, art, music, and special foods. You might not believe, but you participated. Serafina, the woman who worked in our home, adored my oldest daughter Sarah, and suffered because we hadn't baptized her. The thought of that beautiful child not being saved kept her in a constant state of anguish. And so one day, I told her to take my baby and do the deed. It meant nothing to me and so much to her. This was religious practice as an act of kindness, not belief.

It was in Mexico, though, that other religious beliefs began to encroach on my personal life, and I learned that a particular system was not the only one I found insulting. The man who was then my husband, raised as a Catholic as most of his countrymen and women were, had long since rejected that faith. But at a certain point in our relationship, he became interested in other religious manifestations: first in the teachings of George Ivanovitch Gurdjieff and later in a variety of Japanese Buddhism. These explorations opened important doors for him. Perhaps they were necessary to his spiritual development. They also began to define his life in ways that helped to create a distance between us, philosophically and also practically.

By this time, feminism had begun to inform my thought and shape my life. For the first time, I understood—viscerally as well as intellectually—that problems I had believed my own were socially conditioned and shared by women as a group. The moment my husband declared, one day, that women could not attain Nirvana was definitely a turning point. It wasn't simply a personal affront but also a statement that got me thinking about religious authoritarianism generally.

Every religion, just like most political organizations, includes an authority figure to be blindly obeyed. I felt reconfirmed in my rejection of religious hierarchy, even when a particular group might claim a more horizontal framework, do good work, or fulfill the powerful need to belong that so many experience. There is always someone at the top, almost always a man, whose word is law. It would take me many more years to become wary of political organizations for the same reason.

By the time I moved on to Cuba, that husband and I had gone our separate ways. I was living with a North American whose attitude toward religion seemed much the same as my own. He too had Jewish roots, and although his family didn't suffer from the shame that afflicted mine, in terms of belief he didn't consider himself a Jew. We weren't destined to experience religious conflict, though eventually our attitudes toward other hierarchical structures differed to an important degree. Gender has so much to do with the ways men and women experience authority.

The Cuban Revolution reinforced my rejection of religion. The materialist state came into early conflict with upper-class and upper middle-class Catholicism and made cultural use of, but didn't really respect, the more popular African religions so rooted in the Cuban psyche. Although religious persecution never took the severe forms it did in the Soviet Union, during the revolution's first decades religious believers were prevented from joining the Cuban Communist Party, the only road to real power within the new political system. It wasn't until liberation theology, so important to social change on the Latin American continent, made its mark on the island that the Cuban Communists began to change their position with regard to the issue of political participation and religious faith.[3]

My children were raised in Cuba and received materialist educations; such that my youngest daughter, Ana, was fearful at age ten when she and I moved to Nicaragua and she was invited to a birthday party that included a Catholic mass. For the first time, I observed how virulent antireligion can be as frightening as intense religiosity. Both were limiting extremes. Although the Cuban Revolution talked a line of religious tolerance, in practice nonbelievers had a powerful advantage over believers.

Nicaragua was a different story. In that country, the revolution had been fought by people of faith and by Marxists—by those to whom their religious practice was important and by those who had none. Progressive religious sisters and priests educated a generation of socially conscious revolutionaries. I came to know Catholic nuns and ex-nuns who were among the most committed people I had ever known. Some of the women had entered convents because they wanted to be involved in social change and couldn't conceive of living their lives in subservience to men. Some eventually came out as lesbians.

When the Sandinistas took power, several of their leaders were Catholic priests. Although constantly challenged by Rome, they saw no contradiction between their religious faith and revolutionary commitment. Vatican II had produced a revolution within the Catholic Church, and liberation theology had taken hold throughout Latin America and in other parts of the world.

I remember my first year in Managua. During the early December season of devotion to the Virgin, I saw more than one image of Mary with the red-and-black Sandinista kerchief around her neck. The syncretism was profound. Liberation theology churches displayed stations of the cross in which counterrevolutionary forces attacked the Calvary of Jesus with tanks and guns. Within the Catholic Church, as within every other major world religion, a class struggle was taking place. The hierarchy was almost always conservative, while parish priests, more intimately in touch with the people, often worked diligently for social change.

My first year in Nicaragua, I worked at the Ministry of Culture, headed by Ernesto Cardenal: Sandinista, Catholic priest, and one of the Spanish language's greatest living poets. We had known one another since my years in Mexico, when the literary magazine we edited published his poems. Now his position as minister of state took him to many parts of the world. I remember one day, standing in a small group beneath one of the giant laurel trees in the ministry's garden. Ernesto had just returned from Lebanon and was telling us about the holy wars raging among Christians, Muslims, Hindus, Jews, and undoubtedly every other religious configuration. It was the class struggle, he said, splitting hierarchies from ordinary people just as was happening in secular society. This was 1981. It was the first time I heard the analysis that would later explain so much of what was to come.

In Nicaragua I was fascinated by the role Catholics and, to a lesser extent, members of other religions had played in radical social change. I researched and wrote a book, for which I interviewed members of a base community on the island of Solentiname as well as an urban parish in Managua.[4] Both groups had come to political conviction through biblical study. Both provided soldiers to the revolution, and both lost members to Somoza's fierce repression. I was interested in documenting a revolution that had not shied away from religious belief, as had been the case in Cuba, but embraced it as another reason why the struggle for justice was an imperative.

In the introduction to that book, I said I was an atheist, interested in the phenomenon from a sociological rather than religious point of view. I remember a man with whom I worked at the time questioning that self-definition. Why the need to identify yourself, he asked, why not simply tell the stories? Oral historians were beginning to define themselves as a way of situating their own personae with relation to those they interviewed, and I felt it was important to do this in that book. My colleague thought it politically unwise. He understood his people's deep faith and believed my book might not be received as positively if I revealed my position in that regard. Interestingly, although the book appeared complete in English, the Nicaraguan edition was published without the introduction.

Throughout my years in Nicaragua, despite my avowed nonbelief, I found much to like about the *misas campesinas* and other popular rituals that took place each Sunday morning at Managua's liberation theology churches. I continued to frequent them long after my book was out. I loved the music, the camaraderie, and the fact that discussions in the religious venues included a sort of questioning that was beginning to be absent from the more orthodox political gatherings. A certain sense of humanity was present. It was that humanity that had abolished the death penalty, when the Sandinista Revolution came to power, and permitted a range of opposing opinions in the press. This was very different from what had gone down in Cuba, and I felt it was healthy.

By the time I returned to the United States in 1984, change was on the horizon. And it wasn't a change that embraced justice. It would be five more years before the Sandinistas would be voted out of office in Nicaragua, with strong financial help from the United States. We had yet to witness the implosion of the Soviet Union and European socialism. Yet Ronald Reagan, Margaret Thatcher, and even Mikhail Gorbechev were pointing the way. The more-egalitarian societies we had built with so much sacrifice were about to go down in defeat.

Organized religion had a great deal to do with that defeat. The power exerted by the Vatican, by the rapidly expanding protestant denominations such as the Mormons and others, and in fact by every stripe of religious fundamentalism would wield great power in the defeat of socialism and in the defeat of other forms of social justice. The class wars within the world's major religions had taken their toll, and the dominant classes were emerging victorious.

Socialism, in its various forms, also bore some responsibility for the failure. It had become stratified and hierarchical, in other words too much like religion. And some measure of error could be ascribed to how it handled race and gender issues as well as religious belief itself. In condemning people's need for spiritual expression, it created a vacuum that traditional religion was quick to fill. One need only look to the subsequent history of Eastern Europe and those republics that broke away from the Soviet Union, to understand that taking people's religiosity by force is doomed to backfire.

As the twenty-first century dawned, religious fundamentalism achieved a frightening level of power. Those who would point only to the attacks by Muslim madmen on September 11, 2001, in New York and Washington, as emblematic of the new holy wars forget how fundamentalist Christianity spread its tentacles throughout the world for centuries, promoting conquest under the guise of conversion. They ignore the Promise Keepers and other groups of misogynist fundamentalists whose enormous rallies relegate women to second-class citizenship. They fail to make the connections between conservative Christianity and the Tea Party and other manifestations of right-wing political power.

They also forget the Zionist takeover of the Palestinian homeland, through which fundamentalist Jews continue to fuel years of killing. They forget decades of English-Irish conflict, the ongoing wars between Hindus and Muslims in parts of India and Pakistan, and the sharia law that deprives women and children of their rights in many Islamic countries.

In our own United States, Christian fundamentalism has made dangerous inroads into the political arena, reversing forward-looking legislation, reintroducing creationism into public education, and keeping this country trailing most other modern societies with regard to education, medical research, gay rights, hate crime legislation, and a general recognition of equality among peoples. Drummed up fervor around what they call the social issues—abortion, gay rights, school vouchers, and the like—excites great numbers of people to a strange frenzy from which they routinely vote against their own best interests.

The Mormon Church spent $17 million to overturn gay marriage in California.[5] Extreme religious dogma supports every backward social stance. Those who murder abortion providers do so in the name of a vengeful God. Despite centuries of scientific research, Christian fundamentalists teach that the world was created in seven days, four and a half thousand years ago, and that the Grand Canyon was carved by Noah's flood. During the George W. Bush administration, I saw a book written from this point of view on sale at a Grand Canyon National Park bookstore.

Powerful churches also protect their own, often at the margins of the state's system of justice. For decades now, Catholic priests have engaged in the widespread and long-term sexual abuse of minors. Those priests have been protected by their bishops. And the Vatican overlooked the situation until victims and their advocates proved too powerful to ignore. What finally forced the church to act, albeit inadequately, wasn't the trauma suffered by innocent young people but the threat of economic devastation. The church's legal defense cost so much that parishes began having to sell off their assets, including the church buildings themselves, in order to pay for lawyers, court fees, and appeals. Some parishes have disappeared altogether. Religious hierarchies have only admitted wrongdoing and made some attempt at restitution when they had no other choice: a classic example of authority defying the evidence until it could no longer do so.

Evangelical ministries have also been overcome by scandal in recent years.

Great megachurches, with congregations numbering in the tens of thousands, have seen powerful leaders and televangelists go down because of suddenly revealed misappropriation of funds or extramarital affairs, some of the latter involving homosexual liaisons or prostitution. The homosexual liaisons have been particularly dramatic, since evangelicals consider homosexuality an abomination and a sin. Yet these leaders' authoritarianism often wins the day. In many such cases, they explain their missteps as human frailty, ask God's forgiveness, and continue to enjoy the allegiance of their congregations. Forgiveness is, after all, a Christian virtue.

Given my history and my understanding that tolerance is always the wiser path, one might expect me to stand against only such extreme religious manifestations, not religion per se. Yet I find it increasingly difficult to separate the two. Authoritarian belief systems inevitably lead toward cowering before authoritarian order. Although many of my good friends, people I love and respect, hold religious beliefs, I admit to experiencing religion itself as a source of conditioning that discourages curiosity, creativity, independent thought, and social change. So while I appreciate the difference between fundamentalist madness (of any stripe) and the more open-minded religious manifestations, it's still hard for me to understand why an intelligent person would subscribe to either.

It may be the systems themselves that most annoy me. I retain an open mind toward what may happen after death. Perhaps it's the end, or perhaps our spirits do live on. We won't know for sure until the time comes. But the moment people try to explain what they believe by means of a system of whatever sort, I want to laugh. It just seems utterly absurd. Whether it involves karma, the rapture, salvation to some heavenly plane, eternal marriage, or any other configuration or scale of "good" and "evil," I want to ask: do you really believe all that?

I am curious about what the healthy individual needs and finds in organized religion. One thing is most certainly community, a place to come together with friends and neighbors for a sense of unity and solace, especially in hard times. But what is it about churches that provides this more than, say, social clubs or cultural organizations? Maybe it is the ritual that appealed to me when I was young or a structure where quiet and contemplation offer momentary escape from the overload of noise and motion that have become so much a part of our contemporary life.

None of this seems to fully explain the phenomenon, though. Faced with corporate criminality, unrelenting poverty, war, sickness, homelessness, environmental disaster, economic crisis, and the litany of lies that protect the whole sick panorama, people everywhere feel less and less in control of their lives. Religious belief seems to be gaining converts as the chasm widens. The relief many experience at not having to think for themselves, at being able to place themselves in the hands of a higher power, is clearly endemic to the human condition. Although it cannot fix the problem, it doesn't seem to be going away anytime soon.

In Albuquerque we have an institution we call Church of Beethoven.[6] It advertises itself as "not church . . . more than Beethoven." Every Sunday morning, when many in our community attend religious services of one kind or another, some three hundred people crowd into a loft building for an hour and a half of live chamber music, a short poetry reading, and a cup of excellent coffee. Two minutes of silence is the Church of Beethoven's concession to contemplation. We have found a beautiful way of coming together to celebrate community and art—with neither a higher power nor an earthly authority figure. I suspect other communities have similar programs.

Religion has gotten a (well-deserved) bad rap, and so another move that seems popular among some religious configurations today, at least here in the United States, is for the group to claim it is not a religion. I don't know if this is meant genuinely, or in reaction to the fact that the idea of religion does make some uncomfortable. There are different criteria by which this claim to secularism is made. A big one is when no belief in a higher power is involved. Without God, the reasoning goes, there is no religion. Yet the group in question generally follows all the other tenets found in religious bodies. Invariably, there is a minister, guru or leader of some kind. There is a physical building that must be cared for through the economic support of its congregation. And there are rules that must be followed. Exclusion is favored over inclusion.

When I hear the pope, dressed in his vestments of silks and gold brocades, urging his flock to care for the world's poor, I am appalled that flock doesn't see the contradiction. When radical Muslims send young people out as suicide bombers to murder innocent citizens and die themselves, I have to question allegiance to a dogma that permits much less encourages the practice. When a revered Buddhist teacher knows he has AIDS and has sex with young devotees without divulging the danger and then some of those faithful still defend the man, I wonder to whom they have given their sense of self. When a West Coast guru looks more like a Vogue model than a shepherd leading her flock, I wonder about that flock as well. And while the northern Arizona strip continues to harbor fundamentalist Mormon men who marry dozens of young women and impregnate them because God tells them to, I suffer for those young women and for the young men expelled from the community so they won't be competition.

All in the name of religion. Not sane religion, you may argue. But where is the line drawn? Once faith is blind, it has free reign. Many of the followers of Jim Jones were poor people of color drawn to a man who preached racial equality and urged them to move to a place where they would be free of the poverty and class stigma they were burdened with in San Francisco. The original message sounded sane indeed. Once he had them in literal isolation, the serious brainwashing began. By the time almost a thousand of his followers drank the cyanide-laced Kool-Aid, it was too late.

What I am left with is a deep love and respect for my friends who are believers. For myself, the whole range of religiosity leaves me angry. At a time when disaster follows disaster—some "natural," others criminally engineered, many a combination of the two—it is clear we need to learn to think for ourselves. To stop taking orders from those who have shown themselves over and over to be unworthy of our trust. To turn away from the "magical thinking" that would strip true magic from our lives.

It may seem strange, after this diatribe, when I say that I am a deeply spiritual person. My spirituality comes not from some imagined god or institution constructed in his name but from the rich desert landscape of the U.S. American Southwest or whatever natural setting where nature's harmony remains untouched. It comes from nature's fury, too, from witnessing that force of wind or rain or tide before which we can do nothing but stand in awe and watch, conscious of how insignificant and yet unique we are. And it comes in equal measure from realizing our significance—for example, when we love or give birth or read, or better yet write, the perfect poem. It comes when we immerse ourselves in a painting that speaks in a range of registers or listen to music so complex yet elemental it could only have been created on another plane.

Religion seems to me an obstacle to enlightenment; spirituality, its living map.

The Courage It Takes

In 1960, living in New York City, I opted out of a trip with the Fair Play for Cuba Committee to the recently liberated island, with the excuse that my son was only a month old and I didn't want to leave him at that early age. The truth is I didn't have the courage to go to a place already in the crosshairs of U.S. government disapproval.

Fifteen years later, had I still been living in the United States rather than Cuba, would I have accepted an invitation to travel to North Vietnam? I want to say "yes" but fear "no" is the honest answer. By the time of that second invitation, I had a broader comfort zone, largely because I now resided in a place where I was able to acquire a better sense of the world. And so I went to North Vietnam in the fall of 1974. Traveling to countries deemed off-limits by the U.S. government no longer posed the same sort of problem.

Looking back, I understand that courage became more natural to me not necessarily because I was older or more practiced in its art, and certainly not because of any romantic implications attached to the concept, but because I had grown in my ability to juggle political realities and my personal response to those realities.

I want to explore that intangible we call courage, the malleable stance we are all asked to assume from time to time, sometimes unexpectedly. I will begin with trying to remember what I was like at different moments in my life—the real me, not my public image. At this age or that, would I have had the courage to make such and such a decision or take such and such a step? One of the first conclusions I come to is that being courageous involves our ability, at each point along our journey, to access and use reliable information, to understand the world and our place in it.

Growing up, I heard a great deal of rhetoric about honesty, fairness, and justice. My parents—good people from conservative backgrounds, who were traveling their own road toward a more liberal outlook and often spoke about the values they wanted to cultivate in their children—proclaimed the evils of racism and the desirability of equality. I was convinced. But their words proved to be more attractive than their actions.

I remember the time I wanted them to rent a small apartment to my college friend from Ghana, who in our provincial southwestern city couldn't find off-campus housing in the racist 1950s. Although they had always proclaimed themselves accepting of people of all races, my mother and father refused to rent their vacant room. They argued that having a black man living at their house would bring down the street's property values. What would the neighbors think?

I was stunned and angry. My response was not to speak to my parents for several months. I definitely felt their courage had failed them. I even questioned whether they really believed what they taught. As a rebellious young woman, I only understood practicing what one preached or failing to do so. I conceived of no middle ground. I couldn't really decipher the forces that had shaped my parents' lives, their fears and insecurities. All I knew was that they had taught my siblings and me that all people are equal but that they were unable to act on that teaching themselves. I saw this as an egregious failure of courage.

Lately I have come to understand that the positions we assume most effortlessly have to do in some deep way with our ability to make connections. I think of it as a sort of global intelligence: how able we are to see the world around us and our place in it, how holistic our comprehension is.

Even at a relatively young age, I acquired a healthy mistrust of reality as presented by the public school education I was given, by lying politicians and a thoroughly biased mass media. I'm not sure how this came about, because my parents and most of those around me pretty much accepted the prevalent social values, even those obviously rife with hypocrisy. Many of my peers espoused a virtuous line but mostly just wanted to fit in when it came to what they said or did.

Perhaps because I sought out people with truly inquiring minds, perhaps because I was a voracious reader, I came to understand that the power structure routinely produces misinformation disguised as information and that the "democratic" notion of an impartial press serves as an effective cover-up for the defense of powerful interests. As a young woman, I wasn't able to explain this in so many words; my incipient values were instinctive rather than analytical.

Still, I learned to see through the control mechanisms used by major religious configurations, self-help movements, mainstream political parties, and even some of those closest to me—like family and friends. It took me a lot longer to develop a similar distrust of left-wing alternative ideologues and their organizations. My growing rage at the capitalist system's lies and manipulations led me to accept the lies and manipulations sometimes put forth by those with whose stated objectives and proposed solutions I agreed. My position, as a young woman before the advent of feminism's second wave, also kept me from asking too many questions.

I studied Marx and Lenin, Rosa Luxemburg and Ho Chi Minh, Wilhelm Reich, Samora Machel, and Fidel Castro and believed—still believe—their ideas point toward a social organization that is more just and egalitarian for the vast majority of people. Later I began to read many of the great feminist thinkers and was able to add a critique of patriarchy to my understanding of class and race.

What was more difficult for me to accept was the self-aggrandizement and eventual corruption of some of my revolutionary and feminist heroes. And like so many of my peers, I still compartmentalized. I had learned that an analysis of gender must be added to our analyses of class and race. But I didn't yet understand that the intersections of all these categories are where the important answers lie or that power itself holds the key to deciphering social, political, and economic relations.

I've written elsewhere that the Cambodian genocide was my generation's Stalin trials. It took the shocking Communist claim that Pol Pot's Killing Fields were an invention of Western journalists to stop me in my tracks. Following the revelation of that lie, I began to question everyone and everything. Never again would I take anything put forth by anyone I admired at face value. I learned to do my own research. Often I took a devil's advocate position, just to test my doubts and instincts.

In the highly stratified patriarchal time in which I came of age, it wasn't always easy for me to trust my intuition, especially when faced with male worship of almighty reason. For quite some time arrogance passed itself off as right.

Slowly, though, I learned to defend my perceptions and feelings. And more slowly still, I began to honor their artistic as well as intellectual aspects.

A few years into Nicaragua's authentic Sandinista period (the first half of the 1980s), I saw some of that movement's leadership lie about their personal enrichment and sexually accost any woman who struck their fancy. Some of my idols began to fade and fall. At first I continued to defend them publicly, believing the revolution was more important than a few individuals and allowing myself to be convinced that "washing dirty laundry in public" would hurt the cause. Slowly, I came to realize that the end never justifies the means. The values we wish to see in the new society must be incorporated into the struggle itself.

Toward the end of that decade, the Cuban Revolution's show trial and execution of Arnaldo Ochoa also gave me great pause. I had participated in many of the most beautiful achievements of both the Cuban and Nicaraguan revolutions. But I had also learned that social change is made by human beings and that many of them may be as power hungry and devious as the most ardent defender of capitalist inequality.

Feminism, because its most cogent thinkers have given us an important tool for looking at power, has remained a major source of strength and analysis. Even there, though, some major icons have disappointed: theoreticians who have given us interesting and even useful ideas, such as Mary Daly, Catharine MacKinnon, and Robin Morgan. Eventually I found the claims and stances of these and other feminist foremothers one-sided, lacking in the complex understanding that would have made them viable or life changing in the context of overall change.

Some revolutionaries, feminists, and other social scientists have stood the test of time for me. Their work continues to inform my own, and I will always be grateful. These geniuses continue to push my own thinking and feeling processes forward. Some, although by no means all, of those I continue to cherish are William Carlos Williams, César Vallejo, Nazim Hikmet, Fidel Castro during the first several decades of his leadership, Haydée Santamaría, Nelson Mandela, Ho Chi Minh, José Benito Escobar, Agnes Smedley, Elaine de Kooning, Meridel LeSueur, Adrienne Rich, Howard Zinn, Joy Harjo, Roque Dalton, Susan Sherman, Eduardo Galeano, Subcomandante Marcos, June Jordan, and V. B. Price. Although some of these names belong to twentieth-century political leaders, many belong to artists and writers. Many were, or are, poets. Imagination occupies a central place on my horizon.

I feel immensely fortunate to be a poet myself, to see the world and exercise much of my talent in it with and from a poet's sensibility. Perhaps it is this condition that ultimately rescued me from the dogmatic party-line mentality that at certain points in my life could so easily have carried me onto sterile, unimaginative, and dangerous terrain. As I grew older and nurtured the artist as much as the agent of social change, I was able to perceive truths more complex and nuanced than those that fill a variety of scriptures, policy statements, or political platforms. Feminism also helped me see through the authoritarian structures so endemic to religious and political movements. It enabled me to develop the ideas about power that are the basis of my worldview today.

With increased knowledge, courage became more accessible.

I have sought to surround myself with thinkers—artists, writers, unorthodox multidisciplinary scientists, and agents of social change—who value the process as much if not more than the product. This requires intentionality and no small amount of humility in a consumer-oriented society. Ongoing discussions with these good friends—who include my children, grandchildren, and very centrally my life companion, Barbara—are a continual source of growth.

I have learned to value the meaningful question ever so much more than the answer, no matter how brilliant the latter may seem. This brings me back to my earlier statement about how understanding the world and correctly situating ourselves within it make it easier for us to take courageous positions without stumbling over our choices.

I started this essay talking about courage, quickly retreating to the world of ideas. But I don't want to abandon courage or its close cousin, which is youthful improvisation and impetuosity. As a young woman, I did a number of things that many have regarded as courageous. In fact, they were little more than the result of throwing myself into the fray without a nuanced sense of why or an understanding of the consequences that might accrue. At times, I'm sure I did this to appear more courageous than I was—as if the act itself might bring with it the character trait. At times, I might simply have been exercising my decisive nature. I tend to distrust those who hesitate too long before choosing to move in one direction or another. Fence-sitting annoys me.

I engaged in the first of a list of what some have referred to as courageous acts when, living as a provincial young poet in New York City in 1960, I decided to have a child. I wasn't married or even in a steady relationship. Back then, polite society referred to such a birth as "out of wedlock." *Lock* now seems as relevant as *wed* in that strange description. Family members judged my decision as unwise, but I had the support of my artist friends on Manhattan's Lower

East Side. I never regretted bringing my son Gregory into the world. I never understood how the word *illegitimate* could be applied to a child. How can anyone judge the love between mother and child as anything but profoundly magical? Having my first child in that way never seemed courageous to me. It felt entirely natural.

Later decisions may have been a bit more rash. When I acquired Mexican citizenship in 1967, as the mother of three small children, I was married to a Mexican and knew that taking my husband's nationality would make it easier for me to work in my adopted country. What I didn't know was how relinquishing my U.S. citizenship would impact my later life (at that time, one couldn't hold dual nationality, and taking out Mexican citizenship implied I no longer had U.S. citizenship). In the 1980s, when I came home and was forced to fight the U. S. government for the right to reside in the land of my birth, I wished I had understood the consequences of that decision made so many years before.

In my youth, I also did things that were considered brave by others but responded more to the guilt I felt because my government was oppressing so many people around the world than to any carefully considered decision. I didn't gravitate toward options based on sufficient information about their pros and cons. One example is the time I casually agreed to smuggle a Guatemalan guerilla fighter across Mexico's southern border.

A friend had contact with representatives of the Guatemalan revolutionary organization that requested our help. They told him they needed someone to drive to the border city of Tapachula, retrieve the man in question, and bring him to Mexico City. My friend thought of me: the young U.S. American woman with a dependable car. Surely I would be beyond suspicion. I was glad to help. I'm not sure whether I refrained from asking the pertinent questions because of the well-established protocol regarding "need to know," or simply deferred to my friend's judgment because he was the man, and someone I trusted.

So, was participating in that act courageous or utterly foolish? We made the arduous trip, took all the suggested precautions, and still were stopped on our way back by local border officials. Our human cargo was heavily armed, something he had not thought it necessary to reveal. Only our on-the-spot creation of a pretty ingenious story saved him, and us. We delivered him as promised. I have often thought back to my willingness to be used in such a way as indicative of my youthful ignorance and gravely misplaced faith. That trip was only one of many involvements from which I am fortunate to have escaped with my life or, at the very least, my freedom. When you are young and believe completely in a cause, it is often hard to tell courage from foolishness.

In an unrelated incident, I once spent the night in the holding cell of a Mexico City precinct station. Anticipating a scene that he clearly thought he would enjoy, one of the policemen put an accused murderer in the same cell, then sat on a chair just outside its bars. I knew he hoped for action. I looked hard into the eyes of that man who shared the small space. Wordlessly, I tried to communicate to him that, at least in this particular time and place, we were on the same side. Then I curled up in a corner and went to sleep. My cellmate never touched me. My confidence in him was rooted more in what I hoped would be a shared code of honor than in courage per se.

This brings me to the issue of fear. Those who haven't had the experience may think that revolutionaries or others involved in David and Goliath struggles are fearless. Nothing could be further from the truth. A battle-worn combatant once told me that if a revolutionary claims not to feel fear, he or she is lying. I can attest to the truth of that statement. Courage is not a product of fearlessness, but the conscious decision to risk danger despite being afraid.

When I returned to the United States after nearly a quarter century in Latin America, my acquisition of Mexican citizenship in the sixties made me vulnerable to the sort of punishment our government metes out to those with whom it disagrees politically. In 1985 the U.S. Immigration and Naturalization Service ordered me deported based on the content of some of my books. Under the McCarran-Walter Immigration and Nationality Act of 1952, I was accused of being "against the good order and happiness of the United States." During and since the five years my struggle for reinstatement of citizenship lasted, people often called me courageous for standing up to U.S. governmental authority.

But that decision to fight for my rights never seemed courageous to me. The obstacles thrown my way were irritating, sometimes outrageously so; but I always felt fighting that particular battle was a logical outgrowth of my politics and, as such, quite simply what I was supposed to be doing. I believed I had the right to live in the land of my birth, to be close to my aging parents, and reclaim the landscape and cultural milieu so important to my creativity. I also knew the history of U.S. immigration law and how many lives it continues to destroy, lives of people who have access to far less support than I was able to attract. I was fighting to help change the law—for myself and for them.[1]

I define courage as the ability to make a particular decision or take a particular stand even when it may be far from comfortable—because you know it is the moral thing to do. The act may be small, almost insignificant in the eyes of some, such as stopping the telling of a racist, sexist, or homophobic joke or challenging a remark that is insulting to anyone's humanity. Or it may be huge, such as defending someone who has been wronged even when doing so means you too may be vulnerable to repression. Courage is the ability to stand up for what you know is right although you may be alone in that position. It requires a very complete and confident sense of self.

I want to get back to the more complex idea that the more holistic a sense one has of the world, the easier it is to take positions that may seem unusually courageous to some but in my mind more accurately respond to a deep understanding of where we stand in relation to the whole. Recently someone I love and admire asked what I thought is going to become of the planet. She meant what will happen to it in the wake of human-caused global warming, climate change, the greed-based and/or irrational acts of governments, and the inability even on the part of those who understand how we are shitting our nest to reverse the process.

The answer seems evident to me. The polar icecaps are already melting; the oceans, rising. Countries at or below sea level will cease to exist, and current coastlines will be radically reconfigured. Millions of people will be displaced. Hundreds if not thousands of species will disappear; a few may be able to change and adapt. Economies will collapse. Goods and services will become even more skewed than they already are. The differences between those few who own everything and the billions who have nothing will not be simply dramatic; it will have become unsustainable.

This immense and immensely complicated alteration of intra- and interspecies relationships will make for a very different balance, one that won't be able to sustain life as we experience it today. We are probably headed for a sixth major die-off. Studies of fossil and archeological records over the past 30 million years reveal that between 15 and 42 percent of the mammals in North America alone disappeared after the arrival of humans.[2]

Some die-offs, such as the extinction of the dinosaurs, were probably caused by natural phenomenon. The one we face now will be the result of bad citizenship. So the earth itself will continue to spin along with the other planets in our solar system. But our great-grandchildren, perhaps even our grandchildren, may not be around to witness the mind-boggling demise. (As with the implosion of economies, we don't really know how long it will take the earth to rid itself of those who are destroying it.)

We are so thoroughly conditioned to believe that life as we know it will always exist that such change is impossible for most people to comprehend. Even the increased frequency of devastating natural phenomena—such as earthquakes, tsunamis, great clusters of tornados, or a proliferation of destructive fires—seem more like discrete events than signs of change. And I'm not talking about the warnings proclaimed by Bible-thumpers or other apocalyptic terrorists. The science behind climate change and what it is doing to our lives is still shrouded in special interest doublespeak.

A similar veil has fallen over the more obviously human-made tragedies, such as the nuclear disasters, wars and holocausts, genocides and other large-scale repressions some groups of humans wage against others. All manner of inquisitions, apartheids, and ethnic cleansings have plagued our human history. The decimation of indigenous peoples, the Nazi's extermination of European Jews, Israel's oppression of the Palestinians, the Khmer Rouge's Killing Fields, Latin America's mass disappearances, Rwanda's grotesque mass murder of one tribal people by another—all have ended with the phrase "this must never be allowed to happen again." People meant this affirmation, and many worked hard to prevent repeat performances. And yet these holocausts did and do continue to be perpetrated, over and over and over.

In each of these terrifying scenarios, and others, courageous individuals have resisted. They have hidden potential victims, helped them escape (often at great personal risk), gotten the news out, lobbied for change, or in other ways fought against the terrifying status quo. These acts of courage have been extraordinary, moving, and powerful—each in and of itself and also in the positive energy they release. But collective courage has generally lagged far behind individual courage.

Now the courage—collective as well as individual—required to turn this around may in fact be unobtainable. It isn't easy for someone like myself, who for so much of my life believed we could create a better world, to admit that the time for such courage may be past. As I move through my seventies, I often ask myself if I am able to keep the idea of annihilation at bay because I have already enjoyed the privilege of a long life. Then I think of my children and grandchildren. What sort of future do they have?

Widespread misinformation, education that privileges memorization and testing over thoughtful investigation, blind religious fervor, the correct-line tendencies of political movements on both right and left, and the authoritarian teachings of prophets, priests, and gurus—all favor follow-the-leader mentality over in-depth analysis. In an increasingly complex world, abdicating to neatly packaged "systems" is more and more attractive. Why bother to think, when readymade answers are available for the taking? Group adherence to a figure believed to have the answers can seem so much easier than searching for the relevant information and making up our own minds. We are deliberately conditioned to intellectual laziness.

We live in a world in which success is measured by where we go to school, with whom we align ourselves, what clubs we join, whom we marry, how much we earn, and consequently what social status we acquire. Compliance with convention is rewarded.

Mixed messages—TV commercials touting fast food alongside those advertising diet plans, or ads for medications with a list of side effects that should make the most adventurous think twice before taking them—are everywhere. Even attempting to research most products on the Internet becomes an obstacle course, because so many of the available studies are paid for by the companies that manufacture the products in question. With this sort of corporate sleight of hand, it isn't easy to find the truth. Succumbing to the commercial designed to convince us that if we buy or ingest or use the product being advertised we will look like the model on our screen can so easily become the line of least resistance.

Courage happens when we realize we have a choice and when that choice posits taking an unpopular, even dangerous, position against tradition, social acceptability, familiarity, and personal safety. History is filled with examples of men and women who chose to do what they knew was right rather than hide within the folds of convention. Breathtaking are the thousands of cases of non-Jews during World War II who, risking imprisonment and even death, hid Jews persecuted by the Nazis. Photographer Gay Block and writer Malka Drucker spent several years documenting these rescuers of the Holocaust.[3] They wanted to know what compelled those who were not in physical danger to risk their lives in that way. The answers were invariably the same: "It was the only thing I could have done."

This is my definition of courage.

Every genocide, every great attack on human integrity and well-being, has its rescuers, those with the courage to move beyond their safety zone in order to save people they may not even know. Sometimes they get away with it, sometimes not. And every period in history has its almost indefinable moment, before which life is lived as it always has been and after which everything has changed. Knowing when to make the choice can be difficult, often almost impossible to calculate. It helps to have a moral framework that makes the right decision all but automatic.

Sometimes the decision may not present itself in such a life-or-death way, but it's nonetheless dramatic, its consequences also life changing. In El Paso, Texas, in 2007, the city council voted to provide citizen tax dollars to erect a monumental statue immortalizing the sixteenth-century war criminal Don Juan de Oñate. Powerful sectors of the community wanted Jon Hauser's seven-story statue; working-class and poor constituents, many of whom descend from his victims, did not. A single councilman, Anthony Cobos, voted against funding the statue. His courageous stance cost him reelection.[4]

More recently, the state of Arizona launched a ferocious attack on Mexican American studies in its public schools and universities. Arizona House Bill 2281 set the guidelines for comprehensive war against the people of Arizona connecting to their history. It isn't just against current law for educators in that state to teach anything but thoroughly sanitized white-bread history and literature. Dozens of books have already been banned. This list includes many of the most important Native American and Hispanic writers and also such classic authors as historian Howard Zinn, pedagogue Paulo Freire, award-winning novelist Leslie Marmon Silko, and political activist Winona LaDuke.

In January 2012 the Tucson Unified School District board voted four to one to uphold the Arizona ban. Across the country an immediate and defiant response came from educators, artists, writers, activists, and ordinary citizens who know that book banning is the first act toward all-out mind control. I think of that single dissenting voice on the district school board. It belongs to Adelita Grijalva, who called for the district to continue to defend in court the existence of Mexican American studies and to challenge the new law's constitutionality. Fox News quotes Grijalva as saying, "This is an issue that is not going to go away by this vote. When bad laws are written, they are usually picked up by other states. This is an opportunity to fight a bad law."[5]

How long will Grijalva remain on the job? What punitive measures does Arizona fascism have in store for the lone councilperson courageous enough to defend freedom against such odds?[6]

Courage is intimate and monumental. It may be evidenced by a woman who manages to escape her battering husband or by someone willing to reveal that his beloved parish priest sexually abused him fifteen years earlier. From time to time totalitarianism demands humanitarian response. Choosing courage may mean something as momentary as disrupting an otherwise easygoing social interaction, or it may risk breaking with family or community. Sometimes we have time to make our decision, while at other times we may be called on to react spontaneously, in the moment.

Courage can be lonely. Some of us find it easier than others. What is irrefutable is that it is something we can cultivate. We all need it and ultimately benefit from its grace.

Mirror, Mirror on the Wall

for Tineke Ritmeester

Queen: Mirror, mirror on the wall
Who in the land is fairest of all?
Mirror: Snow White is the fairest of them all.
—*Brothers Grimm, "Snow White"*

So goes the conversation between a vain woman and her mirror in one of the many versions of the German fairytale collected by the brothers Grimm in the mid-nineteenth century.[1] All versions have as their antagonists a woman obsessed with being beautiful and preserving that beauty forever and a daughter or stepdaughter more beautiful than she. All have in supporting roles a contingent of male dwarfs who protect the beautiful younger woman from the jealous and murderous older one. And all introduce at the story's climax a young prince or some other full-size male savior who rescues the hunted beauty—undoubtedly so she may also service him.

If mirrors could really speak.

But of course they do, although their voices may be distorted or hold forth in a language we do not understand. Almost all women, in our commodity-oriented societies, stand before them hoping to see ourselves as we have been conditioned to want to be: young, thin, unblemished, thin, demure, or confident, thin, thin, thin. Today's key to personal and social success is to be waif-like, and there is rarely such a thing as thin enough. This is hardly news. Still, it cannot be overly explored. For women in the United States, this desperate yearning to reduce our physical presence—the amount of space we occupy—crosses class, racial, and cultural lines.

It contributes, consciously or not, to our erasure.

It wasn't always this way. Peter Paul Rubens (1577–1640) painted an ideal woman who was fleshy in the extreme; *voluptuous* was the joyful adjective of the day. The images of Minoan women in the frescos we still admire are robust, with pendulous breasts and strong bodies. In Africa and countries with large populations of African origin, women with ample curves are considered desirable, and allusions to a hefty silhouette are meant to favor the recipient. In many poor countries, where food is at a premium, *How fat you are!* is a compliment.

When I lived in Cuba during the early years of that country's revolution, Alicia Alonso's ballet school was just establishing itself. Dance experts saw the full-hipped Afro-Cuban body as genuine and beautiful rather than as something to be starved into an emaciated figure resembling that of a prepubescent boy, and dance moves were especially designed with this body type in mind.

But here and now, in the United States, every message urges women toward being thin and toward a heterosexist subservience to the male. And each of these messages is a piercing high-pitched solo against a mixed-message chorus: the plethora of fast-food ads, medications rife with weight-increasing side effects, and a lifestyle from which even healthy walking has disappeared.

Size zero is the prize.

Thanks to the hard work of many feminists in many different fields, girl children now have a bounty of books in which they can read their variety of realities and dream of limitless potential. Still, tales such as "Snow White" are archetypal classics, embedded in our very culture, and they continue to shape our sense of self. All of us are prey to the stereotypical imagery, and few believe we make the grade.

This is where the mirror comes in. It rarely responds to our gaze with anything resembling truth but shows us an image comprised of a complex of distortions. The "perfection" each of us was taught to covet may be there somewhere: fleeing violence, disassociating from unwanted touch, hiding from abuse, trying to disappear when faced with the aggression of those with power over us, creating a place of invisibility and safety. Or that "perfection" may in fact stare back at us from within the glass, no matter what size and shape we are. Both these perceptual distortions come from the same social objectification, and both sleights-of-hand interest me.

Layered on the unobtainable or skewed early image may be a succession or mix of later images: the flat-chested model, the figure most desired by spouse or partner, a particular fashion currently in vogue, or some other look utterly foreign to our individual body type. Depending on who we are and the demons with which we do battle, we may actually see the desired image when we look in the mirror—or bemoan the fact that it will forever remain beyond our grasp.

Mirrors are magic, often in its cruelest incarnation. Rather than show us what others see, they give back imposter beauty or exaggerated failure. Weight, while a common indicator of acceptability, is far from the only one.

The glass surface speaks a complicated language, and we ourselves must provide the code through which we decipher its meaning. I know women who stop and look in every reflecting surface they pass, from shop window to three-way or magnifying makeup aids. I know others who avoid mirrors at all cost, refusing to contemplate their own physical image even when they prepare to step into their day.

As I say, there are those of us for whom mirrors invariably return an altered image. Not necessarily "better" or "worse," simply different. We look but may see someone older than we are, or younger. Thinner or fatter. Ready for the next moment or so tired we may doubt there will be a next moment. It's never *what you see is what you get.* No wonder that when Alice walked through the looking glass, she entered another world, one filled with double takes and realities that were not what they seemed to be.

Dictionaries tell us a mirror is an object that reflects light or sound in such a way that it preserves much of its original quality prior to contact. Some mirrors also filter out certain wavelengths while preserving others. This makes them different from other light-reflecting objects that do not retain much of the original signal other than color and diffuse reflected light. The most familiar type of mirror is the plane, which has a flat surface. Curved mirrors are also used to produce magnified or diminished images, focus light in certain ways, or simply cause image distortion. Side mirrors on automobiles are designed to warn us of approaching dangers, while a caveat lettered along the bottom cautions that what we see in them is even closer than it looks. The mirror in camera optics facilitates right-side-up observation of an object the lens views upside down. Fun-house and carnival mirrors play with these propensities, turning fragmented or exaggerated reflection into a game that delights some while frightening or horrifying others.

The first mirrors were probably pools of dark, still water or water collected in a vessel of some sort. The earliest manufactured mirrors were pieces of polished stone such as obsidian, a naturally occurring volcanic glass. Examples of obsidian mirrors found in Anatolia (modern-day Turkey) have been dated to 6,000 BC. Polished stone mirrors from Central and South America date from around 2,000 BC. Metal-coated glass mirrors are said to have been invented in Sidon (modern-day Lebanon) in the first century AD, and glass mirrors backed with gold leaf are mentioned by the Roman author Pliny in his *Natural History*, written in 77 AD. In China people began making mirrors with the use of silver-mercury amalgams as early as 500 AD.

From this brief overview of the fabrication and history of mirrors, we might surmise that they have developed in a purely utilitarian way: a device in which we can see ourselves and/or reflect other beings and objects, improving as technology advances. If we cannot look into them metaphorically as well as practically, though, we ignore a source of deep and provocative meditation regarding not only what we see but who we are and what keeps us from knowing who we are. Mirrors, as I say, are magic. And their magic powers may be disastrously damaging as well as excitingly revealing and creative.

Photographic portraits often provoke similarly confusing responses. Both mirrors and photographs involve reflections of light on a surface; but with those in a mirror, movement also plays a role, in which we have the prerogative of trying for a more acceptable angle. A single moment stretches to become a parade of moments, extending to give us a trail of repeats and returns.

In a photograph, we are stopped in time and place. Light and shadow are captured by a mechanical instrument. Someone looks through a viewfinder, glass plate, or digital monitor. The movement of a finger pressing a shutter determines the result. The intention of the person making the photographic image adds another layer of meaning.

I once visited a remote mountain village where none of the inhabitants had ever seen him- or herself in either mirror or photograph. I made some portraits and returned several months later, bearing pictures for those whose images I had taken. Not a single person recognized him- or herself. They had no idea what they looked like. To whom, then, were they introduced by my portraits?

Not all mirror mythology is as gender biased and focused on constructions of female physicality as *Snow White*. Obsidian mirrors and other objects held power in pre-Columbian cultures throughout North and South America, reaching significant intensity with the Aztecs to whom obsidian was a sacred stone. Coatlique, mother and "earth monster" in the Aztec creation story, was first impregnated by an obsidian knife, resulting in her giving birth to Coyolxanuhqui (goddess of the moon) and to a group of male offspring who became the stars.

The Aztecs also used obsidian to create images of their god of sorcery and divination, Tezcatlipoca, or "Mirror that Smokes." The antithesis of Quetzal-coatl, the Feather Serpent who stood for life, love, and luminosity, Tezcatlipoca represented darkness. He was god of the nocturnal sky, of ancestral memory, and of time. Another manifestation of this dark god was Itzpaplotl or Itzlaco-liuhque, translated as "Obsidian Knife Butterfly" (itself a description that holds dualities). She was the lovely female goddess of fate, stars, and agriculture.

Mother. Life. Luminosity. Darkness. Ancestral memory. Time.

Life and darkness may seem to be in contradiction with one another in today's simplistic or clichéd rendering. But duality is always present in myth. I am interested in the juxtaposition of time and ancestral memory in these legends, and in how both inhabit the mirror simultaneously. Duality of meaning is always powerfully present in our archetypal symbols.

I began with the Snow White story because it is such an apt metaphor for women in our society: how we perceive ourselves, how others perceive us, and where we are taught to turn for the solutions to our problems. There are vari-ations in the way the story has surfaced in different countries, its translations into a variety of languages, and how it has been rendered in other mediums (including the Broadway play staged in 1912 and the family-friendly Walt Dis-ney animated film of 1937). Each of these representations reflects social stric-tures of time and place, in turn influencing women's yearnings and the choices they have made at each historic moment.

The following is as faithful a rendition of the original story as I have been able to put together:

Once upon a time a queen sat sewing at her window. She pricked a finger on her needle, and three drops of blood fell on the snow piled on her ebony windowsill. Looking at the scene, she wished for a daughter with skin as white as that snow, lips as red as the drops of blood, and hair as dark as ebony. Soon after this, the queen gave birth to a daughter with precisely these characteristics. She named her Princess Snow White and almost immediately died. The unspo-ken implication is that she died in childbirth: a mother's ultimate sacrifice.

The king took a new wife, also beautiful but excessively vain. This new queen had a mirror, an animate object that answered any question asked of it. The queen frequently asked, *Mirror, mirror on the wall / Who in the land is fairest of all?* The mirror always replied *You, my queen are fairest of all.* That is, until Snow

White attained unmatched beauty at the age of seven, at which point the mirror began telling her *Snow White is the fairest of them all.* The jealous queen then ordered one of her huntsmen to take the beautiful child into the woods, kill her, and return with her heart as proof of the deed done.

The huntsman was loath to complete the heinous task. He told Snow White to flee from her stepmother, shot a doe, and delivered its heart to the queen. The palace cook prepared the heart, which the queen then ate believing she had vanquished her competition. Meanwhile, in the forest, Snow White came upon a small house inhabited by seven dwarfs. They offered to take her in and protect her, in return for her cooking, cleaning, sewing, and otherwise caring for their every need. The next time the queen asked her mirror, *Who is the fairest of them all?* she was horrified to hear the name Snow White once again.

The story continues with the queen disguising herself on three different occasions and visiting the dwarfs' cottage, where she tries a number of unsuccessful ruses in order to do away with her beautiful stepdaughter. In one of these, she helps the young girl into a corset and then pulls its laces so tight that the child faints. A more extreme example of forcing the female body into complete submission is hard to find.

The Queen's last attempt to do away with her stepdaughter involves getting her to eat a poison apple. Snow White ingests the apple and falls into a deep sleep. The dwarfs, believing her dead, place her body in a glass coffin. Time passes, and a prince traveling through the land sees the coffin with the princess inside. He falls in love and begs the dwarfs to let him have her—apparently even dead beauty has its allure. With the dwarfs' consent, the prince's servants carry the coffin away. But they stumble and fall, causing the piece of poison apple to dislodge from Snow White's throat. She wakes and finds her prince charming, who, once and for all, rescues her from her evil stepmother.

But the story doesn't end there. The vain queen, still believing Snow White dead, once again asks her mirror, *Who is fairest in the land?* The mirror responds, *You, my queen, are fair; it is true. But the young queen is a thousand times fairer than you.* Not knowing that this young queen is her stepdaughter, the jealous one arrives at the wedding. When she realizes the truth, her heart fills with dread. As punishment for her wicked ways—and as the moral of a story whose intention is to teach young girls about goodness and reward—a pair of heated iron shoes is brought forth with tongs and placed before her. She is then forced to step into them and dance until she dies.

In gendered Western culture, the mirror that proclaims Snow White the fairest of them all is a perfect, and insidious, metaphor for the tyranny of women's external characteristics and the process through which we judge ourselves—what our own mirrors tell us. I don't believe I have ever met a woman whose mirror tells her the truth. The truth is relative, you may say. I agree. Still, there is almost always a vast difference between what we see in a mirror and anything resembling what others see when they look at us.

Age is one of the most interesting variables. I once asked hundreds of women I knew what age they see when they look at themselves in the mirror. None saw a woman her age. Many saw a reflection commensurate with how they felt inside—in most cases, younger than their chronological years. Although I am seventy-six, for a long time now I have seen myself as somewhere around forty. I am always surprised to look down and note my gnarled hands or the loose skin of my neck and upper arms. In the mirror, I remain a full three decades younger. My mother, not long before her death at ninety-six, continued to view her mirror image of around sixty.

As we approach the mirror's surface, many of us strike a certain pose, holding our bodies in ways that we've been taught display it to its best advantage. We may stand straighter, suck our bellies in, lift our chins to pull sagging skin taut, turn to the three-quarter view for a slimmer image, or arrange our faces at their most favorable angle. My mother used to tell me to cover my parted teeth with closed lips, as a way of making my nose appear smaller. She was the one who considered my nose too big, not me. It is as if the mirror is, indeed, alive and responsive to what we consciously bring to it. Like the evil queen's mirror, ours talk to us, and they don't always tell us what we want to hear. Depending on our personal histories and expectations, their discourse may push us in different directions.

Consider other aspects of the Snow White story. To begin with, what expectant mother thinks first of her newborn's physical beauty? Every mother knows our only and fervent request is for a child healthy in mind and body. In the fairy tale, beauty is a life-and-death proposition.

Then there's the nature of that beauty, not unique or interesting but stereotypical: white skin, red lips, and ebony hair. Like Barbie dolls and other popular toys, this reinforces the racist assumption that the whiter a woman's skin, the fairer she is. And the prince falls in love with a woman who is completely passive, lying in a coffin. This story also pits one woman against another, in line with that insidious female competition rigged at all levels of our social interaction.

Perhaps most important of all are the various ways in which the princess's life is saved: first by the compassion or pity of the huntsman, then by assuming all housewifely duties for the dwarfs, and finally through the love of a prince who is smitten by her beauty even when he presumes her dead. Nowhere in this story is Snow White encouraged to resort to her own intelligence or creativity. Never is her life saved because she herself takes a risk or commits an act of courage or ingenuity.

There is the interesting bit about her heart, through history and cultures a symbol of power. If the jealous stepmother had in fact been able to devour it, the implication is that she might have been able to take that power for herself. I am reminded of the hearts of Aztec prisoners cut from their bodies with obsidian knives, the obsidian in that case playing a very different role than it did when fashioned into a mirror. Removing those hearts was clearly a way of taking the enemy's power—en masse.

I think, too, of the Mexican painter Frida Kahlo and her mirror-image self-portraits, in which blood often runs from one dual heart to the other, telling a ferocious story of suffering, rage, and reclaimed identity.

And then we have the end of the Snow White story with its peculiar punishment for the evil queen. Not the abused young princess, not even her prince charming, is given the satisfaction of deciding what should happen to the jealous stepmother. Instead, she is made to dance in red-hot shoes until she dies, presumably of burnt feet—yet another powerful image of wild abandon (in this case dancing) causing a woman's death.

Snow White, long analyzed by European feminists, remains an excellent fable for mainstream women and the mirrors in which we search in vain for an image that speaks our deepest truth. That truth may be psychic or emotional; or it may be physical, which in our social structures has ever more forcefully become a stand-in for every truth—especially for women. We look in the mirror hoping to find ourselves. Instead, we find an image that tells us we aren't good enough: too fat or too thin, too old or too unfashionable, too dark or with the wrong kind of hair—out of sync with today's prescription for success, whatever that may be.

I have said I am interested in the juxtaposition of time and ancestral memory, and how these inhabit the mirror and also the photographic image. These elements are present but remain unseen by those of us who internalize society's patriarchal messages about what constitutes beauty, acceptability, and success. With the photograph we also have that fixed moment, a person inhabiting a particular landscape at a particular time and in a particular way that will never be repeated. The instant holds clues we can decipher only if we use our experience—our learned understanding of class, culture, gender, and the other elements of identity that construct and define our lives.

Our ancestral memory—who we truly are and can be—is erased by a time that has been flattened by patriarchal values, wars, disdain, and ignorance. I believe time is circular or spiral, with neither beginning nor end. In our societies it has been commercialized and commoditized until it has become a linear equation, as if it does not build on itself, and until it can no longer bear our weight and we ourselves cannot partake of its healing powers. Rather than the embodiment of our journey, time then becomes our enemy, that which wrinkles our skin, adds inches to our girth, grays our hair, and renders us old or inadequate or broken as that image we see in the mirror.

I am left with these questions: Is time a mere organizing principal, or can we reconceptualize it so that it will not drag us to our doom? And how may we restore memory to image, in order to reclaim a self that empowers?

Lord Power

What we know about the highly publicized case of a powerful man raping a powerless woman is this: the man is Dominique Strauss-Kahn, a millionaire and influential figure in the world of international finance. Until the event about which I write, he was president of the International Monetary Fund (IMF) and a likely Socialist Party candidate to the presidency of France. The woman is Nafissatou Diallo, a poor, defenseless, undocumented immigrant from Guinea and a maid at New York's Sofitel Hotel. On the morning of May 14, 2011, she entered his room to clean it. He frightened her by coming out of the bathroom naked and forced her to perform oral sex on him. If there is anything unusual about what has been reported, it is that any notice at all was taken of a powerful man attacking a powerless woman.

So far, both sides agree to the general facts of the case, except that Strauss-Kahn predictably says the act was consensual and Diallo says it was not. She claims she tried to argue with him, push him away, and even tell him her floor supervisor was right outside the door. He disregarded her pleas and charged ahead in his attack. She was sickened—afraid of losing her job and even, as she later explained, of hurting him (she was taller, although he was stronger). His abuse caused her to pull a shoulder ligament. She had bruises on her vagina, and her stockings were ripped. He achieved his goal of oral sex, after which she spit his semen out on the rug and ran from the room. Despite the motto of most hotels that "the customer is always right," she dared report the incident to the Sofitel's authorities. At the time, she had no idea the man who assaulted her was an internationally known financial figure.

Interestingly—because tens of thousands of such cases end with the abuser getting away with his *droit de seigneur*—the Sofitel contacted the New York City Police Department. Strauss-Kahn, about to return to France, was pulled off his departing flight, arrested, put in jail, and obliged to remain in New York to stand trial.

In the United States, feminists were outraged and loudly rallied to Diallo's defense. In France, at least at first, most women (including feminists) thought the whole affair overblown and laughed at the puritanical social mores operative in a country they generally see as amusingly unsophisticated. Men are like that—powerful men even more so. It just wasn't something worth getting excited about. In the immediate aftermath of this event, approximately half of France's population—women as well as men—faulted the U.S. legal system for having arrested and charged Strauss-Kahn. They thought it especially inappropriate that such an illustrious individual had been presented to the media in handcuffs.

Strauss-Kahn himself vociferously denied the charges against him. It was clear from his demeanor, even while in handcuffs, that he believed he had done nothing wrong. Several weeks into the series of resulting stories, *Newsweek* reported that the Sofitel's records revealed that nine minutes after the incident, he was on the phone making a lunch date with his daughter. Strauss-Kahn's wife stood by her husband but made no public statements. Presumably, his conduct was acceptable or at least didn't surprise her—although this is the first time it had landed him in this sort of trouble. Perhaps she, too, felt the Americans were making much ado about nothing.

Not surprisingly, leading up to Strauss-Kahn's trial, the wheels of influence surrounding male power began to turn in his favor, and the humiliation reserved for poor and powerless female victims resulted in Diallo being depicted as unsavory, opportunistic, and a liar. A picture quickly emerged of Diallo as an uneducated "illegal" immigrant with convicted drug dealer friends, someone who, when she discovered her attacker's identity, was rumored to have set out to make money from the incident. The police interviewed her, by interpreter, in her native language, a dialect of Fulani; and a later review of the transcript showed that a good deal of mistranslation had taken place.

Although for a brief while it seemed Strauss-Kahn would, in fact, have to stand trial for rape, the stories released about Diallo began to affect the prosecution's case, and his prominent highly paid lawyer soon got him off. Until she consented to doing some prime-time TV interviews and press stories, in which she acquitted herself quite well, doubts continued to be cast on Diallo's integrity and good faith. Following these interviews, however, highly respected mainstream journalists expressed their opinions that she was telling the truth. As is so often the case, these mostly male pundits were believed while she hadn't been. Slowly, the aura surrounding this story began to shift yet again.

At this point Strauss-Kahn was placed under house arrest. At first the U.S. authorities kept his passport so that he couldn't leave the country. Soon, however, he was released and returned to France, where, as you will remember, women mostly just took his known seductions of women in stride.

But wait.

All of a sudden a discussion broke out in the French press. If not surprised by the fact of male philandering, some of that country's feminists now began to question the power inequity in this particular case. And then Tristane Banon—who was neither an immigrant, a prostitute, or a hotel maid, but a respected journalist—stepped forward and accused Strauss-Kahn of attempting to rape her in 2003. She had gone to him for an interview, she said, and he had received her in an apartment clearly set up for his extramarital affairs; it had been furnished only with a bed and a few chairs. He had ripped her bra and panties while they struggled on the floor, but she had managed to fight him off. She hadn't reported the attempted rape at the time, for fear of bringing bad publicity to the Socialist Party; back then Banon's mother had encouraged her daughter's silence. Today the mother confirms the daughter's story.

It seemed that although Strauss-Kahn was able to avoid a criminal trial in the New York case, he would still have to deal with civil charges here. And in his native France he faced this new accusation. He was forced to resign from his post at the head of the IMF, and his chances of becoming future president of his country may have been damaged beyond repair. Only time, the tenacity of prosecutors and defense teams on both sides of the Atlantic, and the influence men like this can garner will determine how this case ultimately unfolds.

I am, of course, much more interested in the larger picture than in Strauss-Kahn's fate, or even in whether or not Diallo will obtain a measure of justice. How is our society shaped by the attitudes toward powerful men forcing themselves on less powerful women? Should every act of sexual transgression or malfeasance committed by a male political figure be reason enough to strip that man of his position—in other words, does a man's personal conduct necessarily affect his work on behalf of the public? When the powerful take advantage of the powerless, especially through violent means, what does that say about the victimizer's general attitudes and actions? Should married and unmarried men be held to different standards? Should the rules be different for males and females in public positions?

Throughout much of the world, including France, the public and private spheres are kept separate, especially for men. This may advertise itself as social sophistication, but most often it hides significant male privilege. In some countries women who stray outside marriage are stoned to death, while men are able to take refuge in every sort of religious or secular loophole.

Here in the United States, until not that long ago, the private lives of men in high offices were off limits to the press. Among U.S. presidents of recent memory, Franklin Roosevelt and John Fitzgerald Kennedy come to mind. Everyone knew about their mistresses; but as long as an opponent didn't decide to capitalize on the issue, it remained a private matter. Italy's President Berlusconi is infamous for his philandering; but to date, even a tryst with an underage girl has failed to bring him down.

And religion plays an important role here. I translate *droit de seigneur* "lord power" intentionally. Almost every major religion places men directly below a male god figure and women below men. Each has the right to manipulate the next in line. Religious dogma reinforces male status and control.

In the United States, where a puritan ethic reigns and women have long been expected to play supportive roles, most wives of well-known men caught having extramarital affairs have stood by their husbands in their moments of disgrace. This stance seemed to gain the women a measure of dignity—or martyrdom (always attractive in women)—as they endured the unwelcome spotlight. Jacqueline Kennedy was spared public humiliation because the press protected her husband: everyone knew of his trysts, yet no one spoke publicly of them. Doing so would have been considered disrespectful to the office of the presidency back then.

By the time it was Hillary Clinton's turn, impeachment hung in the balance. After Bill Clinton's affair with Monica Lewinsky, it seemed every woman in the country had an opinion as to whether or not Hillary should stick by her man. She was permitted a period of visible distance. But in the end, she had her own ambitions. Who knows if it was love, genuine forgiveness, or political expediency that caused her to reconcile and remain married to someone who had so flagrantly caused her private pain and public embarrassment?

More recently, the list of male public figures caught in flagrante has become longer and longer; here in the United States not a month goes by without the press or some political adversary gleefully announcing that so-and-so has been caught with a prostitute, in a secret relationship with someone of the same sex, sending improper e-mails to an underage intern, impregnating another woman while his wife is dying of cancer, or advertising his "charms" via the Internet or Twitter—in a world where instant digital communication erases any semblance of privacy. Republicans make sure they mention the party affiliation of Democrats. Democrats return the favor.

The public attitudes displayed by the wives of these men have begun to vary somewhat. Eliot Spitzer lost the governorship of New York after his identity as an expensive call girl's Client Number Nine was revealed. His wife, Silida Wall, a successful lawyer in her own right, did more than stand by him. She took public blame for her husband's transgression. In several news stories, she told reporters, "The wife is supposed to take care of the sex. This was my failure; I was inadequate." Wall's statement seemed shocking to many women. Some philandering public figures seek solace in religion, claiming God has forgiven their sin. Their wives may adhere to the marriage vow "for better or for worse" and believe that if God has forgiven their husband, they should too. But a modern woman with her own career publicly admitting she was sexually inadequate?

No longer is it assumed all wives will stand by their men so supportively, though. At first it was simply the facial expression that changed: instead of a dignified silence, some women appeared angry—or didn't appear at all. Several have wasted no time in filing for divorce, such as California governor Arnold Schwarzenegger's wife Maria Shriver, who discovered her husband was having a long-term relationship with their housekeeper who had borne him a child.

Ex-presidential candidate John Edwards's wife, Elizabeth, maintained her belief in her husband even as rumor became proven fact and it was clear that he was still having an affair with a campaign videographer who had given birth to his child. Finally, at whatever breaking point, Elizabeth stopped defending him and sought a divorce. A year or so later she died of cancer. The public uniformly applauded her response throughout this ordeal—both while she stood by her man and after she left him. Perhaps it was the incurable cancer that earned her such role model status. Our culture loves women who die with dignity and grace.

And so it goes. Some women refuse to take public humiliation easily. Others may feel they have more to lose by leaving than by staying. We have the case of New York representative Anthony Wiener, who in June 2011 first denied sending lewd photos to a young woman online and then admitted he had done so—to her and a number of others. Wiener was a hardworking and effective Democratic politician whose constituents loved him. But the revelation proved too much, and he was forced to resign. His wife, Huma Abedin, preferred to remain out of the spotlight. A longtime aide to Secretary of State Hillary Clinton, she was also pregnant when the scandal broke. One can assume that her boss and mentor had some advice to share with her assistant.

In the United States the honesty factor is critical. Most of the men mentioned above at first denied their transgressions, often vehemently. For a few days or even weeks, we were treated to the bad playacting, the devious dance in which the guilty party tried to maintain his innocence. We remember Bill Clinton's defiance, his repeated insistence that he "did not have sex with that woman" (note his refusal to dignify his victim with a name), and the spate of jokes around the meaning of the word *it.*

Not until Clinton was forced to testify under oath did he come clean. Many regarded the president's lies as being worse than the act perpetrated against the young intern. Still, I saw quite a few bumper stickers proclaiming "Clinton lied and nobody died!" Few public transgressors have lied more extravagantly than South Carolina governor Mark Sanford, who in June of 2009 claimed he was hiking the Appalachian Trail, when he was actually visiting his mistress in Argentina. His wife moved out when the truth was discovered, and divorced him soon after.

I am less interested in the changing social mores that now allow the wives of public figures a range of individual responses than I am in the issue of power itself: its gendered nature in a patriarchal society and whether a lack of honesty about one's personal conduct necessarily denotes a lack of honesty in public office. Power inequity, wherever and however it occurs, prejudices the subservient group in ways that reverberate through our society as a whole. It also warps the perpetrators, holds skewed values up as model conduct, and pushes truth down a dead-end street.

Although Nafissatou Diallo's story was substantiated by the evidence, she had been immediately made suspect in all other areas of her life when she was thought to have lied in an attempt to gain entrance into the United States. It momentarily invalidated her accusation and caused the U.S. court to back away from its case. Dominique Strauss-Kahn, on the other hand, has a long history of lying about his personal life and perhaps his business dealings as well. Lying to at least some degree is the acknowledged currency of such men. Yet arresting him, bringing him into the courtroom in handcuffs, and otherwise treating him like any other person charged with a crime was considered unacceptable by his defenders. He is, after all, an important and powerful man. Diallo suffered all sorts of gratuitous attacks in the press. Because she is a poor immigrant woman, and perhaps most shockingly one who has dared to accuse a man such as Strauss-Kahn, few questioned the way she was treated.

That there is a deeply entrenched double standard is nothing new in a class-stratified society. That this double standard almost always accrues to the benefit of men is nothing new in patriarchy. On university campuses male professors routinely seduce their female students; and dependent as they are on grades, only occasionally do such students dare to report their victimization. Even more rarely does the university support the student's right to redress. Within the Catholic Church, for far too long, male bishops have protected male priests against accusations of blatant and widespread sexual abuse.

Great writers, to whom we continue to look for moral example, have themselves also written with pride about their droit de seigneur. Victor Hugo kept a secret diary in which he went into great detail about his illicit activities with female servants in his later years. In fact, he called these activities consensual, claiming that the women in question charged him a few cents to glimpse their breasts, half a franc to view their naked bodies without being allowed to touch, one franc to caress them, and a franc and a half—or even two!—for "full service." Male Hugo scholars have delighted in this diary, without a word about the unequal power relationship between the famous writer and the poor women who were the objects of his seduction.

Fast-forward, historically. A few years before his death, the great Chilean poet Pablo Neruda published his autobiography, *I Confess I Have Lived*. In an overall fascinating book, I won't forget the chapter in which Neruda confesses to raping a chambermaid from the untouchable caste during his tenure as his country's ambassador to Ceylon. The poor woman entered his room each morning to retrieve his chamber pot. He described her as exotically beautiful. One morning, he grabbed her and without a word had his way with her. She too was silent throughout, no doubt incapable of thinking she had the right to protest. In his book, Neruda follows this admission, which exudes a sense of entitlement, with a pitiful mea culpa, as if his acknowledgment that it was wrong somehow made everything right. I found this story shocking. Most readers of the autobiography, female and male, excused the poet based on his literary contributions and communist concern for the poor.

In almost every country—Western or traditional, rich or poor, capitalist or attempting a transition to socialism—men feel entitled to use and abuse women, justifying their entitlement by custom, religious dogma, class status, racial dominance, or simply because they get away with it. And society as a whole goes along with this assumption. Parents—even mothers—teach both daughters and sons that this is the natural way of things. Schools reinforce these teachings, religions authorize them, the corporate media deploys messages that support the status quo, and popular culture makes it all seem perfectly normal.

And I want to say something more about entitlement. Were it not so deeply engrained, so much a part of what men perceive as their birthright, surely fewer public figures would engage in illicit activities that, if discovered, could bring them down. In the United States so many men have had to retreat from public office because they have been caught at these activities that one would think politicians would refrain from such behavior. They must truly think they are immune. Or they don't think at all, so pervasive is their sense of entitlement.

This is the tension that concerns me, highlighted each time we have a news story about a powerless woman sexually abused by a powerful man, whatever the response in public opinion or legal resolution may be. These are but isolated examples of an ongoing war that rages in almost every culture everywhere on earth. And believe me it is war: male against female, power against powerlessness, glorified and protected soldier against abused and vulnerable victim.

Rape is a product of war. But societies have a hard time defining war. Most people agree that nations fighting nations are engaged in wars, but those same people may not accept the fact that other endemic sorts of war exist everywhere there is a misbalance of power: between abusive men and the women they control, between abusive parents and their children, between the religious or political hierarchies in which men generally dominate a membership subject to their privilege, and between any group and those who are able to manipulate that group.

All these situations of inequality are wars of one sort or another. All have victors and victims. True, some produce thousands or tens of thousands of victims in bombings or battles featured on the nightly news, while others hide just as large a number behind the secrecy cultivated in the presumed "sanctity of the home" or in the privacy of organizations that refuse to make their everyday abuses public. Some produce their victims in dramatic conflagrations, while the victims of others remain mostly hidden from view.

Rape has long been a feature of both types of war. It is one of the oldest weapons in conventional warfare but until recently was treated much like looting, as regrettable collateral damage rather than as a war crime. Clearly, this is because most victims are women, usually second-class citizens in their respective societies. The raping of women has been so effective, in fact, that men have taken to raping men as well; in Latin America during the 1970s and '80s, this was a favored method of torture that broke the spirits of more than a few rebel prisoners.

Throughout history, armed conflicts and military occupations have produced their share of rapes, often committed by the defending as well as the invading soldiers. Sexual slavery is also a tragic aftermath of war, often causing generations of shame and damaged lives; the Japanese comfort women of World War II are a notable example.

Rape in the context of armed conflict was first recognized as a crime against humanity when the International Criminal Tribunal for the former Yugoslavia issued arrest warrants based on the Geneva Conventions and the Violations of the Laws or Customs of War. Specifically, it was recognized that Muslim women in Bosnia and Herzegovina had been subjected to systematic and widespread gang rape, torture, and sexual enslavement by Bosnian Serb soldiers, policemen, and members of paramilitary groups after the takeover of the country in April 1992.

This indictment was of major legal significance and was the first time sexual assaults were investigated for the purpose of prosecution under the rubric of torture and enslavement as crimes against humanity. A 2001 verdict issued by the International Criminal Tribunal in The Hague confirmed the indictment for the former Yugoslavia. This ruling challenged the widespread acceptance of rape and sexual enslavement of women as an intrinsic tactic of war—the old collateral damage argument.

The International Criminal Tribunal for the former Yugoslavia found three Bosnian Serb men guilty of the rape of Bosnian Muslim women and girls—some as young as twelve and fifteen years of age, while many others were grandmothers. Two of the men were found guilty of sexual enslavement for holding women and girls captive in a number of de facto detention centers. Many of these women subsequently disappeared.

Mass rape and other sexualized crimes against women and girls have long been prominent features of war. They were medically documented practices in the Nazi concentration camps, and Elie Wiesel even describes rape perpetrated on the trains on the way to the camps. Rape and other sexual misconduct occur as well within a country's own military, usually vastly underreported and rarely punished (stories about this in the U.S. armed services have been frequent in recent years, although most of the cases have been dropped, the victims often forced to leave military service and the perpetrators receiving little more than a slap on the wrist). Still, it wasn't until June 2008 that the United Nations finally declared rape to be a war crime. And like most UN declarations, enforcement lags far behind the establishment of the decree.

In fact, almost half a century after the earliest consideration of rape as a war crime, prosecution and conviction remain almost nonexistent. According to the United Nations Development Fund for Women, an estimated 20,000 rapes were committed in the war in Bosnia, yet they resulted in only twenty-seven convictions; 64,000 rapes in Sierra Leone yielded six convictions; and 500,000 rapes in Rwanda, eight convictions.

Nevertheless, in terms of sexual assault in the context of war, some progress has been made. There has been a profound change in the way sexual violence is regarded in international law, from something acceptable that soldiers do, to a criminal act. In 1998 the International Criminal Tribunal for Rwanda declared rape an act of genocide, committed in that case with the purpose of destroying the Tutsi ethnic group. And a decade later, the UN Security Council adopted a resolution recognizing rape as a "tactic of warfare" that is a crime against humanity.

But what about that parallel war, the one that rages in and outside marriage and other sorts of intimate relationships throughout patriarchal societies? When a particularly violent incest or rape is uncovered, the victim is a very young girl, or the context is unusually sordid, public opinion generally rushes to the defense of the woman or girl (or, occasionally, young boy). The press and community take satisfaction in prosecuting the victimizer and upholding the victim's honor. Until quite recently, in fact, the victim's name was often withheld to preserve her privacy, and many women are still unwilling to testify against their abusers because of the shame they are made to feel, their fear of losing custody of their children, and economic considerations. The era of "your skirt must have been too short" is not entirely behind us.

While these individual cases often garner widespread publicity; convictions are more frequent than they once were; and sentences, longer—few connections are being made between these incidents and the power inequality inherent in patriarchy itself: how its very nature continues to set the stage for this sort of widespread abuse. "Boys will be boys" and "men will be men" are still deeply engrained in our popular culture. And they continue to be reinforced through media messages, song lyrics, advertising images, video games, and the false patriotism and idealization of violence and war that have been so much a part of our post-9/11 world. Today we know more about the connections between mass and individual conduct and between the public and private spheres but continue to live our lives as if we didn't.

In the end, justice did not result in the Dominique Strauss-Kahn–Nafissatou Diallo case. The tide of public opinion among French women and that nation's general population may or may not have been permanently affected. Wives of U.S. politicians who are caught having affairs may continue to stand by their men or leave them in greater numbers. And in the larger venue of armed conflict, international agencies may continue, very slowly, to take specific violence against women seriously and just as slowly prosecute and penalize some of the worst offenders. The Catholic Church began prosecuting some of its guiltiest priests after it was forced by its own constituency to do so. Economics often tip the balance in one direction or another.

I don't see a meaningful change on the horizon in the tragically unacknowledged and underreported arena of violence against women, sexual or otherwise. As long as society is structured so that women have fewer opportunities, earn less, and often depend on men for their and their children's support, too many women will remain in unsafe relationships—some until they have been murdered by their abusers. As long as a girl's or woman's sense of self-worth is determined by her connection to a man, too many women will put up with too much—often until it is too late. As long as reporting sex crimes continues to bring more disgrace to the victim than the victimizer, the majority of such crimes will go unpunished. And as long as "lord power" remains an ingrained part of our culture, men will feel entitled and women, as if they have no redress.

As for the questions posed at the beginning of this piece, I believe men and women in the public trust should be honest in all their dealings, no exceptions. Males and females should be held to the same standards. But we must recognize that in patriarchy it is overwhelmingly men who enjoy "lord power," and this is where our attention should be focused. How we manage our private lives—whether straight or gay, married or single, in a monogamous or open relationship—is entirely our business. But we have a right to expect that our public officials tell us the truth and also that they not engage in acts of violence, especially against those less powerful than themselves. I have no more use for a domestic abuser than I do for a serial killer or a preemptive strike.

Diallo and Straus-Kahn are only the tip of a very large iceberg. The problem is a cancer that corrodes individual relationships as it does the relationships between nations.

There's Plenty of Time for That Later

March 9, 2011. It's been more than a month since rebels, led by mostly young organizers fed up with thirty years of dictatorship, ousted Egypt's president Hosni Mubarak. Western media used words like *spontaneous uprising* and spoke with thinly disguised paternalism about the need for *democracy*. Social media like Facebook and Twitter rallied thousands and then millions to points in Cairo and other Egyptian cities, from where they marched in peaceful protest against symbols of the authoritarian regime. Early on, the armed forces refused to fire on their own people. Mubarak gave a defiant speech. The next morning, he fled.

Middle Eastern upheaval had started in Tunisia little more than a month before. There, too, peaceful demonstrations achieved governmental change with relatively little bloodshed. After Egypt, grassroots rebellions flared in Yemen, Bahrain, Oman, Kuwait, Algeria, Jordan, Iraq, Iran, and even the Saudi Arabian kingdom. Libya's conflict quickly rose to the level of civil war.

Meanwhile in Egypt, even with a long road ahead, everything points to a real change in the power structure. And evidence of years of careful planning and organization has also become evident. Women were among the Internet-savvy youth leading this new type of liberation struggle.

One eighty-year-old woman, Nawal El Saadawi—the psychiatrist, writer, and longtime feminist activist—was mentioned as someone who had long been meeting with the new generation of revolutionaries, guiding their courageous moves. As I listened to an interview,[1] in which she spoke of gatherings at her home over a many-year period, I thought: yeah, spontaneous. Not really. I had several times taught El Saadawi's *Woman at Point Zero*, an extraordinary book that depicts the life of Firdaus, a prostitute who faced execution for having murdered her pimp.[2] On several occasions, El Saadawi spent time in Mubarak's prisons for her defense of women's rights and other "crimes" against the regime.

This isn't an essay about liberation struggles in northern Africa. By the time you read this, many of those struggles will have been settled in one direction or another. In some countries, fundamentalist religious sectors may try to gain control, and life for women will become more restrictive. In others, rebel forces inspired by successes in other parts of the region will prove no match for the regimes they hope to topple. In yet others, third-party intervention may settle the dispute—for now. In all cases, the complex job of reconstructing society will be longer and more difficult than the struggle that toppled the previous regime.

The rest of the world, especially the United States and European Union countries, will conspire behind closed doors, peddling their influence and attempting to move outcomes to best support their economic and geopolitical interests. While talking loud about people, freedom, and democracy, their behind-the-scenes greed has always been, and will always be, for political control and for oil. Since global dependence on this resource, the Middle East—a group of oil-rich countries—has been wooed by Western governments that talk democracy out of one side of their mouths while pandering to tyrants willing to supply them with the black gold out of the other.

Each of the countries in upheaval has its own history, culture, and organizational possibilities for change. Some will make it. Some won't. Again, this is not an essay about geopolitics in the Middle East. There will be plenty of those. What I want to write about here is women: their role in social change in countries where they have been punishingly oppressed, repressed, and kept from social agency to varying degrees and where their participation follows curves that women in the West are often hard put to decipher.

March 8, 2011, wasn't just any International Woman's Day, but the hundredth anniversary of its worldwide commemoration. In Cairo's Tahrir Square—the place where, a month before, hundreds of thousands of men, women, and children climbed onto army tanks and hugged the soldiers who opted to protect them instead of the dictator—women began to gather. They approached from different directions. They were old and young, housewives and professionals.

They wore hijabs and veils, or dressed in jeans and T-shirts with their heads bare. Many had young children with them. All carried signs.

In the spirit of what had happened in their country only weeks before—the overthrow of a brutal dictatorship by means of peaceful protest—these women took the opportunity of the holiday to make their demands known. They wanted simple things: greater and more equitable representation of women in parliament, harsher punishment against sexual harassment, the possibility of a woman as a presidential candidate, and other rights long achieved by women elsewhere. They had participated in the revolution, and now they wanted it to address their concerns.

The United Nations' 2010 World Gender Gap Report lists Egypt as 125 out of 134 countries; it has performed worse than most others in terms of women's political empowerment.

Revolutionary fervor is like wildfire. It can blow in any direction. During Egypt's eighteen days of public protest, women were at the barricades with their brothers, husbands, and children. Old and young women prepared food and cared for young children. They tended wounds but also attended political meetings, spread the word, mapped out strategies, and involved themselves in all phases of the struggle. Many reported an astonishing absence of sexual harassment during the demonstrations.

But the moment Mubarak stood down, this harassment—which has long been pandemic in Egypt—started again. The very night of the dictator's resignation, numerous cases of sexual assault, groping, and slurs took place. Women were spit at and kicked. Verbal attacks were routine. One female foreign journalist was corralled and gang-raped. She was saved by a group of women and more than twenty soldiers, showing that not all Egyptian men engage in woman abuse as a matter of course.[3]

The March 8 attack on the women demonstrating in Tahrir Square is evidence of just how deep and ingrained in the Egyptian social fabric disrespect for women runs. I was in Egypt a couple of years ago. Even as a tourist at the margin of ordinary social interaction, I remember the rude stares and other aggressive behavior by men in public places.

Once, when I tried to exit a market stall without buying, a man physically barred my escape. I had to push my way past his large body. Since this harassment most often came from men trying to sell me something I didn't want, I chalked it up to desperation on the part of people only trying to support their families in a society with almost 50 percent real unemployment. I didn't think of it primarily as virulent sexist behavior. Still, even in many sexist societies a woman of my age would be given the respect bestowed on older mothers and grandmothers.

The women protesting in Tahrir Square asked only for gender equality, a demand that should be a part of revolutionary change wherever it occurs. For their attempt to be heard, and so soon after they had been part of a massive human outpouring that resulted in almost immediate regime change, they were charged by hordes of angry men, physically and verbally attacked, shouted at to return to their homes, and violently dispersed—without any group of male citizens coming to their defense.

Glen Johnson, a New Zealand journalist based in Cairo, quotes Farida, an editor at a local magazine who was shouted out of the demonstration. She says her day began optimistically: "It was going to be like a school trip. We made our funny signs and wanted to be there to stand up for women. I did not expect such hatred, not after we had all stood together in Midan Tahrir," she said. "Some men told us that the closest we would ever get to a president would be giving birth to one. There were so many men we couldn't even see the women. They got so aggressive with us saying: 'What the hell are you doing here, you should go home.' They started pushing women, some got kicked, had their cameras taken. They were saying 'no' to us. Couldn't they have given us a couple of hours? What is the problem? In the future I hoped things would get better. After today, that's bullshit."[4]

I'm in my midseventies at this writing. My early involvement in the struggle for social change took place in the early 1960s. In the United States the movement for civil rights was at its most intense. Within a few years, blacks demolished Jim Crow. Southern schools, busses, and drinking fountains were integrated, and the next long phase of racial justice work began. The U.S. American war in Vietnam raged. Tens of thousands of young soldiers refused to fight, and gradually the nation as a whole rejected that imperialist war.

I moved to Mexico in 1961 and began learning on the ground about dependent capitalism. Marxism informed my thinking. Marx, Engels, and Lenin had all talked a good line with regard to women's rights. Engels had even written that the level of freedom in a society could be judged by how it treats its women. My comrades and I talked the same line, but movement men acquiesced to the Marxist dictum that class contradictions were the most important and that other problems—such as racial equality and women's rights—would be dealt with once liberation was achieved. We women acquiesced to the men.

In 1969 what we now call the second wave of feminism caught my attention. Position papers, other documents, articles, and essays came from the United States and Europe. Reading this material changed my life. I began to study patriarchy, that system by which men have controlled women for millennia. For the first time, I understood that issues I had seen as personal were in fact social problems shared by women everywhere. Feminist analyses became important to my worldview, and feminist consciousness took up residence in my daily interactions. Still, I was influenced enough by classic Marxism, and by the men who espoused it, that I continued to defend the class contradiction as most important to political struggle.

I advocated for women, yes, and for people of color, and eventually also for those of differing sexual identities long before coming out as a lesbian myself. But I still subscribed to a hierarchy: the overthrow of egregious dictatorships first, class as the central contradiction, and then all the other contradictions, many of which I agreed at the time would have to wait until political power was won. I couldn't see that the values implicit in the struggle itself would exert an indelible influence on the way the new society looked, that the means would inevitably shape the end.

Along the way, I met and argued with a number of brilliant feminist theoreticians. Some insisted that patriarchy, a state preceding capitalism by centuries, was what we needed to be looking at. These women saw the contradiction between men and women as central to a just distribution of power. I was able to appreciate bits and pieces of their argument but stuck to my view that class trumped gender.

Poor men, I and many others argued, had more in common with poor women than those poor women had with women of the owner class. Women of my generation and my persuasion pointed to Margaret Thatcher, Jeane Kirkpatrick, and others as examples of women who couldn't possibly have working-class values. Of course those male-oriented figureheads didn't take the interests of ordinary people to heart. But easy sloganeering obscured the real issue.

That issue is power: its distribution and abuse. What I couldn't see at the time was that power itself is a political category, the most important of all.

I lived in Mexico from 1961 to 1969. There, as I say, I learned about the relationship between a superpower like the United States and a nation that shares its southern border and, since losing half its territory to its northern neighbor, has found itself mired in the unfair strategies of dependent capitalism. As a poet and editor of a bilingual poetry magazine, I came in contact with Latin

American poets, who helped me emerge from the chill that McCarthyism had placed on creativity in my country of origin. The Mexican Student Movement of 1968 taught me how far a government will go to defend itself against citizens fighting for their rights.

Cuba, where I lived from 1969 through the end of 1980, proved a moving experience in the struggle to build a society equitable for everyone. The Cuban Communist Party's Marxist orientation reinforced my perception of class as primary to social change. The Cuban Revolution talked about women's rights and racial equality. It did a lot to attend to both those issues. But when either group's demands conflicted with the economic or political goals of the country as a whole, or were even perceived to do so, those demands were invariably seen as divisive.

Women and members of other social groups were told they mustn't do anything to get in the way of national unity, especially when the revolution was being attacked on every front. The Federation of Cuban Women, Cuba's massive women's organization, labeled feminism a brand of "bourgeois deviancy." And a dangerous nationalism obscured the need to look at profoundly important issues such as gender.

By this time, I was searching, hard, often outside prescribed political lines. I began to interview women, write about women, and most of all listen to women in different parts of the world, women who were involved in a variety of gender-based struggles. My failure to accept the official answers often marked me as suspect; and throughout my years in Cuba, I was sometimes forced to defend myself against accusations that I was a U.S. feminist, an outsider, or otherwise out of sync with accepted policy.

I listened harder, wrote more, and tried to put it all together. It was clear to me that the Cuban Revolution had its logical priorities: national sovereignty and defense, the right to succeed against the ongoing U.S. embargo, a need for unity in the face of such a many-pronged attack. But I was troubled by the fact that, despite their great advances in terms of education, healthcare, work, and social services, women continued to occupy far fewer positions of power than men.

I moved on to Nicaragua at the end of 1980 and lived there until my return to the United States in 1984. The Sandinistas took power in Nicaragua in 1979, twenty years after the end of the Cuban Revolution. Those twenty years had witnessed the global rise of feminist analysis and action. Sandinista women had participated in the armed struggle to a degree impossible in Cuba. Many among the female leadership proudly called themselves feminists. In Nicaragua, throughout the early years of the Sandinista decade, women tried hard not to let the revolution's male leadership erase their prospects for real equality.

For a while it seemed they might succeed. But patriarchy everywhere is entrenched; and despite some poetic declarations on the male leadership's part, the men had no intention of letting the women share power. They used all sorts of excuses, those that have become tired mantras as well as a few that were new and innovative. Whenever a woman rose to a position of ideological influence or threatened the status quo in some way, unless she was willing to go along with the patriarchal recipe, her downfall was dramatic and immediate. As the Sandinista Revolution came under more severe attack, the old national-unity argument took center stage. By the time I left Nicaragua in 1984, it was clear that men were firmly in charge. It was also clear that the Sandinista Revolution as we'd known it was on its way out.

After the Sandinistas lost the 1990 elections, an independent women's movement in Nicaragua surged. Many of the women involved had been important FSLN (Sandinista National Liberation Front) cadre. Some had held positions of relative power in the revolutionary government. I had interviewed a number of these women for *Sandino's Daughters*, a book I wrote at the very beginning of the period of social change.[5] At the time, they credited the party with their political education. But after the defeat, when I interviewed many of these same women for *Sandino's Daughters Revisited*, they revealed stories of crass inequality and abuse that a misplaced loyalty had encouraged them to keep hidden the first time we'd spoken.[6]

These women and others began organizing themselves into a strong and innovative movement for gender equality within the overall struggle. They saw gender issues as linked to, and interrelated with, all aspects of change. As abuses ranging from merely painful to criminal came to light and were openly discussed, patterns emerged. The Nicaraguan independent women's movement remains today among the most intelligent and forceful in Latin America.

Back in the United States, my own ideas about class, race, gender, and other social contradictions were also beginning to change. I expressed my disappointment with several revolutionary movements in a book called *Gathering Rage: The Failure of 20th Century Revolutions to Develop a Feminist Agenda*.[7] In hundreds of personal conversations and public lectures, I began saying I thought socialism and feminism needed one another. And I began to envision what that need and interdisciplinary interaction might look like. I also began to understand the sexist control to which I had been subject and how that control had delayed my understanding of the issue.

Around this time, I discovered an experience of incest in my early childhood, abuse I had successfully blocked from memory. Coming home created a context in which I could begin to examine areas of my life that would have seemed self-indulgent to consider when I lived where we were trying to change whole societies. Slowly, painfully, I began to understand that only changed human beings are able to change social structures. Psychotherapy around the incest led me to new ideas about memory, collective as well as individual. I realized that when, so many years before, we had said *the personal is political,* most of us hadn't really known what that meant. More to the point, we didn't know how to live what it meant.

A friend, writer and activist Judith McDaniel, wrote a book about the U.S. sanctuary movement in solidarity with immigrants from Central America who were seeking refuge in the United States.[8] I wrote a book about incest.[9] Our books appeared from the same publisher at the same time; and we realized that she, who was known as a feminist writer, had tackled what was then thought of as a more overtly political subject, while I, known as a political writer, was dealing in a subject considered to be highly personal. We saw the absurdity of those distinctions.

Even many of the women who had coined the phrase *the personal is political* found it difficult to understand that Judith and I were talking about two versions of the same patriarchal abuse. The invasion of a child's body by a man who wields control over her life has a lot in common with a powerful nation invading a smaller one. The scale is different, but so many of the mechanisms are the same. In both cases humiliation, damaged dignity, shame, physical disease, loss of memory, and a sense of inferiority result.

Judith and I saw the connections our work made. We tried to take a joint reading on the road. But the public wasn't ready for us. We did two programs, at both of which there was a moving response, but we received no further invitations. In subsequent years, I was able to think a lot more about how gender is reflected in society and how power—in every social system in which I have lived—has been invariably held by men. It is not the individual man who is at fault. From before birth he has been conditioned to take on the dominant role. Patriarchy damages women, but it also damages men, robbing them of their humanity and sense of justice.

I think about the women who demonstrated this past March 8 in Cairo's

Tahrir Square. Just a few weeks earlier, they had taken part in a mixed movement that shocked the world with its apparent suddenness, power, and success. The truth is they and their brothers had prepared for years. What we saw from outside Egypt was a largely peaceful struggle unfolding over an eighteen-day period. The women must have gotten enormous energy from their participation. I could not imagine the men, their eyes focused on the common goal of unseating their country's dictator, sidelining those women in any definitive way.

But then the major battle was over. They had won. And true to their patriarchal mindset, most Egyptian men, I'm sure, believe they had been the ones to achieve this victory. The more progressive among them may have considered their women as having helped. When the women protestors massed in Tahrir Square, their simple demands scrawled on hastily made placards, their countrymen easily reverted to the values and prejudices that have always seemed to them to be the natural order of things.

This patriarchal value system is not unique to the Arab world or to the Middle East. With cultural variations, men hold power almost everywhere. Sometimes they exercise it brutally, sometimes more subtly.

Men continue to push us into horrific wars. Men head the banks and corporate boardrooms that have thrown us into economic crisis. Men make the decisions to continue developing nuclear energy, stockpile nuclear weaponry, ignore the obvious fact of climate change, and sacrifice education and health. Today, in a few isolated countries, some women have taken leadership roles; and in a few of those countries, they are rejecting the old male values and trying out new ideas rooted in different views of human relationships and how we must inhabit the earth.

Iceland is one such country. In January 2009 the first nation to be devastated by the global depression was the first to elect someone with very different values and charge her with extraditing it from the morass. Johanna Sigurdardottir was sworn in as her country's prime minister. Sigurdardottir is not only a woman but a lesbian. In her nation of 300,000, neither of these facts seemed relevant to the electorate. The population wanted someone in charge who could turn things around. After only a few months in office, Prime Minister Sigurdardottir had earned an approval rating of 73 percent.

Perhaps it is unfair to counter the indignities suffered by the women in Cairo with the election of a lesbian prime minister in a country long known for its progressive social policies. I make the leap because I believe women throughout the world are battered by prejudice and disrespect. The abuses to which the women of Cairo were subjected are emblematic of what women endure almost everywhere. Sigurdardottir shows what is possible when patriarchal values give way to progressive power sharing.

Throughout my long activist life, when feminists have voiced their demands, I have heard male political leaders in a variety of cultures and contexts assure us *there's plenty of time for that later*. In whatever language, in whatever situation, this is the answer given to women when we demand our basic human rights. They take advantage of our brilliance, skill, and loyalty, as they woo us with promises of a more egalitarian future. And if and when they win, we still find *there's plenty of time for that later*.

It is clear to me now that no one of the social contradictions alone is more important than the others. Class, race or ethnicity, gender, sexual identity, culture, ecology, and much else must be examined in relation to all the others. Only when we understand and are able to address life in all its complexity will we be able to shape a society that works for everyone. If and when that happens, I believe everyone will defend that society.

The thing men always seem to forget is that everywhere women are slightly more than half the population. As we throw off old taboos, become better educated, and acquire more experience in the political sphere, we will accept nothing less than full participation.

In the long run, no revolution will succeed if it won't share power with half the human race.

What Are They Afraid Of?

After legislative defeat several years earlier and months of closed-door meetings in which Governor Andrew Cuomo waged a meticulous campaign to win over powerful Wall Street interests, reluctant Democrats, and Republicans who were expected to oppose the bill, late on the night of July 24, 2011, the New York State Senate voted to legalize gay marriage. Moments later, Cuomo himself strode into the chamber to sign the bill into law. Thirty days hence, his state, the most populous in the nation, would become the sixth to give lesbians and gay men the right to legally honor their relationships like heterosexual citizens have long been able to do.[1]

To date, a growing number of our fifty states have authorized same-sex marriage. California is still moving back and forth: between legalization, the right's well-funded campaign in support of Proposition 8, and the law's journey through courts that finally seem headed toward reestablishing tolerance. By the time you read this, several more states will probably have joined this number.

Thousands of gay Californians who married during their state's window of opportunity wait to learn if their nuptials stand, while men and women in states with civil unions or domestic partnership benefits wade through the rights they have and those that remain to be won. And nationally, two powerful lawyers—an unlikely team, previously on different sides of the political spectrum—are aiming even higher. They have been moving surely and steadily toward pleading their case for federal gay marriage before the U.S. Supreme Court.[2]

All this at a time when Argentina, Belgium, Canada, Croatia, Denmark, Finland, France, Germany, Hungary, Iceland, Ireland, Luxembourg, the Netherlands, New Zealand, Norway, Portugal, South Africa, Spain, Sweden, Switzerland, Uruguay, and the United Kingdom have adopted same-sex marriage rights. In Uruguay, homosexuals have all legal rights except the right to call their partnership marriage, and a law that would add that is likely to pass this year. Israel resists passing its own law but recognizes gay marriages performed in countries where it is legal. Several years ago Mexico City moved ahead of Mexico as a whole by legalizing marriage between partners of the same sex. And a number of other countries have stopped short of sanctioning marriage but have legalized same-sex unions of one sort or another. To say nothing of the broad diversity among nations regarding allowing gays to serve in the military, and even around the issue of gay identity itself—is it natural or unnatural, should it be legal or illegal, punishable by prison or death, and other medieval positions still tragically in effect in some of the African and Muslim nations.

I am a seventy-six-year-old woman who lived almost my entire first half century of life identifying as heterosexual, came out a few months short of my fiftieth birthday, and now call myself a lesbian. For the past twenty-six years, I have been with a woman and have every reason to believe we are joined for the duration. Before she and I got together, my longest relationship with a man lasted eight years. I do not deny the years I lived as a heterosexual. I loved some of those men and am immensely grateful for the four children and ten grandchildren who came into this world as a result. But I do believe that, given a more level sociopsychological playing field, I might have discovered my lesbian identity earlier. And I am one of the lucky ones. Although somewhat late, I came to a realization about this part of who I am relatively unburdened by fear, shame, or negative pressure from family and community.

The fear is what interests me most. I often find myself asking the question that gives title to this essay: what are they afraid of? When it comes to rejecting gay equality, I know there is a gamut of attitudes. These range from denying that the identity exists to nervously tolerating homosexuals, and include many religiously or politically based positions. Organized religion's primary weapon is fear. Fundamentalist dogma plays a huge role: be it Muslim, Christian, Jewish, Buddhist, or other faiths.

And this brings me to a subtext in the New York victory, having to do with this country's uneasy separation between church and state. Before the gay marriage bill could pass, Republican senators insisted on a provision protecting religious organizations and affiliated groups from lawsuits if they refused to provide their buildings or services for same-sex marriage ceremonies. The provision also insists such organizations and groups be spared penalties by state government when they fail to follow state law. It is all about the tenuous relationship between the tax breaks churches enjoy and those churches' adherence to the laws of the land.

Once again we are reminded of the growing distance between church hierarchy and congregants. Interestingly, while 53 percent of those polled in the United States now approve of gay marriage, this figure rises to 60 percent among members of the Catholic Church. The New York State gay marriage bill clearly troubled the hierarchy more than it did ordinary Catholics.

Legal quibbling aside, in every one of religion's manifestations of denial or rejection, I sense fear. I see it. I hear it. I smell it.

Conservative ideology teaches fear of anyone who is not white, middle-class, heterosexual, and unquestioningly patriotic—which these days means going along with the very un-American policies of warmongering, corporate criminality, and duplicity. It is fear of difference, of the loss of pure patriarchal power, but perhaps most difficult to admit and hardest to pinpoint, it is fear of self.

How do we name ourselves? What part does sexuality or gender identity play in who we perceive ourselves to be? What of our own hidden desires? Where does each of us stand along the broad arc of sexual identity? How much easier to subscribe to an acceptable category rather than question the categories themselves or admit to participation in one that is socially proscribed?

And the fear comes with powerful props to back it up. Believers of whatever religious persuasion will point to their scripture of choice as the basis for what they call taking a coherent position. But these scriptures were written down by human beings, often hundreds of years after oral transmission. They date from eras when social mores of every sort were different from those we observe today. And they are open to a range of interpretations.

Many, including the books of the New Testament, were also selected from among others that were rejected, at conclaves of a highly political nature. Who was in power at the time? What interests were at stake? Men decided which books would be called sacred and which, relegated to oblivion (although the oblivion didn't always last). I hold contemporary belief systems accountable for the dictums they set forth, and their devotees accountable for what they choose to believe.

I am fascinated by the fear element more than the political or quasi-religious posturing, and I don't necessarily equate these, although I recognize that they are linked in a great deal of contemporary rhetoric. In the United States these days, moral posturing is often quite fluid and only skin deep. Politicians defend the positions they believe important to the majority of their constituents, those they think will get them elected or reelected. If verifiable polls show a shift in support for one position or another, many claim to be "for something after they are against it," or vice versa. For this reason, I will avoid speaking here about political positions, as fickle as those are when expressed in electoral campaigns.

Asking what they are afraid of brings to mind so many of the myths they invent to explain their flimsy positions. The recruitment myth, so laughable I will not give it the validity of discussion. The abuse myth, which, although disproven by study after study, continues to be held up as justification for anti-gay fear. Important sectors of the Catholic hierarchy still claim that homosexuality is to blame for the legions of priests who have sexually abused young boys and girls. There is no scientific proof for this claim. Abusers are abusers, gay or straight; and those covering for them, criminals. Rather than looking to enforced celibacy as a possible reason for some priests seeking sexual pleasure where they shouldn't, the institution of the church finds it easier and more expedient to blame a sexual identity they call deviant. In the general population, as well as within the Catholic Church, the vast majority of sexual abuse crimes are committed by straight men—albeit sick straight men—against vulnerable women and children.

When I come up against the different manifestations of gay hatred—from rude comments, stereotyping, and antigay jokes to social ostracizing, workplace bias, religious diatribe, restrictive legislation, shunning, hate crimes, or the punishments ranging from imprisonment to execution still being handed down in too many parts of the world—in my mind it all reduces to fear.

I understand the thing about different strokes for different folks. I accept the fact that some people feel comfortable living by a particular set of rules, while others identify with another, or none at all. As long as it is not based on hatred or mistreatment of any group, I find difference interesting and exciting and love exploring cultures where almost everything is foreign to my own experience or belief. What I can't accept is proselytizing: the idea some people have that it's their way or no way, that everyone else must think and act as they do. Nothing like a pair of missionaries knocking at my door to raise my ire.

Which is why the marriage question in particular fascinates me.

Marriage is a legal contract to some, a sacrament to others. But the two seem hopelessly confused in public discourse. The second interpretation is religious, and there are denominations in some religions that extend the sacrament of marriage to their gay members. Most of the world's churches, though, still deny all but heterosexuals the right to marry, and the issue has caused schisms in several major denominations. This is fine by me. I say let churches—functioning, after all, as private clubs—play by the rules that make them happy. States that recognize gay marriage, however, should be able to demand tax revenue from all their institutions, and an institution that does not obey state law should not be able to obtain tax-free status.

Although family tradition plays a role, most people belong to or join churches with which they identify. If they find a congregation limiting, they can always search for something that more accurately reflects the beliefs by which they want to live, or avoid religious dogma altogether. I believe churches should be free to defend their beliefs.

Marriage contracts, on the other hand, are drawn up by states. And most states, at least on paper, proclaim the equality of all their citizens. They stipulate that candidates for marriage adhere to certain requirements, such as a minimum age for men and/or women, that the two people not be closely related or currently married to someone else, and that they submit to rudimentary tests to determine freedom from sexually transmitted diseases. These regulations are required across the board, not for a single race or gender. Only same-sex couples are routinely denied the benefits of legal marriage.

And the benefits are many. Gay men and women may not need the state to place its seal of approval on their marriage in order to legitimize their love; my partner and I, for example, feel thoroughly "married" although our commitment ceremony took place in private very early one cold winter morning huddled in a car on the south rim of the Grand Canyon. But we would very much like to have the legal rights that go with state-sanctioned marriage.

There are numerous benefits heterosexuals in our society enjoy that homosexuals lack. Inheriting Social Security income or pension payment is an important one. Tax and health care equality are others. Involvement in a partner's illness or end-of-life decisions, something that is automatic for straight spouses, can be a source of wrenching frustration for gay couples. In many cases, estranged and judgmental family members have more of a legal right to make such decisions than a same-sex life companion of many years. Adoption; guardianship of underage children raised by two mothers or two fathers; child support in the event of separation; and inheritance, property, and insurance issues are only a few of the other areas regulated to the benefit of married heterosexuals and are sources of anguish for those who are gay.

There is the human spillover as well: privileges that do not pertain to the legal rights obtained through marriage but are socially accepted when a relationship has the backing of the state. For example, families uncomfortable with homosexuality may balk at having a gay son or daughter's partner at a wedding or other important event, while a straight partner—no matter how obnoxious—is welcomed. I am astonished at how far the simple sanction of the state goes toward legitimizing situations that should be recognized simply by paying attention to authentic feeling and loving relationships.

What are they afraid of?

In no particular order: what other people may think, guilt by association, the threat of eternal damnation, the taunts and/or bullying we know so often accompany the perception or reality of homosexuality, an imagined need to explain oneself in relation to one's gay friends, and more. But I believe the greatest fear around gayness is always fear of self. Who am I?

Social pressure is such that people are afraid to externalize difference, whatever that difference may be. They are afraid that truly acknowledging who they are will bring rejection and stigma. Until they have the courage to make the leap, they won't experience the immense relief of no longer having to hide—most importantly from themselves. Coming out of any closet also frees up other manifestations of well-being: physical as well as emotional. New talents may emerge. Old ones may develop in new directions. We relax into who we are meant to be.

As someone who came late in life to the realization of my own lesbian identity, I am well acquainted with the internalized homophobia most of us inherit from birth. It is analogous to our internalized racism, classism, able-bodiedism, consumerism, greed, and so much else. We naturally participate in and reproduce our society's values. To become fully thinking and feeling human beings, we must consciously unlearn many of them. In our most formative years, most of us want nothing more than to fit in. Difference of any kind can be uncomfortable.

And so, fear of gayness in others is often a cover-up for our unanswered questions or doubts about our own sexual identities.

To those who need well-defined categories to feel safe, it can be particularly unsettling to be confronted with men or women who do not fit the prescribed patterns or dress in ways that blur gender lines. My partner, who exudes an aura of androgyny, has suffered particularly in Muslim countries, where men and women are supposed to follow precise models of behavior and dress. On more than one occasion she has been forcibly shepherded out of a public women's restroom because someone thought she was a man. Even generous breasts and earrings don't seem to establish a clear enough distinction. So far she has been able to explain herself out of these uncomfortable situations. But it hasn't been fun.

Most striking to me are lawmakers and other public figures who insist they favor equality for all while voting against the rights of any group. Some even go so far as to announce that they really have nothing against gay people. Of course they don't: "some of my best friends," etc. Yet they cling to the tired mantra that marriage should be between a man and a woman, and act as if that is reason enough to vote against progress. It's true because it's true. I find it especially curious when black men or women—so recently denied their own civil rights—put forth this argument.

This brings up two other lines of "reasoning," both of them tendentious. One is the matter of propagation of the species: unless we continue to reproduce (which, despite all evidence to the contrary, can only be accomplished by heterosexual couples), the race will die out. Or if gay people are allowed to marry and raise children, another half-brained argument goes, those children are likely to be gay.

In most countries, the problem is overpopulation, not a diminishing birthrate. And every serious study demonstrates without a shadow of a doubt that most gay children are born into straight families and that same-sex parents raise vastly more straight than gay offspring. In a population in which only between 10 and 20 percent is thought to be gay or transgender, how could it be otherwise? Still, fear repeats the mistaken assumption until it is considered fact.

The other related and equally erroneous claim concerns teaching about sexual difference in the schools. Those who fear difference say that teaching about gayness may "make" children gay. Yet we teach about other cultures and religions without presuming a similar contagion. Rather than inducing copycat identities or otherwise leading malleable minds "astray," knowledge only brings greater understanding, tolerance, and real and healthy options.

In fact, it is not teaching about homosexuality that does such immense harm to our children and young people—especially those who may already suspect they are different, wonder about their sexual identities, and feel horribly alone. These young people are taught to be invisible and therefore remain the feared

Other, even to themselves. What is so harmful is not teaching children about every human condition.

The outrageous amount of bullying that is tolerated in our schools—often ending in self-mutilation or worse, like the rash of suicides that shook our society throughout 2010 and 2011—could be prevented if differences were respected as viable and presented as one among many lifestyle possibilities. As a society, we allow uninformed fear to determine the values we pass from generation to generation.

In a few states, a respect for gay lives has trumped the previously entrenched fear. Currently, same-sex marriage is legal in Connecticut, the District of Colombia, Iowa, Massachusetts, New Hampshire, New York, Vermont, and most recently Maryland. Domestic partnership or civil unions exist in Hawaii, Illinois, New Jersey, Washington, Maine, Nevada, and California (where marriage is still being debated in the courts). While this progress has been made in roughly only a fifth of the states, the trend seems clear. I no longer consider it completely out of the question that during my lifetime we may see a change in federal law—which would, of course, provide the greatest equality for gay men and women in all areas of our lives.

The fear still rages, though. We hear it in the rapacious rhetoric issuing from the mouths of televangelists and other fundamentalist preachers. We read it in skewed reports about "gay choice." We are besieged by organizations that still use aversion and other questionable therapies in their claim that they can turn gay people straight. We experience it in the hate crimes that continue to target lesbians and gay men across this country, and in the resistance to passing hate-crime legislation. We feel it in the still-strong resistance to change.

This is why I found the backstory to what took place in New York State particularly interesting. The day after that state's senate voted to legalize same-sex marriage, the *New York Times* ran a lengthy article detailing the steps Governor Cuomo followed in his successful campaign to get enough of the powerful on board to achieve the votes he needed to change the law.[3]

This article demonstrates several things. First of all, a strong politician, convinced he is morally right, will still occasionally put himself on the line for something in which he believes. Secondly, a true appreciation of what freedom is can overcome entrenched religious dogma and irrational fear. The *Times* piece takes us step-by-step through months of expert organizing. Perhaps most poignantly, it allows us a glimpse of individuals who, ultimately, were convinced to put personal relations above political haggling.

Some of the lawmakers had gay family members or friends. They knew them as real people, and these connections helped them overcome their fear. There is nothing like discovering that the person you knew and trusted before you found out he or she is gay is still the same person—still trustworthy, still your friend. This scenario played itself out in one life after another among the New York State lawmakers who went on to legalize gay marriage. Governor Cuomo appealed to their sense of right and wrong, their obligation to support legislation that would be fair to a broader range of constituents. He may have indulged in some of the usual quid pro quo political maneuvering, but his final argument was "do what's right."

Fear is a powerful and devastating weapon. We can only combat it with courage.

Too Late Because

Written following the January 8, 2011, shooting in Tucson, Arizona, when a young man crazed by hate shot a U.S. representative, a federal judge, a young girl, and a dozen others. The nation's vitriolic political discourse provokes more and more such events.

Too late for Christina, nine years old and fascinated by government. Her neighbor took her to the rally, thinking she would be interested in seeing how adult politics works.

Too late for the immigrant whose body lies on the desert beside a black plastic bottle. Black so it wouldn't be seen at night. The bottle smells of urine, just a slosh of liquid at the bottom, not a mile from the wall.

Too late for the woman who waits for a kidney in a system that erases the names of the poor from its transplant lists. Too late for her.

Too late for the bride and groom whose wedding looked like a terrorist training camp on a computer monitor in Idaho. The soldier who pressed the remote is sorry. The Pentagon sincerely regrets.

Too late for the man who spent eighteen years on death row, insisting he was innocent, and was then executed pre-DNA. Too late for the man twenty-three years on death row and then was freed because of DNA.

Too late for the young gay boy who might have thrilled audiences with his violin, the middle school girl who preferred taking her life over suffering another day of cyberhate.

Violence, American as apple pie.

In single file we walk along a narrow ledge, sway on the edge of a precipice where old winds howl and earth disintegrates beneath our feet.

Will we retreat from the ledge or fall?

Because.

Because is the meaningless retort when a wall goes up and the people in charge find nothing better to say. A word like a sneer, a gaseous overblow of ignorance dressed in the emperor's new clothes.

Because is not an answer that satisfies.

Because is too much noise. Too much air sucked from our lungs. Too much adrenalin that's lost its way. Too much titillation wrung from the blood of children, too many expensive trinkets fabricated from dreams that dared to dream their dreamers.

Because is too many unwritten poems, primed canvasses yearning for paint, cello bows waiting to be pulled across the strings.

Because is that lifetime together you couldn't have because he was a he, or she a she.

Because is a history of power greed, taught as patriotism and Might Makes Right.

Because is the serious schism, embraced in fear when it might have been held in humility.

Because is invading armies rotting in wards of men and women without limbs, or in the hallowed ground of military cemeteries, their bullet-riddled chests choked with medals for Valor or What Else Could I Do?

Because is neighborhood gangs, vilified in hospital ERs, morgues, and prisons.

Because is waves eating away at the shores of island nations, and polar bears retreating, confused, when the ice beneath their feet breaks and splinters or disappears.

Because is a forgotten species of frog, a birdsong no longer heard.

Because is banks counting their money while families lose their homes.

Because is the family pet eating from a crystal bowl, while the child in the alley claws through garbage.

Because is the Twinkie defense become the mad cow defense or the salmonella defense.

Because is films and video games, song lyrics and TV programs: the bad guys as good. A reality show to top all reality shows.

Because is guns and more guns. Everybody has a right to defend his home and family. And the guns are bigger and faster, blowing away the battered wife, the man watering his lawn, the woman who happened to be walking at just this moment along that street, the child sleeping in her bed. Her mother kissed her and tucked her in before she turned off the light.

Because is a light that never goes on again.

A map of little white circles, crosshairs positioned above the names of elected officials who favor reason over hate. Only seventeen more to go. You betcha!

Because is bigger and better. There is always another torture method, another concentration camp for another group of people, another extraordinary rendition, another loophole to keep our crimes from oversight. Another distraction to make us forget.

Until It's Too Late bursts to the surface, breaking through chainmail and breastplate, flak jacket and fabric of tight-knit lies.

Because is James Brady slumped in his wheelchair.

Because is a seventh circle of hell, where Charlton Heston's ghost is forced to eat and sing and sleep with the ghosts of Columbine, the Twin Towers, Fort Hood, Tucson's ravaged street corner, Sandy Hook Elementary School, or any U.S. post office.

Because is Gomorra, Rome, Tenochtitlán, Auschwitz, Hiroshima, Mai Lai, Sarajevo, Kigali, the house on a Buenos Aires street, or a secret Guatemalan prison.

Because is the memory of a new holocaust erasing the one before, one murder erasing an earlier murder, one or a thousand child rapes ignored because oh, you know, in such good standing, prominent, pillar of the community.

Because is secrets. The priest telling the boy not to tell, the father telling his daughter.

Because is not telling.

Because is the expert who says it is in our DNA: man's tendency to fight and conquer man.

Boys will be boys. Men will be men.

Because is we're too tired to care. Or too sad to care. Or think it won't matter.

Because, despite what we want to believe, it really can get worse.

Because, as a man who knew once said: I wasn't a Jew or a Catholic or a Communist, so I didn't stand up. And when they came for me, there was no one left to stand up.

Keeping Us Safe

Be safe. We say this to people when they get into a car and buckle up or when they take off on a trip. When we place an infant in her child seat. When we make sure the safety on a gun is in place or the dial on a safe is positioned as it should be. When we spend a few moments making sure that all the safety features are in place before using power tools or that our fingers are safely out of the way when wielding a hammer or preparing to saw a board in two. The directive has become a formality, often uttered without much thought.

Safety first. The routine introduction to an airline flight, a quick course in rock climbing, or even something as mundane as cooking. We rather automatically want the appropriate precautions to remain present for the person taking on the task, and especially for the first time learner. I wonder how often I have told someone to be safe, without considering the ways in which my own unthinking actions may be making her less so.

It's not safe. Here an assumption takes center stage, often more relevant to the person speaking than to the remark's recipient. People are warned against embarking on adventures for many reasons, not all of them having to do with physical safety. My mother used to say this as a matter of course, whenever one of her children proposed to do something even a little bit risky or out of the ordinary. She was afraid for us and didn't understand that her well-intentioned admonition might be making us timid or hampering our creativity.

A safe place to fall has become a common description of a spouse or lover who understands and consoles out of unconditional love, someone who has one's back as a matter of course. Mass media one-size-fits-all therapist Dr. Phil popularized this phrase on the small screen. While his program is geared toward the mass audience and privileges high drama and TV ratings over serious psychology, there's no question most of us want and need a safe place to fall.

"Making It Safe for Charles" is a poem written many years ago by my friend Judith McDaniel.[1] The title took up residence in me and never left. It was the 1970s or early '80s, and some of us were involved in the struggles of Nicaraguans, Guatemalans, Hondurans, and those from El Salvador to free themselves from U.S.-backed terrorism. In my memory Charles becomes Carlos and then Charles again and then once again Carlos. Or Carol or Carla or Caroline. Any child, there or here, to whom we as adults surely owe a world free of violence and terror. We desperately want to be able to make a future in which children aren't hungry, homeless, cold, or on the receiving end of a bullet made in USA.

In Judith's poem, Charles, a four-year-old neighbor boy, says, "*I got a secret place back there, my own / place where nobody else can go and today / we're cleaning it up, we're making it safe / for me . . .* " The poet evokes one child's excitement as he and his father ready his own secret haunt and then moves out to consider other children in other unsafe spaces. She speaks of El Salvador and a South Africa still in the grip of apartheid. Toward the end of the poem, she writes:

Charles is three times

more likely than his friend Mark to die a violent
death because Mark is white, six times less
able to find a job, ten times more

likely to live in poverty, to go to jail, to overdose
on drugs, and I want to know how to go beyond
the statistics, go beyond even

the question of how this child can learn to be a man
who is not afraid . . .

That's it in a nutshell: safety versus fear, and the way both are manipulated in a society where skewing the issue of safety helps to control people through fear.

Danger is everywhere in our societies, from the proliferation of street violence to sexual perversion at the hands of sick family members or pillars of the community, from alcohol abuse to drug deals gone bad, from a psychopathic loner who decides to shoot up his school or workplace or shopping mall to what we like to think of as the sanctity of the home.

Danger also comes in more mundane but ultimately devastating forms when we continue against all warnings to use our cell phones while driving, or to get behind the wheel when we've been drinking, or smoke cigarettes, or get obese, or ingest a medication sold by a pharmaceutical company that cares more about making money than effective testing.

In poor countries and the poverty-blighted areas of rich ones, people are routinely endangered by being forced to live near toxic waste sites; to endure unsafe air and water and food, or having no food at all; or to try to outmaneuver the violence that threatens their lives. Increasing numbers of people confined to prisons throughout the world are endangered by the system itself, a system more interested in keeping presumed offenders off the street than in any sort of rehabilitation. In communities where people still have work and believe they can expect a certain level of social protection, they are endangered by hypocritical and inadequate social policies, by the lies of corporations that put profit before safety, and by being coerced into serving as cannon fodder in a succession of criminal wars.

Here I want briefly to reference the equation used by almost all corporations to decide if a dangerous product should continue to be sold or be taken off the market. It's called cost effectiveness. If companies can increase their profit margin by continuing to promote and sell the product in question, that's the call they will make. When the legal challenges from the injured and dead begin to cost them more, they will reaccess and—without admitting any wrongdoing—may remove the product from the shelves. Not to keep consumers safe, but to protect their bottom line. These same companies want us to believe their advertising mantras: they are "a family company" or have our best interests at heart.

Millions are spent on studies that tell us the obvious, and millions more on campaigns to get us to live in ways that keep us wanting what we don't need. Millions are also spent on advertising that entices us to smoke and drink and devour cheese-stuffed pizza. Mixed messages, told in all sorts of seductive ways, make it difficult for those of us with tendencies toward addiction, or unfulfilled hungers of any sort, to consistently make decisions that will truly serve us.

Keeping America Safe. This is an idea that has been at the forefront of every political race since September 11, 2001. It's been grossly distorted and profoundly mythologized, to the extent that military might and preemptive-strike political policy have replaced sanity.

Under the banner of Keeping America Safe, our government—not just the George W. Bush administration but the Obama administration as well—has sent hundreds of thousands of men and women to wars that have nothing to do with the terrorist attacks of 2001, causing thousands of dead, tens of thousands of wounded, and hundreds of thousands who will suffer from post-traumatic stress disorder for the rest of their lives. To keep America safe, this country has invaded, indiscriminately killed, and destroyed the infrastructures and decimated the millennial cultures of peoples who never invited our belligerence.

Over the past decade, keeping America safe has been the excuse for every intentionally misleading foreign and domestic policy decision, an explanation for our dangerously high national deficit, and a ready pocket for all manner of subterfuge, deception, and graft. Billions have been spent on new security systems—in homes and gated communities, at military establishments, in airports, at the entrances to important buildings, and elsewhere. Metal detectors, highly sensitive X-rays, and well-trained dogs are only some of the modalities used. Whether or not these systems can really keep us safe is debatable and, of course, impossible to prove.

Have we not suffered another major attack since September 11, 2001, because of all these measures, or because the terrorists have not had the capability to strike again? Or has it been simply a matter of luck? A great deal of money, as well as an immense investment of lives, has gone into making us believe our safety depends on governmental policy and those policies' costs. The idea that our national security is at stake has led us to allow our tax dollars to underwrite such obscenities as a nonworking electronic wall along our southern border and several ongoing wars.

As a people, we have systematically been robbed of the ability to think for ourselves or analyze the pros and cons of a situation or its solution. We have become docile citizens; if we are told we are safer, we feel safer.

In the name of this presumed safety, we have been willing to give up a long list of rights once considered the bedrock of our democracy. The Patriot Act—a sweeping conservative law reminiscent of the Cold War era, passed virtually without discussion under Bush and then extended under Obama—makes a mockery of our right to independent thought and of our ability to debate and disagree with official policy or to demand due process and a jury of our peers. As a nation, we have accepted the necessity of wiretapping ordinary citizens, the preemptive strike, extraordinary rendition, and torture.

Under the guise of national security, all sorts of crimes are committed every day. National security has also been used as an excuse for racial profiling and other acts in which the perpetuation of racism has gone unchecked or been encouraged. Popular discourse, however, is such that we are constantly reminded of the dangers that will surely destroy us if we don't keep our national security beefed up. We are led to believe that it is the Other, never we ourselves, who will suffer from racial profiling, illegal search and seizure, unfair imprisonment, or any number of other problematic practices sanctioned by the Patriot Act.

Sadly, many of us discover much too late that letting go of rights that once made our nation unique renders us less safe in all sorts of ways. Generally, only when we ourselves become the Other do we realize that "keeping us safe" results in our being more vulnerable—in other words, more routinely endangered. Beyond the obvious importance to our integrity of such rights as freedom of thought, speech, dissent, organization, and resistance, there are a number of more mundane issues implicit in some of our security measures.

Take, for example, the elaborate safeguards that have become routine at all U.S. airports. We all support real and effective efforts to keep us safe. But when we are X-rayed as we pass through security checkpoints and told the amount of radiation we receive is not a danger to our health, it reminds us of all the times we've been told the same thing about mammograms, chest X-rays, and the like—only to discover the accumulated radiation is in fact harmful.

There is a troubling dichotomy in the United States between public safety and what we think of as our private lives. The first involves citizen safety on the streets and in other public places. We depend on our police, firemen, national guard, and during natural disasters and man-made emergencies even on the military to provide for our collective safety. There's no doubt that all these agencies do heroic work, and we are grateful when they protect us. But members of these institutions also often overstep their limits. In Albuquerque, for example, we have had nineteen "justified" deaths from police shootings over the past year and a half. Citizens have asked for a meaningful investigation of police brutality, while a conservative mayor and the police force itself have defended themselves against such an investigation.

The conveniently named private sphere has been much more difficult to regulate, or even talk about honestly. For centuries, all sorts of public crimes have been prosecutable by law, while crimes committed in the privacy of homes, churches, and other protected venues have gone unreported and unpunished. A man's home is his castle, so the saying goes; and as long as it doesn't concern the community, he can go on beating or raping his wife and children without fear of legal reprisal. Shame and secrecy effectively keep the domestic sphere hidden. "Don't wash your dirty laundry in public" is the mantra that protects legions of perpetrators.

Even as we gradually enact better legal safeguards for women and children, patriarchal custom and the failure to speak out maintain millions in situations that lead to thwarted lives or even to death. And as these laws are being implemented more thoroughly in a greater number of communities, money and social status is usually enough to keep the most powerful offenders from being tried or punished.

Slowly, very slowly, this is changing. Today many U.S. states have effective safeguards against domestic violence, hate crimes are taken seriously in some places, and a few businesses even discourage workplace harassment. Widespread sexual abuse of young parishioners by priests within the Catholic and other churches finally reached the point where sheer numbers gave victims the courage to speak out. The Catholic Church could no longer continue to cover its sins by hiding behind the supposed sanctity of its mission. Still, as with other powerful institutions, those at the very top have managed to escape prosecution.

So are we really making the world safe for Charles, Carlos, or Carla?

Not as long as we refuse to do anything about climate change; continue to poison the air we breathe; genetically alter the food we eat; taint our water; favor nuclear energy and run coal mines based on profit rather than the safety of the miners; privilege the powerful; allow the fat cats to get away with robbing us of home, health, and future; and support wars that inevitably lead to other wars—trading precious life for dogmatic and poorly thought-out principles. Not as long as we fail to come to terms with classism, racism, sexism, homophobia, and all the other fears and -isms that favor some humans over others. Not as long as we ignore the dangers that haven't yet victimized *us*. And not as long as we tell ourselves there's time for all that later.

Passports and Me

My partner, Barbara, and I had to send our current passports in to the National Passport Office in order to obtain extra visa pages (many countries now demand at least six completely blank pages upon entrance; it was precisely for lack of that number that Barbara was stopped several years back on our arrival in South Africa and threatened with being sent back to London). So in late May 2011 we mailed in our passports, both in the same envelope and with the hefty fee now required for this service. The passports were received and entered the agency's routine processing operation on May 31. Less than two weeks later, Barbara's was returned with the additional pages.

Mine wasn't.

Passports are official documents used by a minority in our country—because relatively few people are able to travel abroad and because the document itself is expensive: over one hundred dollars last I checked. Sources vary, but from several I gather that only between 18 and 25 percent of U.S. citizens have them. This is roughly half the percentage of Canadians who possess passports and lower than that in most of the developed nations. For many reasons, including the small percentage of travelers, a majority of U.S. citizens are somewhat insular and unfamiliar with, and even disinterested in, other lands.

In fact, obtaining a U.S. passport may become even more difficult in the near future. According to David Edwards in an article for the Raw Story, the State Department wants passport applicants to reveal their lifetime employment histories and much more data when applying for the identity document.[1]

Edwards's article states that in February 2011 the State Department published a request in *The Federal Register* allowing sixty days for comment before the new rules go into effect. These new rules would require that "the Biographical Questionnaire for a U.S. Passport, form DS-5513, be used to supplement an application for [same] when the applicant submits citizenship or identity evidence that is insufficient or of questionable authenticity."

This would be reasonable within certain circumstances. No one would question that applicants for an identity document should be able to prove they are who they say they are. But the proposed law also requires some applicants to submit information about the mother's prenatal and postnatal care, her residence one year before and after the birth, those persons in attendance, and religious or institutional recordings of the event. I would argue, as the Consumer Travel Alliance does, that "this form vastly exceeds the statutory authority of the Department of State, is unconstitutional and in violation of U.S. obligations pursuant to international human rights treaties to which the United States is a party."[2]

Passports have their history.

And I have my history with them.

The earliest mention of an object we might recognize as a passport letter or book appears in the Bible, in the often-overlooked book of Nehemiah. Wikipedia states that in the month of Nisan in the twentieth year of the ancient Persian king Artaxerxes (around 450 BC by our calendar), the prophet who was working as a royal cupbearer was given letters from the king requesting that the governors of the lands beyond the Euphrates grant him safe passage to Judah. The purpose of Nehemiah's visit, incidentally, was to rebuild the walls of Jerusalem. In more modern times, in Britain the earliest surviving reference to a safe conduct document appears during the reign of Henry V in 1414.

Throughout the world, passports came into use in each country in accordance with that country's history and culture, although the documents were not generally required for international travel until the First World War. War always changes the nature of human relationships, whether by enacting a law aimed at preventing spies from crossing borders or through the massive displacement of persons and vast migrations they cause, requiring whole new ways of labeling people and facilitating their refugee status, removal, arrival, or continued claim on a place they may call home.

The term *passport* itself is believed to refer not to sea travel, from port to port (ports in ancient times were considered open trading points), but to documents needed to pass through the gate or *porte* of a city wall, or to pass through a particular territory in medieval Europe. Early passports included a description of the passport holder, such as "complexion," "shape of face," and "features." Some travelers found this offensive, probably in response to whatever form of racism was rampant at the time. The United Nations held a travel conference in 1963, which failed to unify guidelines. It wasn't until 1980 that standardization finally came about, under the auspices of the International Civil Aviation Organization.

Passports are ideal repositories for digitalization and other advanced technologies now overtaking our lives. The passports of the future will undoubtedly feature embedded microchips and biometric data such as photographs, fingerprints, and iris patterns. Malaysia was the first country to introduce this technology, and Australia, New Zealand, Japan, Sweden, the United Kingdom, the United States, Germany, the Republic of Ireland, and Poland—among others—have followed. But no nation is more remarkable in this regard than Nicaragua. The second poorest country in Latin America boasts that its passport contains eighty-nine separate security features (including bidimensional barcodes, holograms, and watermarks).

The passports of some countries remain unrecognized in others; for example, the Israeli passport is not accepted by twenty-three Muslim nations or North Korea. Pakistan requires a Muslim citizen who applies for a passport to subscribe to a declaration that includes affirmation that he or she is a Muslim, believes in Muhammad as the one and final prophet, and similar stipulations. The Vatican has no immigration controls but does issue passports; the pope, among other honors, always carries Passport Number One. Medieval religious strictures, as we know, continue to exert great influence in the modern world. Passports are sometimes largely ceremonial or symbolic, existing even where there is no sovereign territory. Two examples of this are the Iroquois League and the Sovereign Military Order of Malta.

All these quirks and exceptions aside, however, almost every country now issues an identity document of some kind, most often called a passport, and many require visas be stamped on the visitor's passport when the bearer crosses their borders. Thus, modern-day passports identify travelers; provide a source of income to the countries of origin and those they wish to enter; and, in increasingly limited ways, may also offer consular protection to the holder in the event of need.

Today there are some groups of countries, however, that are making it easier rather than more difficult to cross their borders. The European Union, South America's *Mercosur*, the Caribbean's CARICOM, and others have issued single documents to be used by all persons in these multination groups. This modest easing of international restrictions points in the welcome direction of a world without borders, but this is a dream we probably will not see materialize within our lifetimes.

To explain a bit of my own harrowing relationship to passports, I should say something about my history with the identity document. My father was a public school music teacher with three months of summer vacation each year. We were an adventurous family and, in my youth, traveled quite a bit—collectively planning excursions aboard freighters to South America, traveling down Alaska's Alcan Highway when it was still an unpaved two-lane road, and camping out in English poppy fields. My brother, sister, and I were included on our mother's passport—the way it was done back then. Eventually, I graduated to acquiring my own, and my childhood experience as well as an innate and insatiable curiosity caused me to move eagerly from country to country more often than most people I know.

In this context, throughout the 1960s I lived in Mexico, married a Mexican citizen, and in 1967 took out Mexican citizenship. Although the U.S. government later tried to make it appear that I had done this out of political allegiance, this wasn't the case. With three young children at the time and a husband who rarely had steady work, obtaining the citizenship of the country in which I resided was helpful in the search for a decent job. Mine was an economic decision. After obtaining Mexican nationality, in fact, I went to the U.S. consular office in Mexico City and assured them I did not want to lose my original citizenship. I was told it was too late; I already had.

And so for the next two decades, I considered myself a Mexican—at least legally. I have written elsewhere about those times and tribulations. I had no idea that what to me had been a simple act enabling me to better support my family would, in time, come back to haunt me.

Like many thousands of young people, I took part in the great Mexican Student Movement of 1968 that quickly spread nationwide. This was the year of the Paris Spring and of the uprising at Columbia University in New York City. Around the world, young people were taking to the streets, protesting authoritarian government rule and limits to freedom of thought and action.

In Mexico the movement began to jeopardize that country's plans to host the 1968 Olympics. Large numbers of expected visitors were beginning to cancel their hotel reservations; and ten days before the games were scheduled to begin, the government felt it had to come down hard on the mass protest that continued to gain momentum. On October 2 government and paramilitary forces fired into a peaceful demonstration, killing hundreds. The Mexican Student Movement was over, and with it our political innocence and youthful dreams.[3]

Following this crackdown, Mexican students tried to regroup. It wasn't possible. And when the first anniversary of the uprising came around and we wanted to mourn our losses, the repression started up again. My Mexican husband and I had divorced by this time. I was living with a North American poet, Robert Cohen, and had just given birth to my fourth child.

One morning, when my new daughter was three months old, a pair of paramilitary operatives came to our home. They were disguised as people working for Social Security and said they were investigating an accusation that I, a foreigner, was operating a sweatshop at the house. When my partner ushered them in to show them there was no sweatshop and argued as well that I held Mexican nationality, the two men asked to see my passport as proof. When Robert produced it, they made a rapid exit—guns suddenly in evidence and my passport in hand.

No routine reportage of the theft or appeal to high places proved successful in getting my Mexican passport back. At the time, repressive acts were rampant. Children were being kidnapped to punish their activist parents; some of those children's bodies began to appear abandoned on the *pedregal,* a rocky expanse at the edge of the huge city. My first thought was to protect my children. We immediately removed the older three from school and from everything that constituted life as they'd experienced it to that point. We felt we had no choice but to leave the country.

But without my passport, how? We explored a number of solutions to the problem and, for their safety, ended up sending all four children to Cuba—a country with whose poets we had developed a strong relationship, and one that took in many children in similar circumstances, then and for years to come.[4] I had to go into hiding while I figured out how to get out of Mexico. Three months later we made it to the Caribbean island. I had bribed my way to possession of an illegal Mexican border-crossing document (which didn't look anything at all like a passport) and traveled with it to my destination, via the United States, Canada, France, and Czechoslovakia.

That border-crossing document, in fact, had turned out to be a disappointment, a misunderstanding between two people trying to help me in a long chain of such efforts. When I saw it, I realized it was something of a relic: unusable, almost humorous. The light-blue, cardboard-covered, accordion-like document was intended for inhabitants of border cities, who worked on or regularly visited the other side, and had to be stamped by U.S. immigration officials to be valid.

I suspected my problems originated with U.S. rather than Mexican authorities, and couldn't chance this validation. So I ended up making it through the immigration checkpoint hidden in the back of a refrigerated meat truck. From then on, my old U.S. birth certificate got me across borders until I landed in Prague, where Cuban officials were waiting. They took care of shepherding me through the last leg of my journey.

This, then, was my first dramatic passport event.

For the next twelve years, I was literally a woman without a country. As I write these words, I am reminded of Edward Everett Hale's story, "The Man without a Country," first published anonymously in the *Atlantic* in December 1863. I read this story in high school, during the rigidly patriotic 1950s. I remember feeling deep pangs of anguish for its protagonist, Civil War lieutenant Philip Nolan, who develops a friendship with Aaron Burr.

When Burr is tried for treason (an event that actually happened in 1807), Nolan is condemned as an accomplice. In the fictional version, Nolan renounces his country, crying out angrily, "Damn the United States! I wish never to hear of it again!" The judge sentences him to this wish, ordering that he be confined to navy war ships for the rest of his life and that no one ever mention the United States in his presence.

Throughout his long sentence, Nolan misses his country more and more; and more intensely than family, friends, nature, art, or culture, he seems to miss the idea of country itself. Without it, he feels he is nothing. At the end of his life he shows his little stateroom to an officer named Danforth; it has become a shrine of patriotism. The Stars and Stripes are draped around a picture of George Washington. Over his bed, Nolan has painted an eagle with lightning blazing from his beak and claws grasping the globe (the spoils of war and U.S. expansionism are very much part of this story). At the foot of his bed is a dated map of the old territories. Nolan smiles, "Here, you see, I have a country!"

Patriotism, in all its guises, and a sense of personal identity are often intertwined in complex ways. As history moves in different directions, patriotism may be defined more or less dogmatically. The September 11, 2001, attacks on the World Trade Center and Pentagon upped the ante on U.S. patriotism. Because of the George W. Bush administration's response to the tragedy, challenging or even questioning the rote marching orders of a nation besieged are now considered unpatriotic.

Thus, any thoughtful understanding of nationhood that may once have existed was quickly replaced with one-dimensional sloganeering. Subsequently, the Patriot Act embedded these ideas in our national psyche—making covert surveillance of ordinary citizens, the doctrine of the preemptive strike, extraordinary rendition, torture, nation building in other lands, and other activities that only a decade ago would have been considered suspect seem legal and warranted. Even the U. S. Constitution has not been immune, and any expression of difference is now seen as unpatriotic.

But I want to get back to my personal story.

After leaving Mexico in 1969, my family and I lived in Cuba for eleven years. The Cubans issued me an official document that enabled me to travel when necessary. I kept trying to regain my Mexican passport, but without luck. By this time, most of those in prison or exile as a result of the 1968 movement were once again living normal lives. Some even held positions in the new Mexican administration. I wanted to be able to normalize my own situation.

Finally, almost at the end of 1980, when I was about to leave Cuba and move on to Nicaragua, the newly appointed, left-leaning, and exceptionally principled Mexican ambassador to Cuba, Gonzalo Martínez Corvalán, solved my problem in hours. I had noticed a small newspaper article about his presentation of credentials and recognized his name as that of the man who had been Mexico's ambassador to Chile when the coup against Allende was perpetrated. I remembered how he had risked his life protecting Chilean activists who sought asylum in his embassy and how he had accompanied many of them to the airport when they were finally given safe conduct out of the country. I thought he might be sympathetic to my case, called, and asked for an interview in order to explain my dilemma.

Martínez Corvalán received me immediately and listened to my story with genuine concern. He pronounced me a "national treasure" (he had several of my books in his office, which he asked me to sign) and extended me a new passport within hours. Finally, my years without legal identity had come to an end.

Or so I thought.

What I'd already experienced in terms of withheld, stolen, or muddled identity documents might have been enough for one lifetime. But there was more to come. After four years in Nicaragua, I decided it was time to come home. Psychically, spiritually, emotionally, I had never doubted my origins. My home was the United States, more specifically the high desert country of New Mexico, where I had spent my formative years and where my parents and brother still lived.

With only a Mexican passport, I had to request entrance like any foreign national. I did this at the U.S. consular office in Managua and within minutes was granted a one-year multiple entry visa. When I said my intention was to regain my U.S. citizenship, the consular officer, whose name I still remember, advised me to initiate the process once I arrived. Since my parents and son were U.S. citizens, he said he didn't think I would have a problem.

But I did have a problem, a big one. At one point during what I expected would be a routine process, I was called into an office at the Albuquerque Federal Building where, to my surprise, six or seven of my books were lying open on a table. Passages were highlighted in yellow Magic Marker, and the official who conducted the recorded interview asked what I meant by this or that opinion. These were mostly opinions in testimonies I had taken from Cuban and Nicaraguan women, testimonies that spoke of the horrors they'd endured as a result of U.S. policy in Central America. I said I wanted to write the human history absent from U.S. media. I believed in the freedom of expression I'd been taught existed in my country.

After a year or so of increasingly drawn out formalities, my request for residency was denied. I was ordered deported due to the nature of some of my writings. Invoking the 1952 McCarran-Walter Immigration and Nationality Act, the government deemed them to be "against the good order and happiness of the United States." In October 1985 I was given twenty-eight days to leave the country.[5]

I decided to stay and fight. For one thing, I had come home to be close to my aging parents, to rest and regroup after a quarter century away, to reacquaint myself with the landscape of my childhood and language of my poetry. I felt I had every right to return to the land of my birth. For another, I had come home to *place* in a way that would take a whole other essay to describe in depth. I had been away from the air and light of New Mexico far too long; and these resettled within me as parts of my expressive voice. The state's multicultural mix reflected my childhood ambience and was also an extension of the Latin

American histories in which I had lived the preceding twenty-three years. In my late forties, I needed to pull the threads of my experience together, understand how each of these places had shaped me and what might come next.

I was fortunate to have a great deal of support. The Center for Constitutional Rights in New York took my case, providing me with three excellent pro bono lawyers and a legacy of expertise in this sort of struggle. The center also designed a strategy by which we would not only be able to fight for reinstatement of my citizenship but perhaps put a dent in our country's draconian immigration laws as well. The PEN America Center, individual writers of note, and many others contributed to my case—through concerts, readings, bowl-a-thons, sit-ins, fund-raising parties, and personal checks ranging from five dollars to one thousand dollars. I knew I had the kind of support enjoyed by few of the tens of thousands who are prevented from entering the United States each year. I felt an obligation to fight for them as well as for myself.

So ensued an almost five-year battle to attempt to overturn the deportation order against me. My first trial took place in March 1986, in El Paso, Texas. I lost there and continued to lose at a series of other levels until, just before it would have gone into the federal court system, my case reached the Washington-based Board of Immigration Appeals. And that's where I won, in a split decision. Ruth Bader Ginsberg wrote the opinion that gave me my victory. I was granted full restoration of citizenship in October 1989 and was almost immediately issued my first U.S. passport in many years.

That passport came quickly. I had also been sent an official letter from the Department of State, attesting to my regained status. For years, I traveled with that letter on my person, in case I met with a problem reentering the country. Several immigration officials over the next few years told me my name was still in the system. One kindly said she would take care of removing it.

But ten years later, when it was time to renew, things didn't go so smoothly. More than the usual amount of time passed between my application and the passport renewal; and on one of my periodic calls to try to determine what was going on, I was told there was "a problem." "With me in particular?" I asked. "Yes," the woman said.

So I contacted one of my lawyers, who told me to get in touch with my local legislative representative's office. I called, spoke with the person who attended such issues, and within two days had my new passport in hand. No explanation for the delay, only that there had been a problem. I assumed they had come upon my immigration history and had felt inclined to check it out.

That was four years ago. Since then, I have traveled to many parts of the world, including Latin America, the Middle East, Africa, Southeast Asia, and Cuba. But now, in what should have been a routine request for extra visa pages, here I was again: suffering the unexplained delays and uncertainty of something not being quite right. I would call the number given for inquiries and each time receive a slightly different story. When I asked if I could expedite the return of my passport (a service available at additional cost), the person with whom I spoke said no but stumbled over the explanation of why it wouldn't be possible in my case. Someone would tell me to call back on such and such a date, once even at such and such a time of day, and I would do so—to no avail. And so it went, for six long weeks. The date of a scheduled trip came and went; the trip had to be cancelled.

Here I want to interject something of the parallel universe passports inhabit for me. My history has often made me feel like a woman without a country. Perhaps in some ways like a woman without an identity, at least not one that is officially recognized. And not like the fictional Philip Nolan, who damned the United States, but as someone who loves her country—not always its government policies but deeply its history, peoples, cultures, art, and landscape. (During my immigration case, I remember someone taunting me: "If you hate this country so much, why don't you go back where you came from?" The fact is I love the United States. When you love something a great deal, you want it to be the best it can be. And I come from right here, so where did this person think I should go?)

We each nurture our core identity according to our beliefs and stance in the world. My artist self, my feminist self, and those selves derived from other conditions of character or choice—as a mother and grandmother, lesbian, lover, person committed to struggling for justice, etc.—combine to define mine. But identity is always more nuanced and many layered than a simple list of values and experiences. Even those of us who have given a great deal of thought to who we are may be affected by the subliminal and not so subliminal media messages about identity, belonging, and what awaits us if we challenge the status quo. Home, community, morality, point of view, and, yes, also a number of imposed attitudes combine to tell us who we are.

Beyond all that makes us woman, man, transgender, artist, liberal, conservative, laborer, professional, peace lover, warrior, believer, atheist, young, old, or any other identifying factor, in this world of ours some kind of official document is required for freedom of movement from nation-state to nation-state.

Not having a passport can loom almost as ominous as a prison cell (indeed, in the case of federal crimes, passports are withdrawn when a person goes to prison). Here it is important to note that passports do not belong to the bearer but to the government that issues them. In other words, a document that does not belong to us and over which we have no control nevertheless determines whether or not we can travel freely. Perhaps this is why it is so frightening when such documents are arbitrarily withheld.

At the most dramatic moments in my passport history—such as when the paramilitary operatives came to my home in Mexico City or during the five years of my immigration case—I would be besieged by nightmares of different sorts. Early on, the letter *K* and also a number of objects or ideas beginning with *K* (most prominent among them the Greek *kayros*) filled my sleeping eyes. Looming images, some real and imposing, some fanciful or broken, moved through shadows. I could only partially guess their meanings.

I would wake from those nightmares in anguish. In more recent times, the dreams have returned, especially when I feel threatened by obstacles or delays in receiving a passport renewal or the requested extra visa pages with which I began this essay. In the dreams I have these days, the kayros fragments—pieces of its illusory form—scatter across my path, cutting the flesh of my bare feet.

Freedom of movement is important to my life. Since most of my children and grandchildren live in other countries, it has become more than important. The ability to travel, for me, is also about being able to see my family. The United States lists family ties as the bedrock of its immigration policy but has a long history of flagrantly disregarding those ties when handing down immigration decisions. Although I understand the vast difference between a prison cell and not being able to travel, my body's physical and emotional response is intense.

I should say a few words about kayros (also written "kairos"). When I first dreamed that word and/or object while in hiding in Mexico in 1969, I had no idea what it meant. Subsequent research tells me it can mean "moment of justice," "opportunity," "power," or "eternity." In Greek mythology Kayrós was the son of Chronos. He was the god of time and seasons, presented as a younger son of Zeus and Tyche. In the genealogy of Greek gods, he was seen as a sort of avatar, embracing both intelligence and love. Psychologists have referred to kayros as "insight." What all this has to do with losing or being denied an identity document, I have yet to fully explore, but those long-ago dreams proved both prophetic and ominous.

Clearly, this part of my identity—the freedom to travel when and where I choose—has been important in my life, and continues to be so. When problems of this nature arise, my psyche goes into crisis mode. I try to stay calm and am able to sustain a fairly controlled demeanor. Inside, though, I am anxious, sleepless, and wracked by flashbacks.

So when we sent our passports in for those extra visa pages, the stipulated six weeks were up, and I still didn't have mine back, I once again enlisted the help of my legislative representative, now a different person from the one who had come to my aid three years earlier. I called his office, and the man who deals with such issues among the representative's constituents took all my information and e-mailed me the permission form he needed to inquire about my case.

Once again, two days later I received a call telling me my passport was on its way. "Should arrive FedEx," my contact said, giving me the tracking number, obviously pleased at having been able to solve my problem.

I too was delighted. But I also wondered why my passport was coming FedEx, when the National Passport Office says it mails back documents using the U.S. Postal Service and that is how my partner received hers. In fact, later that same day I received a form e-mail indicating that my request for extra pages had been processed and that my passport would arrive via priority mail in a few days.

My passport did not come priority mail but by FedEx as my representative's assistant had said it would. And it was accompanied by the printout of the government's appeal in *Randall et al. v. Edwin Meese III et al.* from February 1988. This was the dismissal decision resulting from a group of prominent writers suing the state on my behalf in the context of my long-ago immigration case.[6] Clearly, the government is still going back to that case, which I won with full reinstatement of citizenship in 1989.

What's more, it wants me to know it is doing so.

The FedEx packet, containing only my passport with its additional pages and that printout of my case, felt like a warning. We have our eye on you. We will never let you relax. At seventy-six years old and a quarter century after winning reinstatement of citizenship, I must still remember to leave twice the amount of time others need to renew a document or request extra pages. I must still be prepared to ask questions and get no answers, or a variety of different answers, to be strung along without any real information, to be forced to cancel a scheduled trip.

And I must still be prepared for friends—even politically savvy friends—to look at me with incredulity when I tell them my story. The democratic myth remains strong. The Patriot Act facilitates so much needless harassment of U.S. citizens (in the name of national security). And the state is always more powerful than the individual.

Forgiver's Dilemma

for Greg Smith

I believe forgiveness has gotten out of hand. Over the past several decades, the emotion has gained currency in a variety of recovery movements, New Age therapies of different stripes, and in the mouths of such trendsetters as the all-powerful Oprah Winfrey. Whatever undeniable good these movements and gurus may bring—Winfrey has certainly promoted mass understanding of marginalized groups, and twelve-step programs, with their emphasis on forgiveness and accountability, have helped many addicts—the idea that we must forgive in order to achieve happiness or inner peace seems vastly overrated in my opinion. In today's political and economic arenas, it often leads to a completely skewed vision of reality and a failure to hold the responsible parties accountable.

The Stanford Encyclopedia of Philosophy dedicates a great deal of space to defining forgiveness:

> The term "forgive" derives from "give" or "grant," as in "to give up," or "cease to harbor (resentment, wrath)." More specifically, "forgive" refers to the act of giving up a feeling, such as resentment, or a claim to requital or compensation. And the term "forgiveness" is defined as the action of forgiving, pardoning of a fault, remission of a debt, and similar responses to injury, wrongdoing, or obligation. In this sense . . . forgiveness is a dyadic relation involving a wrongdoing and a wronged party, and is thought to

be a way in which victims of wrong alter their and a wrongdoer's status by, for instance, acknowledging yet moving past a transgression.[1]

Note that this definition leaves the victim responsible for both her and her victimizer's emotional freedom. If the victim can forgive, it is said, she can move on, and the perpetrator is also absolved of the weight of his act. Sounds suspiciously like the "blame the victim" mentality that is so pervasive throughout our society. The popular support accorded those capable of forgiveness spreads guilt where it does not belong and reinforces that other New Age dictum that it is somehow wrong for us to judge one another. But if we cannot judge, we cannot acknowledge right and wrong, moral and immoral, or indeed any ethical value.

The Stanford Encyclopedia addresses this as well: "Forgiveness may also go awry, deliberately or inadvertently serving more dubious ends, as when a victim of domestic violence routinely but without good reason forgives her abuser, thereby fueling increasingly violent cycles of abuse. . . . A disposition to too readily forgive may also be symptomatic of a lack of self-respect, or indicative of servility. This recalls Aristotle's idea that the person deficient in appropriate anger is unlikely to defend himself and endure being insulted." We have examples of this in venues ranging from endemic domestic abuse to widespread institutional crime (men of a variety of religious cloths sexually abusing their congregants, or professors taking advantage of their students). In all these scenarios, at some point the victim is encouraged to "forgive and move on."

We also hear "forgive me" uttered in popular discourse ranging from fully intentional to thoughtless or automatic expression. In arena after arena, the plea has become an off-hand and meaningless figure of speech.

Still, the philosophical idea of forgiveness is old and difficult to ignore. The Christian New Testament is full of admonitions in this regard: In Luke 11:4, we read, "Forgive us our sins, for we ourselves also forgive everyone who is indebted to us."[2] In Luke 23:34, Jesus is quoted, "Father, forgive them, for they know not what they do." Forgiveness is linked in 1 John 1:9 to confession: "If we confess our sins, he is faithful and righteous to forgive us the sins and to cleanse us from all unrighteousness."

Clearly, this is where Catholics get their practice of congregants confessing to their priests. The Catholic Church also considers the confessional to be protected by the sanctity of its own laws; what the priest hears is almost never passed on to state authorities, even in the matter of serious crime.

Matthew 6:14–15 claims, "For if you forgive men their trespasses, your heavenly Father will also forgive you. But if you don't forgive men their trespasses, neither will your Father forgive your trespasses," implying the quid pro quo as an implacable feature of God's law.

These Judeo-Christian guidelines reinforce today's tendency to emphasize forgiveness as a point of departure toward achieving mental health and social well-being and toward the desirability of wiping the slate clean and moving on. I have quoted Christian scripture here, but all major religions count forgiveness as a virtue.

How often do we hear politicians, when faced with the irrefutable evidence of heinous crimes, urge people to forget the past and look to the future—as if the first is a necessary prerequisite to the second? What better way to avoid punishing those responsible and perhaps revealing the connections between those now seeking office and those who have wronged us so irreparably?

We are led to believe we have only two choices: to forgive and move on, or to wallow in resentment. There are, of course, other choices, but they are rarely mentioned.

Immediately following the end of World War II, the very public trials at Nuremburg found those Nazi leaders guilty who had been responsible for the terrible atrocities committed. Although it would take several generations for ordinary Germans to acknowledge their role in infamy, Nuremburg provided some relief that such criminality would not go unpunished.

In Latin America, after the Dirty Wars of the 1970s and '80s, each country approached its recent history in its own way. Most sought one or another form of victim restitution. Some eventually brought a small number of criminals to justice. Others preferred various types of amnesty. A particular culture of forgiveness or unwillingness to forgive figured in each solution reached. In Cambodia 95 percent of the population is Buddhist and still uses that practice in attempting to come to terms with Pol Pot's atrocities.

Truth and reconciliation tribunals in South Africa and other countries have further developed our ideas about responsibility, accountability, restitution, reconciliation—and the value of forgiveness. The United Nations' World Court at The Hague has been established as a venue for judging those accused of especially heinous crimes against humanity. Some have stood trial there, but the wheels of justice have been slow moving and, in the eyes of many, inadequate.

Recent emphasis tends away from phenomena such as genocide and other examples of crime on a massive scale to concentrate on the individual. In the case of crimes against humanity, the intellectual or military head of a particular movement or genocidal siege may be sought, captured, charged, and tried. In the everyday context of our increasingly violent society, a murderer or a drunk driver who has taken a life may be scapegoated in order to reduce the level of rage felt by the population as a whole. The single-person human-interest story seems to move the American public more than genocide against millions; we have developed no sense of connection with those Others whom we rarely consider to be like us.

A number of projects have sprung up that work to bring victims and victimizers together, often dramatically and sometimes in ways that have proven useful to both. In London in 2004, Marina Cantacuzino and Brian Moody launched an exhibition called *The F Word*. It displayed ideas and images culled from stories of reconciliation and forgiveness gathered throughout the preceding year. Cantacuzino writes, "I began to see that for many people forgiveness is no soft option, but rather the ultimate revenge. For many it is a liberating route out of victimhood; a choice, a process, the final victory over those who have done you harm."[3]

After the 1979 Sandinista victory in Nicaragua, Tomás Borge found himself face-to-face with the Somoza guard who had tortured him brutally and for a long period of time. Now the tables were turned; the man was in a prison run by his former prisoner. Borge looked at his old nemesis and said, "I forgive you"—a pronouncement more damning than any sentence.

As Mariane Pearl, the wife of murdered journalist Daniel Pearl, said of her husband's killers, "The only way to oppose them is by demonstrating the strength they think they have taken from you." *The F Word* exhibition tells some extraordinary stories, of victims who have become friends with perpetrators and murderers who have turned their efforts to peace building.

Whether aimed at isolated crimes or periods of atrocity enveloping entire nations, forgiveness cuts public opinion down the middle. There are those who see it as an immensely noble and humbling response and others who reject it as too easy, a punishment that does not fit the crime.

An international organization called the Forgiveness Project grew out of *The F Word* exhibition. It works to promote awareness, education, and inspiration; and its goal is to help build a future free of conflict and violence by healing the wounds of the past. Its founders are careful to describe it as secular, because forgiveness is so often presumed to belong exclusively to the world of the religious or to be some magical key to serenity.

How exactly do we heal the wounds of the past?

Right here in the United States, we have a situation that offers an arc of variables in terms of thinking about forgiveness, and yet there has been scant dialogue about it. Those in power—reinforced by the media, the academy, conventional wisdom, and in-vogue assumptions—have succeeded in preventing any meaningful exploration of the subject. Let's consider a bit of recent history.

In September of 2001 a group of Muslim fundamentalist terrorists sequestered commercial airplanes in flight and attacked New York's World Trade Center and the Pentagon in Washington DC. Hijackers who had taken over a third plane, on its way to another East Coast target, encountered resistance from passengers and crashed in a Pennsylvania field, killing everyone aboard. The three-pronged attack was the worst terrorist action on U.S. soil and cost close to three thousand lives.

September 11, 2001, or 9/11 as it's called, marked a dramatic before and after. The nation suffered devastating loss, evident in each life affected as well as in a people's collective sense of vulnerability. How the George W. Bush administration responded would shape our culture for years into the future.

Bush could not have responded more poorly. To begin with, all official discourse concerning the tragedy set it up as a them-and-us situation: the attack was the only crime—no effort was made to explore why anger against the United States and its policies might have raged to the point where a small group of fanatics would choose such a horrific route of revenge.

There could be no justification for the crime committed against us, but there were reasons: reasons twisted by fanatical minds. Decades of U.S. arrogance, manipulation, and invasion of other lands had brought the rage of a few to a crazed point of no return. In effect, a holy war had been declared. Instead of analyzing where isolationist and Big Brother foreign policy had taken us, Bush and company fought back like the proverbial playground bully; we would root out every last one of the forces responsible for the attack and bring them to Old West–style justice.

One of several problems with this decision was that at first we didn't seem to be clear on exactly who the enemy was. Another was that the United States itself—always more interested in short-term gain than long-term coherence—had helped finance and arm those responsible. Another problem was that a hapless administration used the very real tragedy as an excuse to go after personal enemies or attack countries where it wanted to establish control for geopolitical or economic reasons. Finally, nothing was done to differentiate between the extremists who launched the attack and the millions of law-abiding and peace-loving followers of Islam who live among us. Thus the attack provided yet another cover for the racism our leaders find so useful in substantiating skewed power relations and unjust law.

And so we entered an era of national security hysteria reminiscent of our own Civil War days or the period of the rise of fascism in Nazi Germany. Under the pretense of keeping America safe, a hastily passed Patriot Act rounded up tens of thousands of innocent people living lawfully in the United States and detained them, often for long periods of time. It authorized widespread wiretapping of its own citizens and demanded that public librarians submit lists of borrowed books.

Kidnapping people and sending them to countries where they could be tortured freely came to be known as extraordinary rendition. Torture was also revealed in prisons managed by U.S. authorities, and respected academics and others engaged in public discussion about whether torture should be permissible and, if so, under what conditions. Perhaps the worst of what began to constitute "the new normal" was Bush's policy of the preemptive strike: because we had been caught off guard, the administration claimed the right to attack anyone anywhere—before they could attack us.

The preemptive strike policy, supported by lies about weapons of mass destruction, led to the United States going into Iraq, decimating one of the oldest cultures on earth, overthrowing that country's government, and executing its president without a trial. Bush wanted Iraq's oil and had old scores to settle with Saddam Hussein. But Osama bin Laden's Al Qaeda had taken responsibility for 9/11. So Bush also decided to wage full-scale war in Afghanistan. Soon two nations were being torn apart, and tens of thousands of U.S. men's and women's lives were being destroyed by war.

Along with George W. Bush, others responsible for these counterproductive policies had first and last names: Dick Cheney, Donald Rumsfeld, Condoleezza Rice, and John Ashcroft, among others. These men and women made a tragic situation worse. They stripped us of many of our democracy's most cherished values and benefits. They sacked our treasury, bungled our budget, threw us into debt, and covered for the unregulated criminality that created the worst economic crisis since the Great Depression.

Despite the strictures of a national security state, vast sectors of the population rebelled. In 2008, after eight long years of Bush's obstinate charge, the U.S. electorate voted in a new administration it believed would achieve a political about-face. With a groundswell of energy impossible to ignore, much of it from youths who had never voted before, we turned the management of our country over to a young African American president, a man who had run on a ticket of change.

With the new administration in place, what were we going to do about those who had gotten us into such a mess? Obama's rhetoric, or perhaps our own dreams superimposed on what he led us to believe were his intentions, made us hopeful that "yes we can" really meant something this time around. Would those whose criminal policies had cost us so much be brought to justice and punished? Or would we be asked to forgive and forget?

We now know that the Obama administration took the latter course. Once in office, an extreme, almost exaggerated, civility characterized the new president's attitude toward his predecessor and opponents in Congress. His promise to end the war in Afghanistan dissolved in a surge of new troops, and he kept the previous administration's secretary of defense. He also hired the same economic team that had brought us to the brink of insolvency under Bush. Some began to say he was in an impossible situation, that the Pentagon and/or international corporations were in control and the president didn't have the power associated with his office. Some of us looked to his smaller promises, hoping he might at least show some honesty of intention there. Little, if anything, was forthcoming.

As the first black president in a racist nation, Obama suffered indignities that would require a whole other essay to deconstruct. For some of us, this made criticizing him a problem. As a raucous right wing gathered strength, the temptation for thinking people was not to echo its mindless diatribes. As the country sank more and more definitively into economic chaos, though, and hundreds of thousands of people lost jobs and homes, we became more critical. Obama's remedies were tepid at best: no great jobs initiative such as the one Roosevelt brought to bear on the Great Depression, followed by compromise with the Republicans that resulted in their getting and his relinquishing everything, all to the tune of endless platitudes such as "the time has come" and "we must work together."

Most tellingly, we have been coerced into forgiving and forgetting. Not the slightest move was made to hold Bush and his associates accountable for the crimes they committed. International bankers, who oversaw criminal schemes of gigantic proportions, also got away with what they'd done. The most powerful corporations were deemed "too big to fail" and saved by taxpayer money.

Public attention was riveted on the occasional Bernie Madoff, who became the scapegoat for an entire culture of criminality. Moreover, this decision not to prosecute was presented as the moral high ground.

As I write, we wallow in the midst of a worldwide depression. Our pundits may call it a recession or economic downturn or whatever deceptive term they coin; but for the person who has lost his or her job or home, nomenclature is beside the point. The poorest among us are in the street. The vast majority of jobs lost are clearly never coming back. The very future of capitalism is in grave danger, but any alternative has been discarded as undemocratic or unworkable. And the United States continues to push some fantasy of democracy wherever we exercise influence or control.

In a time of global interdependency, most of the developed countries have followed us into disarray, and those considered to be developing are profoundly affected as well. Yet not an international banker, not a statesman of dubious intent, not even a general responsible for the deaths of thousands has been held responsible in any real way.

Forgive, forget, and move on.

Forgiveness, from the largest public arena to the most intimate private sphere, is shaped to fit the interests of those in power. We need only look to the economic crisis for the most dramatic examples of how this works. Those who have lost their jobs or fall one or two months behind in paying their mortgages are not forgiven. The bank will foreclose, even when everyone knows the bank and its partners in crime authorized those mortgages based on false premises that allowed them to make millions betting against people whose payments were much too high for their incomes.

Yet we forgave the individuals and banks, brokers, and mortgage lenders who rigged the system and caused so much collective despair. For to bring them to justice would have exposed their ties to those still in power and threatened the fabric of an already shaky house of cards.

On the underbelly of this political scene, every personal manifestation of crime and forgiveness mirrors the larger picture—just as the larger picture reflects smaller individual acts. Our culture used to excuse men who battered and raped with the expression: "Boys will be boys." Now we have become more sophisticated in our social discourse, encouraging female survivors of male sexual violence to forgive because it is the moral high road or as a way of freeing themselves from resentment so they can move on.

Within the Catholic Church, where thousands of longtime victims of priestly abuse and bishopric cover-up finally succeeded in demanding something be done about the shameful status quo, forgiveness is highly recommended. It is, after all, a Christian virtue. Within the military, it is still the norm to deny the frequent abuse of female soldiers by their brethren in arms; a kind of quasi forgiveness is presumed to benefit the overall morale of the troops—especially in times of war. On college campuses, female students are still forced to forgive predatory professors if they want a decent grade or a ticket to an ever more unattainable profession.

Forgiveness becomes the easy way out, because it is the way protected by power.

In April 2011, in his annual Easter message, the Archbishop of Canterbury in England made an interesting commentary about forgiveness. He told *Radio Times*: "I think the twentieth century saw such a level of atrocity that it has focused our minds very, very hard on the dangers of forgiving too easily (. . .) because if forgiveness is easy it is as if the suffering doesn't really matter. It's not fair to expect victims of abuse, rape or torture to turn the other cheek with ease."[4]

There may be an argument to be made as to whether or not such a victim can be expected to forgive at all, let alone easily. But there do seem to be certain conditions, on the part of both victimizer and victim, that may possibly lift the act of forgiving from meaningless formality to something of use. In the mid-1980s, Terry Waite was sent by the Anglican Church in London to try to negotiate the release of hostages being held by Shiite Muslims in Lebanon. He himself was kidnapped and held captive for more than four years. In 1991 they were all freed. Waite, who has spoken and written at length about his ordeal, has had some interesting things to say about forgiveness. Because he has never had an opportunity to hear an apology from his kidnappers, he describes his forgiveness as incomplete. Presumably, he believes that hearing those words would in some way allow him the grace of full forgiveness.

Others require more than words for forgiveness to be possible. Surely an important difference lies in whether or not the act to be forgiven was intentional. An incident from my own life illustrates this. It was Mexico City, early 1968. I had parked illegally in front of the post office where I intended to run in, retrieve the contents of my postal box, return to my car, and drive off, as I had done so many times before. But this time, when I opened the driver's side door, its outer corner caught an approaching bicyclist in the leg. The kid was ten or twelve. He lay on the pavement, tangled in his wrecked bike, obviously in pain. An immediate crowd urged me to flee the scene of the accident. But

I couldn't leave the kid unattended. So I went into the post office to call an ambulance. When I emerged, the police were already there.

An ambulance did come, and it took the injured boy to a nearby hospital. The police took me to the nearest precinct. I spent several days in jail, during which time one level of graft and payoff led to another and then another before I was freed. The kid's parents showed up at the precinct just a couple of hours into this ordeal. They were poor people, genuine and kind. I had arranged for a friend to see to it that their son was receiving appropriate care, that his medical needs would be met. This was all they wanted, and they had come to speak with the authorities to ask that I be released. They forgave me, they said, and felt it was their moral responsibility to make sure I too was all right.

Their forgiveness, however, meant nothing to the Mexican police, who saw an opportunity to make a few extra pesos. Forgiveness belonged, after all, in the spiritual realm. This was business. I don't believe this pattern has varied over the years, in Mexico or anywhere else.

I want to see if I can deconstruct forgiveness as it is commonly understood in U.S. mainstream culture. On broadly popular talk shows such as Oprah Winfrey and others, in the plethora of TV crime shows, and in newspaper articles about real crimes, there is almost always some mention of forgiveness. An interviewer or reporter may ask a murder victim's mother if she has been able to forgive the person who took her child's life, and an affirmative answer is invariably applauded. It is as if professing forgiveness in and of itself endows the interviewee with moral superiority.

Let's translate this to the arena of governmental crime. Are we to believe that the current administration, in forgiving the crimes of its predecessor, is also superior? Those crimes continue to affect the millions of citizens who have lost their jobs, homes, pensions, and more. Is forgiving and going forward, as if nothing has happened, really the best way of demonstrating that those who lead us today care about their constituents? When this situation is compounded by hiring yet again those who failed us before, the whole idea of forgiveness falls apart.

It is true that the act of forgiving is described in different ways. Many therapists, and even some talk show hosts, emphasize that forgiving does not in any way mean condoning an aggression. One forgives, they say, not as a way of absolving the perpetrator of guilt but as an act that will free the victim from feelings that may make it difficult to live fully. Forgiving doesn't mean forgetting, these professionals insist. In line with certain religious dogmas, on the other hand, to forgive is to follow the example of Jesus or some other figure believed to have forgiven far greater offenses. In these contexts, forgiving becomes a religious obligation rather than something that simply allows the victim to get on with his or her life.

In many of today's social venues, though, forgiveness has become a commodity, one that can be purchased for a price. In Albuquerque a meditation center offers weekly classes in forgiveness at ten dollars for an hour and a half. Like weight loss, eternal youth, and "natural" vitamins, forgiveness is something we are urged to buy to live more fully. The overall social construct leads us to believe, first of all, that these are desirable and, secondly, that they can be gotten on the cheap.

Earlier in this piece, I pointed to a connection between the mandate that we forgive and the one that tells us not to judge. "Judge not, lest ye shall be judged" is popular in much religious discourse and also in a great deal of psychotherapeutic practice. People are attracted to these dictums because they absolve them of the need to make choices, decide what is right or wrong, and take responsibility for their actions and hold others responsible for theirs.

All of this takes courage, in the give and also in the take. This is not to say that I believe errors of judgment cannot be amended or that there is no life after a very serious crime. I do not subscribe to capital punishment, even for the worst offenses, so it stands to reason I believe almost everyone capable of some degree of rehabilitation. I also know that rehabilitation, though it may be the stated aim, is not really the goal in the majority of our country's penal institutions.

I do believe in placing blame where blame is due and holding those responsible for a crime accountable—whether an individual, an institution, or a state. The only way I know of making amends is to stop committing the crime, publicly admit to having been involved, and—if possible—do something meaningful for those who have been wronged.

I also believe in rendering judgments: applauding that which we consider correct and condemning what is not. Judgment need not involve violent retribution or banishing the culpable person from society. In all but the most extreme cases, those who have done wrong should have a second chance. But if we cannot judge good from bad and moral from immoral, how can we construct a value system by which to live? Judgment is a necessary part of human interaction.

As with anything else, forgiveness may work for some in some circumstances. It cannot be a catchall for every time we lack the courage to take a principled stand.

Going Places

At seventy-six it's safe to say I will never climb Everest. Actually, that was safe to say when I was twenty-six. I probably won't be photographing the lemurs on the island of Madagascar, either, or walking through the tragically deteriorating ruins at Pompeii. Because its ruined state is precisely what makes it so interesting, many may wonder why the neglect that destroys it now pulls tight the muscles of my chest, seducing me to see, touch, and feel.

All I can say by way of explanation is to tell of repeated dreams in which those ancient outlines of bodies frozen in configurations of everyday life move in and out among those other silhouettes, the white chalk lines left by police at crime sites involving murders.

Death dies again.

At my age, energy begins to diminish; and in the current economic recession or depression or whatever they want us to call it, it's probably wiser to think about fixing the roof than traveling to some faraway place or accomplishing some long-dreamed-about feat. But the dreams are still there, and sometimes we find ways of bringing them to fruition.

Among the places still waiting, hiking the Inca Trail has long been on my list of things I want to do before I die. I have had the good fortune of walking through Machu Picchu twice, once as a teenager and again close to half a century later with my younger brother, who was seven at the time of our first visit.

In 1973 I spent three months working in Peru, but the intensity of the project left no time for pleasure. Even then, although it would be years before I would be diagnosed with emphysema, visits to the high Andes always ended in an emergency return to the lowlands: I couldn't take the extreme altitude. That is the reason I've been discouraged from making the trek, even now that time and money are on my side.

Too late. Too late as well to walk the Great Wall of China. (Actually I am much more interested in seeing that country's terracotta warriors.)[1] Or hike to the Great Wave, a landscape of swirling rock among Utah's many slot canyons and other dramatic desert landscapes too demanding for my age and physical condition. Grabbing the opportunity while you can is something I've learned the hard way.

I learned it in time to visit Kiet Seel, an Ancestral Puebloan ruin in northern Arizona.[2] Round-trip, that hike is eighteen miles. One has to carry everything needed to spend the night, eat, and drink clean water in a place where that means bringing your own. At a gallon a day, that's two gallons, or sixteen pounds, of water alone.

A friend made that dream a reality by giving me the gift of accompaniment. He hiked alongside me, carried seventy pounds to my twenty, and—having grown up in the South African bush—was expert at deciphering the route when it seemed to disappear. We stashed some of our water on the way in. On the way out, I had no doubt he would be able to remember the rock or bush protecting its whereabouts.

I know I would not have been able to do that hike without Mark and remain deeply grateful. Many of the photographs I made in the ruin itself are slightly out of focus, attesting to hands still trembling from the effort. Images taken by my friend show a deep bib of sweat soaking the front of my shirt. Kiet Seel's uniqueness, among the many ruins that dot the Colorado Plateau, comes from its limited number of visitors and the fact that some items of ancient use remain at the site itself. Gazing in situ at a clay bowl used eight hundred years before is an experience matched by few others.

I inherit my wanderlust from my mother, who definitely wanted to go everywhere and see everything. My father was always willing; his greatest satisfaction, making all her dreams come true. As a public school music teacher, he had summers off, and our family began boarding freighters when I entered my teens. My sister and my brother were three years and eight years younger than me, respectively. Those summer trips were problematic for Ann, as she suffered from motion sickness no matter what the vehicle. John got into the spirit of travel with a young boy's glee. As adults, all three of us love to travel.

And so we went through the Panama Canal to both coasts of South America. We put our old pistachio-green Chevy Suburban on a ship that sailed Alaska's Inside Passage, then drove the still-incipient Alcan Highway back to Albuquerque. I learned to drive on that trip, sitting at the edge of the seat, my feet barely reaching the pedals. I remember struggling to change a flat tire on the heavy vehicle; Dad wisely believed such proficiency a prerequisite to earning a license.

During my teenage years, we crossed the Atlantic on the original *Queens Elizabeth* and *Mary*. Memories rise as I write: of picnicking in the English countryside while Dad read to us from G. K. Chesterton's *Father Brown Stories*, shopping at Harrods for the proverbial basic tweed, and my first glimpses of the world's art in museums such as the Louvre and Prado.

Mother's spirit of adventure was lopsided and vaguely colonialist. She used to make Dad carry a gallon thermos of clean water, so we wouldn't have to drink from the tap in dubious ports of call. I remember him intentionally dropping that heavy thermos off a Caribbean dock one afternoon, then winking at me. We conspired to tell Mother it had been an accident. It wasn't until many years later that I understood how both my parents manipulated their children through the long pain of their relationship, each making us coconspirators in ways that sometimes accrued to our short-term advantage, sometimes not.

In foreign countries, our parents always checked in at the U.S. embassy, a custom that became popular as pleasure travel filtered to the middle classes. In the 1950s the world was still small enough that this might lead to lunch with an ambassador or contact with some other interesting individual. In Peru, embassy personnel warned against traveling to Bolivia because of its recent revolution. This was enough to whet Mother's appetite, and she soon had us on a train headed for Puno, then on a boat across Lake Titicaca. From the windows of a second train, descending over vast sweeps of altiplano into La Paz, we caught sideways glimpses of the death and upheaval still visible along its steep stone streets.

Back in Peru, sitting together on a curb in the high Andean city of Cuzco, Mother invited me to chew coca leaves with her, trying to simulate holding them in one cheek as the Quechua people did. I was repulsed by the taste of bitter saliva, felt nauseous and faint, but the idea of doing something so off-limits made me feel adult and conspiratorial.

As the oldest, I often endured the advantage as well as the responsibility of

Mother's frequent departures from the norm. She would launch into some fairly risky project, then skid to a stop when things got rough—sure someone would be there to catch her in their safety net. Once, she asked me to get her an abortion, still illegal at the time. She was sure I could. Fortunately, by the time I made the connection, she no longer needed the service. As I got older, I became that net holder more and more often.

In 1952 when the freighter we were on was delayed by a sudden order to pick up a cargo of coffee for U.S. troops in Korea, we were forced to spend an extra couple of weeks in Rio de Janeiro. Our money ran out; and while we waited for a bank transfer from home, we were limited to the breakfast that came with our expensive room. We couldn't even check out of the lodging on which we'd splurged for what we thought would be a couple of nights, because we didn't have the money to pay our bill. Morning after morning, each of us would eat half our ration of croissants, then stow the rest in a suitcase. Midmorning Mother and I would don our swimsuits and amble out along the black-and-white mosaic sidewalks that bordered Copacabana Beach until some interested man invited us to lunch.

Our aim at those lunches was to eat as much as we could, while surreptitiously putting something away for Dad and my younger siblings, who waited at a prearranged spot on the beach near our hotel. Toward the end of our lunch, mother always feigned a headache or some other excuse to explain why we suddenly had to bid our host farewell. We would take a rain check on whatever else he had in mind, she promised, making it necessary for us to find different stretches of beach for our subsequent hustling.

I still remember our excitement, back at the hotel, as we unwrapped napkins of delicacies for our waiting family members. The world was not only smaller; it was also safer then. I can't remember Dad ever worrying out loud that the plan might go bad. My parents also allowed me to go out with young men I met on those trips. Some were members of the freighter's crew; others were guys I met here or there. I tried hard to act older than I was, though I don't imagine I fooled anyone.

As I grew into my own ideas and worldview, I continued to remember those childhood trips with affection. But I wished my parents had known more about the places and peoples we visited. I felt I had missed out by not understanding what was happening in those countries at the time, what social and political forces were at work, how other cultures differed from ours, and what role we, as tourists, played in helping to shape or destroy traditions we could hardly imagine. I vowed to find out how my country and its policies fit into the scheme of things and how I might avoid participating in its bully stance. Lines like "The food was good, and the waiter's nails were clean," which I discovered years later in one of Mother's travel diaries, seem shocking in their crass superficiality.

My father's father was a German Jewish immigrant to the United States who arrived on its shores as the nineteenth century ended. I was told he had sixteen dollars in his pocket when he got off the boat. In New York he married a woman of similar descent and eventually made money reproducing the quality full-color prints then popular as greeting cards or on candy box covers. Currier and Ives and Maxfield Parrish were among the artists whose work he featured. A man of Prussian character and few words, he wanted his three sons to succeed at business as he had done. Only the oldest did.

After two boys, Dad's parents really wanted a girl. To that end, they dressed my father in lacey ruffled dresses and kept his blond curls shoulder length until he was six or seven. When it was time for him to enter first grade, the teacher discovered he spoke only German: the result of having been raised by a governess. The sudden adjustment must have been painful. When he spoke of his childhood, which was rare, he always said, "They did the best they knew how."

My father dreamed of playing sports and making music. He told us his father sent him to the University of Pennsylvania's Wharton School of Business, where, at the time, a quota existed for Jewish students. Dad wasn't interested in any of his courses, did poorly, and only graduated because of his father's influence. He tried and failed at one small business after another.

When I was a child, he had a small pipe shop in the Wall Street area of New York City. I loved riding the commuter train in on Saturday mornings, helping him mix the pungent-smelling tobaccos, and then breaking saltines into bowls of canned Campbell's vegetable soup in the shop's tiny back room. I would move the miniature letters around on the soup's surface, trying to form words.

Dad never had the temperament for making money. He was far too genuine and kind. Naïve, some would say. Every one of his business endeavors ended in disaster. His parents would bail him out—something that must have been humiliating—but it was obvious that business wasn't for him. Eventually he began working in retail, selling men's clothing in department stores, where making a go of the enterprise was no longer his responsibility. This had to have been a relief. But evidence of the failures remained. I remember a heavy roll of wrapping paper: diagonal lines of white sleds against a glaring green background. It was left over from the pipe shop. For years, every Christmas present we gave was wrapped in that paper.

Mother and Dad preached thrift and frugality. They never threw anything out and always had neat piles of string, rubber bands, paper clips, used envelopes, paper napkins saved from restaurants, and other items at the ready. Many years later, after Dad's death, my brother and I helped Mother move into an assisted living apartment. One large cardboard box was filled with unused restaurant napkins. We tossed that box, thinking it was the last thing she wanted in the reduced space. But she dragged it right back into the apartment. It was still important to her.

After we left the East and landed in New Mexico, Dad went back to school and got a certificate that enabled him to teach. He became a public school music instructor, traveling from school to school, often having to organize a youth orchestra in an open hallway or the corner of a gym, once even in a boy's bathroom. He also played in the civic symphony and taught private lessons. Our father had finally found his niche. Our mother, too, seemed happy in our new home. For the first few years, she returned to her old love of sculpture, working in clay and then wood. Later she began studying Spanish and became a Spanish–English translator. I remember those early years in Albuquerque as a peaceful time, filled with a sense of possibility.

Mother was from a Jewish family that wished it wasn't, and her parents employed the ruses of the day to distance themselves from their heritage, cultural as well as religious. She was behind our parents' name change, from Reinthal to Randall. When I would ask about that, which I did periodically throughout my childhood, she always said the new name was easier to spell. Interest in such religious manifestations as Quakerism, Unitarianism, or Christian Science erected a useful wall between Judaism and our family life. Mom's deeply internalized anti-Semitism would affect us all. Despite my attempts to come to grips with it and clarify our history for my own children, it is still something I—and they—deal with in different ways.

Our mother's father, who had been a traveling salesman dealing in precious stones and unique jewelry settings, later became a Christian Science practitioner. Some family members referred to him as the Saint. I found him cold as steel, evasive as helium. He was dreamily self-indulgent and had numerous half-hidden relationships with other women, something that drove my grandmother to despair. After many years of psychotherapy and long after his death, I would remember his sexual abuse of me.

While my father's mother was lavish and loving (my grandfather had died before I was born), my mother's mother was long suffering and mean spirited, a less veiled counterpart to her more devious husband. Her classism and racism hovered close to the surface and showed themselves at odd moments. Unable to confront her husband directly, she expressed herself through a litany of self-martyrdom and constant insulting innuendos. She was the kind of woman who, no sooner had a person risen from couch or chair, would run over and puff up the pillows—almost daring them to sit down again. Ashtrays were emptied while the ashes of lit cigarettes still dangled above them. Referring to my grandfather's numerous schemes, which frequently caused him to make a lot of money and then lose it precipitously, she complained about his irresponsibility having forced her to sell eggs door-to-door. The truth was that a liveried chauffer drove her on that egg route in the family Daimler-Benz.

Every family has its secrets and lies. Our societies encourage them while touting the importance of truth. In retrospect, my family's lies were dramatically transparent. Even as they were told, they seemed to reflect a reality I knew enough to question. At the same time, they wove an atmosphere that affected how I would act with my children, a pattern I had to consciously break. Most of the secrets revealed themselves in time as sad longings dressed in see-through disguise. But there were some we never did unravel; these died with our parents, whose lips were sealed to the end.

Mother grew up in a family where making it through must have required endless inventions of determination and cunning. It seems logical to me that her father also abused her, although she never wanted to explore that possibility. Therapy, to her generation, implied mental illness and greater shame than the irrational conduct it might have helped to decipher and heal. For years, her transparent manipulation angered me. Today, long after her death, I see her as a survivor: almost heroic in the face of so much unmet desire and convoluted subterfuge.

One of Mother's dreams, before she died, was to revisit the house where she grew up, a mansion on Long Island Sound beachfront property. When she was in her early eighties, my siblings and I took her there. The house had gone through several owners since her time. Its most recent was William Casey of CIA fame. Now his widow lived in the home, and although elderly and a bit dreamy herself, she welcomed us warmly and showed us through room after room of our mother's childhood.

She even invited us to stay for lunch. My brother, a rare book dealer, perused the Casey library, later marveling that not a single novel or literature of any kind could be found among the hundreds of volumes on war and espionage. My sister and I observed the interior decoration, which seemed to exude a hundred hues of pink and included a number of Catholic religious objects. Mother exclaimed over the curved banister she said she'd slid down as a child. I could see her early years rise seductively in her eyes, as she attempted to square some small nook with space she'd remembered as immense, or great trees with the saplings her parents had planted during her childhood more than seventy years before.

Even as a teenager, Mother wanted to be an artist. She quit middle school to attend New York's Art Students League, where she took classes for a number of years. Sculpture was her first interest. I don't know if her failure to find a strong voice in the medium was finally due to an inability to break through some sort of creative barrier or because of the profound lack of self-confidence that resulted from her upbringing. Eventually, she gave up art for translation, took every Spanish course the University of New Mexico had to offer—several of them two or three times over—and devoted many years to the work of Cuban liberator and writer José Martí. Up until a week or so before her death at almost ninety-seven, she was still going over and refining translations she had finished many years before.

Mom always said she married Dad "on the rebound," when she was jilted by the man she loved. Words like "rebound" and "jilted" describe her era and social milieu for me. She said she accepted our father's proposal because he was from a good family and kind, she thought he would make a good father (he did), and his family had money. Many years later, when I came out to her as a lesbian, she also told me I was "lucky to have been born thirty years later than she was." What she meant by this I could only guess. Mother tended to say what she thought people wanted to hear, so one couldn't always take her words at face value.

Mother and Dad were married sixty-two years, until his death. It wasn't a happy marriage. Although never physically violent, there was an almost constant undercurrent of tension caused by Mom's dissatisfaction and Dad's frustration. The former was exemplified by sarcasm and sideways looks. The latter was mostly muffled, exploding in a shouting match once or twice a year. She taunted him with meaningless affairs with other men. He left her once for a few months, and she begged him to come back, promising she would "be good." He loved her in a way that enabled him to endure such constant rejection. She must have loved him too, insofar as she was able. During the last week or so of his life, she moved out of their apartment and in with a friend. My brother, Barbara, and I were left to care for him. After his death, she rewrote the script, emphasizing how much she had loved and how deeply she missed him. I have no doubt that in her own way she did.

Our father had a sense of commitment that simply could not bridge turning away from his promise to love, honor, and obey. She was the woman he had chosen, in every important way. Ideas for the early family trips always came from her, but he became excited and involved in their planning, and they both encouraged participation from us kids. We spent much of the year pouring over maps and reading travelogues and occasionally something a bit more comprehensive. There's no doubt that those childhood adventures opened me to the world.

And so I was destined to become a traveler. Barely eighteen, I married for the first time.[3] It's clear to me that marriage was my ticket out of the tensions rampant in my childhood home, the only exit available to a young woman of my time and social class. Finally on my own, throughout my late teens and early twenties, I didn't think of my wanderlust as travel but as exploration. I would feel I had gotten what I needed from a place and move on—to another city, another country. In this way, I left Albuquerque, headed for India. My first husband and I coaxed a Lambretta motor scooter from Rotterdam, down through the Pyrenees, into southern Spain, and on to Tangiers, a free port at the time. We hoped we would be able to buy cheap Indian rupees there. But we found no rupees and returned to Spain, where we went broke and ended up living and working in Seville for a year.

Later, on my own again, I moved to New York. By then I knew I would be a writer, and that's where I imagined writers and artists lived. I spent the next few years among the abstract expressionist painters and in the company of poets identified with Black Mountain, deep image, and the beats. Travel in those days and in that city often took place via mind-altering drugs. I used my share, but for me the real journey was the work: getting to know the writing and art of others and developing the discipline needed in order to make that happen for myself. I was beginning a more and more conscious pilgrimage to my core.

Four years after I got to the city, it no longer met my needs. I picked up my ten-month-old firstborn, Gregory, and we boarded a Greyhound for Mexico City. In this new land, I grew politically. I was honing my writing skills but also opening to what was going on in the world and learning about the forces that determined the losses and wins of those years. It was imperative that I, as a young U.S. American, begin to understand the relationship my government established with the nations it controlled. As a result, for the next two or three decades, political involvement and cultural work mostly determined my movements from one place to another.

In Mexico I married a Mexican poet, Sergio Mondragón; and together we founded a bilingual literary quarterly that would enjoy a vibrant eight-year run. *El Corno Emplumado / The Plumed Horn* published some of the most interesting new work from several continents during the decade of the 1960s. Travel began, then, to focus on trips to visit with others promoting creative experience. We journeyed to read and share our work and theirs.

Although cyberspace was a concept of which we couldn't yet have dreamed, we also experienced a sort of virtual travel through our connection with poets and artists from across the Americas and the world. Actual communication in those days was via snail mail and very occasional long-distance telephone calls. But bridges linking consciousness and creativity were traveled instantaneously. And there was a generosity of experience. Artists and writers, with whom we had only had contact through the journal, knew they were welcome to stay with us for a few days or weeks. When we traveled, we also knew we had a place to stay with them.

Our political allegiances and Mexican governmental repression finally put an end to the magazine. Sergio and I divorced, and I soon began living with U.S. American poet Robert Cohen. Because of my participation in Mexico's 1968 student movement, I was forced underground and then out of the country the following year. My family and I ended up in Cuba, whose revolution generously received the four children I had by then as well as my partner and me. After a decade there and once again on my own, I moved on to Nicaragua, where a new revolution had come to power and new forms of social organization were underway.

Taking along the material objects I had collected to date was subject to what was accessible in terms of transport, none of it easy. For example, going underground from Mexico to Cuba meant giving up almost everything I cared about: paintings collected through the years, even manuscripts (in a time before computerized data storage). My children had to leave their favorite toys. We couldn't even say goodbye to many of our friends. Going from Cuba to Nicaragua was easier in terms of material possessions but palpably more difficult in that some of my children would stay behind. After 1980 we would never again live together as a family.

From Nicaragua to the United States may have been the most dramatic move of all. I packed carefully, expecting to fill the container I would send by ship. But those were the years of the Contra War. U.S.-backed forces mined the port of Corinto, and commercial shipping was curtailed for a while. At the last moment, I had to reduce what I would take to its minimum expression; it all had to accompany me by air.

In this move, as in others, I lost irreplaceable items. One I have never ceased to mourn was an eight-by-ten-inch commercial black-and-white photo that had been taken of my father and me going down the Grand Canyon on mule back when I was ten or eleven—souvenir of a trip made many years before. In the late forties and for some time after, every mule train that descended stopped for a moment just below the rim so a photographer from the old Kolb Brothers Studio could snap a picture. When we emerged the following day, we had the opportunity of purchasing a copy for a dollar. This memento accompanied me for decades and was something I treasured, until it disappeared somewhere between Nicaragua and the United States.

During all those years, I also traveled widely to work: exploring the cultural and social conditions of women and reading my poetry in venues ranging from universities to theaters, independent bookstores, and other spaces. I visited Chile, during the Popular Unity government; Venezuela, to attend a conference celebrating the United Nations' International Year of the Woman; and Peru, while working for the UN's International Labor Office (ILO) in 1973–74.

I had the great privilege of traveling the length of North Vietnam, to the province of Quang Trì, just below the seventeenth parallel, only six months before the heroic Vietnamese finally rid their land of U.S. invaders and North and South were reunited. On that trip, I was one of only nine foreigners in the beleaguered North. The images and feelings I experienced have never left me.

Each of these trips was built around specific projects, most of them involving researching women's lives, popular culture, or political situations off-limits to most in the United States. Firsthand I experienced places, peoples, and situations ignored or misrepresented in the U.S. corporate media. It felt important to be able to share my alternative impressions—through letters, journal, articles, and later books and photographs. My travels had made me a bridge.

Coming back to the United States, in January of 1984, wasn't really a trip. It was a homecoming. I had been away from my country for almost a quarter century, during which time I had only occasional contact with my parents, old friends, and the landscape and language of my youth. But my return would be fraught with a drama I didn't expect. Because I had acquired Mexican citizenship in 1967, I had to apply for residency and then go through the process of reclaiming my original status.[4] The U.S. Immigration and Naturalization Service, based on the content of some of my books, invoked the McCarthy-era McCarran-Walter Immigration and Nationality Act and ordered me deported at the end of 1985.

And so began an almost five-year period of being confined to the United States. If I had ventured abroad, to Paris or Mexico City to welcome the births of my first grandchildren, I would have forfeited my right to fight for my change in status. Those years between 1985 and 1989 were filled with hundreds of trips back and forth across the United States, while I engaged in the struggle to remain in the country of my birth. I might fly from Albuquerque to New York for a two-minute segment on *Nightline* or *The Today Show*, or to some other city to be present at a fundraiser or confer with my lawyers.

All the while, I had to earn a living—not easy after years in revolutionary societies, where work depended on where one was needed more than on a college degree, an attractive résumé, or market competition. I decided to teach, but since my hometown university wouldn't hire me—the fallout from my case was particularly virulent there—I was forced to look elsewhere. I did a semester each at Macalister College in St. Paul, Minnesota, and the University of Delaware in Wilmington; and many at Trinity College in Hartford, Connecticut, the school that stuck by me through all the ups and downs of my immigration battle.

This introduced another sort of travel into my life. I would leave the home I shared with Barbara and only come back for an occasional long weekend during my semester away. Some couples thrive long distance. We found the separations painful and exhausting. Sometimes it almost seemed better to forego getting together, because by the time we were once again used to one another's rhythms, we were forced to hug goodbye.

Years passed. I won my immigration case in 1989 and retired in 1994. Barbara and I were finally able to make our year-round home together. That was when we began to travel for the pure pleasure of exploration.

We have been fortunate to have been able to board a dory through the 286 miles of the Colorado River that cuts through Grand Canyon, take our grandchildren to the Galápagos Islands, stand close to Africa's big animals, and walk among the Mayan ruins of Mexico and Guatemala.

When I visited New York's Museum of Natural History and saw an exhibition about Petra, I came home and told Barbara I had to visit that Nabataean site. I remember it was a strange square stone mask that compelled me, more even than the famous photographs of the Siq opening to a sudden view of the Treasury carved in rose-colored stone. Egypt, Greece, and Turkey followed Jordan, making that part of the world one to which we would return often.

My generation was shaped by the war in Vietnam, and I'd always been grateful for that first visit so close to the end of U.S. occupation. Now I wanted to visit a reunified and reconstructed Vietnam and show Barbara the country that also figured in her early political consciousness. Our trip there, twenty-eight years after my first visit, was deeply moving for both of us.

Easter Island was another dream. After two days of travel, via Tahiti, to reach the tiny spot of land in the South Central Pacific, it was stunning to realize we had circled back to Albuquerque's time zone. Our old friend Jane Norling accompanied us on that trip. A brilliant painter, she moved our eyes across its landscape as we explored the island together. Picnicking one day, high on the inner rim of Rano Raraku Crater, we suddenly realized we were eating our sandwiches perched next to a giant stone nose. The great moai are always with me. Those few days on the piece of land its inhabitants call Rapa Nui taught me a lot about resistance, courage, and cultural integrity.

Returning to a place has meant a lot, often more than seeing it for the first time. That sense of recognition, sometimes tantamount to homecoming, is almost indescribable. And so we have chosen to forego some firsts, preferring to return to that magical seam where rock and river join in the depths of the Grand Canyon, the ancient ruins whose inhabitants continue to speak to us, the awe-inspiring experience of watching an African lioness teach her adolescent cubs to hunt, or island-hopping on a small sailboat through the Galápagos.

And when I say "speak," I am not being metaphorical. Language is a big part of it for me: those voices we listen for, those we hear, and how we ourselves communicate. By now it is a platitude that the U.S. American tourist is notorious for not knowing anything but English, speaking it more slowly or much louder, rudely expecting others to somehow understand. Our hosts' patience with us is often sadly related to the money we spend. I am fortunate to know Spanish as well as English; but if I had it to do over again, I'd make learning several more languages a priority.

Yet so much is also communicated by a kind gesture or look. And by wind, a rustle of leaves, the sound of water. A figure pecked into rock by peoples thousands of years before bridges carry meaning from one time to another. Connection travels many roads.

I am interested as well in the experience of almost. How one comes to almost understand or almost make oneself understood. Words in Croatian may sound almost like Spanish. Italian or Portuguese are enough like Spanish that some understanding makes it through. How sound inhabits space, and what that means, rises eager in my throat. Standing before signage in Vietnamese or Arabic and trying to make sense of writing that doesn't resemble any with which I am familiar is an interesting exercise in design. Even German and Turkish have their challenges. Xosa clicks push my tongue to the back of my mouth, and I desperately want to master their music.

Some say the experience resides in the journey itself and not its destination. No matter how many times one makes it, the journey is always new. A different season or time of day brings a different light. A new receptivity reveals new meaning. I've many times discovered the delight in getting lost and then found.

When people travel to remote places, especially when they do so for the pleasure of discovering what they look and smell and feel like, what sounds emanate from them, and what texture the light holds, they often come home with things: souvenirs to remind them where they have been. Something to display on the mantel or show their friends.

We returned from Tanzania with a carved gourd so large Barbara thought she would have to sit with it on her lap for the twenty-some-odd hours of flight. A small handblown crystal glass from Croatia broke the other day. I mourned the loss of the single item I had acquired in that astonishing country. A water puppet from Vietnam looks down at me as I write. That kahao rongorongo board from Easter Island keeps me company. Things, the things that remind us where we have been. The things that are more than things. But as a photographer, I find that my best memories are in the pictures—present even as the words begin to fade.

Some of our greatest joy has come from driving silently through landscapes we know intimately, arriving at places we would recognize with our eyes closed, perhaps discovering a rock art image we'd missed on a previous visit or making a new connection only that particular place at that particular time can give. The texture of shared time is profoundly different from time shared at home.

Then again, love of this space Barbara and I have created together and nurture with our relationship often makes coming home the most fulfilling journey of all.

Cuban Postcards

A continent is a landmass. Its coastline, curves, and teeth remember other ancient coastlines that will forever represent lost body parts. A millennial language. But that language was spoken before time could categorize and order it. The languages spoken today sound small patches of identity—reflect indigenous peoples holding tenaciously to the places of their ancestors, cities that too often speak the conqueror's tongue, destinations where human beings were traded, sold, and sometimes freed.

The American continents are such a patchwork, from polar north to Patagonian south. Between: the riveting majesty of the Grand Canyon, thundering waters of Iguazú, stark desert beauty of Atacama. The secrets of Kiet Seel, Palenque, Tikal. And great modern cities like Montreal, New York, Mexico, Río de Janeiro. Places where anguish and absence are always just below the surface: Santiago de Chile, Buenos Aires, Montevideo, Guatemala. And places where that absence has been redeemed, like today's Bolivia and Uruguay or Cuba's last half century.

Cuba, against every neocolonialist and neoliberal obstacle, chose freedom in 1959. That the Cuban Revolution, with all its problems and forced retreats, still stands is as much a natural wonder as it is the fierce resistance of men and women, a people who continue to respond to "no" with a defiant "yes." And within Cuba there is a space called Casa de las Américas, as old and unique as the revolution itself.

8. Havana's sea wall, or *malecón*

In the first months following the victory of the Cuban Revolution, a vision-ary named Haydée Santamaría was given the challenge of creating an institution capable of breaking the cultural blockade.[1] Not the military or economic or political blockades, those guns lined up against a tiny island nation, but the more amorphous and ever so much more dangerous efforts aimed at silencing the country's artists and writers. Silencing ideas, erasing images, in both directions.

Casa stands at the bottom of G Street, close to the malecón, that serpentine sea wall that protects the city from an ocean embracing and threatening simul-taneously. It is a three-story gray building, once a synagogue, with a large metal-lic map of the continent embossed on its northern face. Inside, galleries, con-ference halls, and the offices of magazines and research centers contain a living history of cutting-edge thought and artistic production from every reach of the Americas and beyond. Haydeé endowed it with a courage and wisdom that live long past her death. What has happened at Casa, what happens there still, is nothing less than the powerful magic of creativity and change.

Along with a couple of dozen other writers and thinkers from Bolivia, Gua-temala, Argentina, Chile, Spain, Peru, Colombia, Brazil, the United States, and Cuba itself, I have been invited to be a judge in Casa's annual literary contest,

9. Casa de las Américas

known simply as Premio 2011, the "Prize." Every year for half a century, literary minds from the Americas gather in Havana to read hundreds of entries in the genres of novel, short story, poetry, testimonial literature, theater, critical essay, literature written by Brazilians, inhabitants of other Caribbean islands, and Latinos living inside the United States, awarding the prestigious prize to the best in each category. I judged poetry in 1970. Now, forty-one years later, I have been invited back to judge testimonial literature.

This prize represents so much more than simply choosing the best book and assuring its publication and attendant monetary compensation. Periodically, the institution has used the Premio as a context in which to establish new centers or programs of specialization in such areas as Caribbean or women's studies. This year the focus is on *culturas originarias de las Américas*, "native cultures of the Americas." And they really do mean all the Americas, from Canada to the southern tip of the South American continent. Casa's library is among the most innovative I have known. Its magazines publish the most exciting new work and retrieve classic texts that would otherwise be lost.

And this is one of Casa's many strengths: brilliant young people work along-

10. Haydée Santamaría

side the old-timers who remain. Cycles of tradition and renovation enrich the physical space and all that takes place within it. I cross the threshold and my skin comes alive with an energy difficult to describe. I am besieged by the faces and voices of those who are gone: Haydée herself, Rodolfo Walsh, Paco Urondo,

Violeta Parra, Roque Dalton, Carlos María Gutiérrez, Laurette Séjourné, Mario Benedetti. I feel their familiar touch on my arm, a conversation surfaces, an image pushes up. I fight back tears or, in some quiet corner, let them come.

Here, over the next weeks, we will work in the spirit of giants, always conscious of our seriousness and commitment. But also of our defiance and humor. The great debates, achievements, mistakes, and personalities of half a century accompany us.

I stand before my old apartment building, trying to recall images of a time more than thirty years gone. Chunks of memory drop away then come creeping back, jostling for a place to stand. I can't find my old neighbor's name on the register but hesitantly press the worn tenth-floor button. A voice comes wavering through the rusted speaker. I say my name and hear a faint metallic click as I push against the glass door and step into the vestibule. Suddenly I am three decades younger. I touch the layers of worn fieldstones on either side of the elevator, trying to find the loose one that once covered the place where my children and their friends hid secret messages.

Inside the worn metal box that is the elevator, I notice a surprising absence of graffiti. Hundreds of coats of paint, brushed over its walls through the years. On the tenth floor, Silvia's door is open, and she embraces me warmly. The interior of her family's apartment, similar to the one we lived in on the floor just below, begins cracking the dense barrier of time. I find myself wondering about buckets of water collected against frequent shutoffs, a stash of used candle stubs for electrical blackouts, cooking oil poured carefully from a refillable bottle, all the machinations in lives that have weathered the revolution's ups and downs but have yet to secure that leap of progress for which so many died— and so many more remain exhausted.

We talk about old times and new, neighbors who are gone and others who still inhabit the eighth floor or the fourth. A son and his wife are there. The last time I saw him he was a child. Now he is a city planner, involved in the magnificent renovation of Old Havana. A thread of genuine caring runs between us, a strong, unbreakable line, dancing from memory to memory, avoiding the entanglements of lives now unfolding in spheres so distant one from the other it would take days or months to retrieve that space in which we might truly inhabit each other's obstinate hopes and failed dreams.

Later Silvia walks me back to my hotel. A couple of dozen blocks shrouded in Havana night. We hold onto each other as we navigate cracked sidewalks and uneven curbs. Groups of young people pass us, arm in arm. A small table where four old men play dominos emerges in a circle of light beneath a rare streetlamp. That 1950s-style building was a Jewish cultural center when I lived here. Is it still? We pass the hulking Américas Arias hospital, referred to as Maternidad de Línea, where I once had an abortion and so many Cuban women still give birth. We turn down G toward the sea, feeling a rise of moist breeze against our faces.

Now we are standing in front of the hotel. Silvia excuses her home attire and says she won't come in. We hug goodbye. We will see each other often while I am here, but I will never feel closer to her than I do at this moment, touching the thin woolen scarf she pulls about her shoulders, the one she reminds me I gave her forty years before, when together we patrolled our neighborhood on a night much like this, convinced we were on the winning side of history.

Cienfuegos. Middle of the island, nestled along the southern coast. This city was settled by French immigration, and many of its buildings conserve their French colonialist architecture and period furnishings, never completely at home in this tropical destination. Casa de las Américas has installed us in the Jagua, a four-star hotel situated on a small tongue of land protruding into the bay. I am in my room, watching from my balcony as a last splash of pink fades to night. The phone rings, and the woman's voice that responds to my "*Oigo?*" wastes no time.

"My name is Rosario Terry García," she tells me, "your daughter Sarah Dhyana Mondragón Randall's third grade teacher." She pronounces Sarah's string of names with perfect recall. "I was fifteen," Rosario goes on to say, "and Sarah was seven or eight. I was one of the Makarenkos, just starting out."

I remember the Destacamento Makarenko, a battalion of young people who stepped up to fill the vacancies left by so many teachers who emigrated in the revolution's early years. Boys and girls themselves, with no pedagogical experience and only the training a crash course of weeks or months could bestow. I think of my son, age eight, whose fourteen-year-old teacher was immensely relieved when his student told him, no, masturbation doesn't really destroy brain neurons as he had warned. In those days, teachers and students learned together.

11. Rosario Terry García

Rosario's voice cuts through my reverie: "I'll never forget that little girl—so smart, so beautiful, so active. One day I was teaching Playa Girón,[2] and I saw she was crying. 'What's wrong, Child?' I asked. And she sobbed, 'No, Teacher, it's the government, not the people, who attack us!' And you came to talk to me the next day. I've never forgotten that lesson. It's served me well, through all my years of teaching. But what did we know back then? We were hardly more than children ourselves!"

Rosario had seen my name on the news and tracked me to the Jagua. Time collapsed as it so often does in Cuba, along with crops and infrastructure and the passionate dream of a different world. I want to see her face, embrace her, learn more about this woman who remembers my forty-eight-year-old daughter when she was seven. She says she lives far from the provincial capital, but if I tell her where I'll be in the morning, she will try to find me. I say I'll be visiting an art school, the Benny Moré. "Why don't you try to meet me there?"

At the school the next morning I hear a voice calling my name. And there's Rosario, a heavyset black woman with a broad grin. "Back then I was just a slip of a girl," she says, no doubt picking up on my astonishment. She must think I remember what she looked like way back when. I don't. I am just very moved by the woman and her story, by the complexity of this web in which both our lives are caught. We talk. We take a few pictures. We hug.

The Benny Moré's principal asks Rosario how she came by her last name, Terry. It is famous throughout the province for having belonged to the plantation owner after whom the city's gorgeous Teatro Terry is named. "Well," Rosario laughs, "most slaves got our names from the family that owned us."

When I tell my daughter about Rosario, she remembers nothing. Not the teacher, not the incident. As a child, spending all week at boarding school was unbearable for her, as it was for many other children of revolutionaries who believed that we were changing the world and that our offspring were getting an education based on the values we hoped would launch the new society.

Did it fail? The revolution, I mean. And how to measure failure? For fifty-three years it has been pulling itself along, a sack full of stones, a hunch between the shoulders, a beautiful garment frayed at the cuffs. Half a century of people wanting only independence, nothing more. Independence from a crude dictator, one of a fraternity at the time. Independence from the puffed up nation to the north and its swindling mafia of casinos, crime syndicate of profit over people. Freedom to make the future of its choice.

When I lived here, through the 1970s, life seemed simple. Everyone worked. Health care and education were free. We paid 10 percent of our salaries in rent

12. Door, Trinidad

and, after twenty years, owned our apartment or home. No matter that someone else had owned it before us and had fled the Communist takeover, sure it
would be a matter of weeks or months before they could return and reinsert
their old key in the lock. Some of those wealthy families hid jewels and silver

services in the walls, walls they hoped would remain mute until they could come back to reinstall themselves in mansions or elegant 1950s high-rises.

There were problems, to be sure. The United States has never given up trying to destroy the revolution. Transportation was difficult. Food was rationed, insuring everyone had enough. After a Sunday spent harvesting potatoes in Havana's greenbelt, Monday morning we'd find proud pyramids of potatoes at our neighborhood market. Simple, that's what we said, and smiled. Simple. Knowing that class divisions were being eliminated was more important than a varied menu or other luxuries.

But in 1989, when the Soviet Union fell apart, Cuba lost its strongest ally. The socialist world disintegrated. Cuba remained defiant, opened itself to tourism, invested in biochemistry, tightened its belt. There was always Vietnam, then Nicaragua and Venezuela. But the monster to the north regained hegemony and intensified its blockade: a point of attack both painfully real and increasingly the excuse for every ill.

Corruption began to corrode. When a construction site or office came up short, the discrepancy was simply *el faltante*: that which is missing. Cubans wrote historic pages of selfless internationalism, sending teachers to Nicaragua, medical personnel to wherever a natural disaster struck, well-trained professionals to those countries where a new society struggled to gain footing. Some say ten thousand Cubans died in Africa—Angola, Ethiopia, Congo. Some say twenty thousand. Cubans are proud of their internationalists.

And proud of their generosity, of the shipload of sugar sent to Allende's Chile when sugar was still severely rationed at home. The shipments of coffee and medicines headed every which way. The schools they built for tens of thousands of children from all over the world. But hardship and shortages carried over from one year to the next. Some asked why the country was giving so much away, when the need at home remained so great. Cuba taught the Vietnamese how to cultivate coffee. Now Cuba imports coffee from Vietnam. Something is wrong with the equation.

I walk along the malecón, a rhythmic pulse of waves crashing over the battered sea wall to my left. To my right, blocks of once-elegant buildings. Their floors of multiple apartments gawk broken and sad. Electrical wires are strung in haphazard disarray. Clotheslines are heavy with faded laundry. These broken buildings are home to thousands who have waited in vain for paint, building materials, relief from a ceiling that threatens to collapse or a flight of stairs creaking menacingly beneath the ups and downs of tired feet.

Farther toward the center of the city is Old Havana, whose exquisite renovation, block by block, has made it a UNESCO World Heritage site. Here the polished cobblestones of some streets alternate with the upended wooden planks of other streets, mimicking original surfaces. Old houses have been restored to their earlier splendor, with attention to every vibrant detail: the wrought iron balcony, dark woods and tile work, the colored glass of the *media luna* above the door, an old-fashioned pharmacy with its shelves of ceramic jars where one can still fill a prescription or buy a tonic.

This whole area functions as both tourist attraction and residential neighborhood. People live in these houses. School children study for months at a time in museums of African or Islamic art. Booksellers stock their open-air stalls with Fidel, Che, an out-of-print novel, or maps of the city when it was controlled by the English or Spanish.

It is Saturday morning, and I am at the beautiful Plaza de Armas, waiting for Mirta Yáñez's book launch to begin. The book is a novel, *Sangra por la herida*. Its author describes it as settling scores for dozens—or hundreds—of talented artists and writers who suffered during what Cuban intellectuals refer to as *el quinquenio gris*, "the gray period." That period, from the late sixties to the midseventies, wasn't confined to five years, and it was a good deal darker than gray for those who opted to emigrate, or who ended their own lives when faced with the shameful repression.

There aren't enough chairs for the crowd that has gathered for the book's presentation. I catch sight of dozens of old friends but also see many young faces in the crowd. There is an atmosphere of anticipation. Around a small table in front, Mirta is flanked by her publisher and a critic—people there to introduce the book.

The publisher opens the event. Then Mirta reads an impressive passage. I look around. There are tears in many eyes. During the launch, several exotic figures appear and position themselves behind the presenters: a mime painted in silver, a woman holding a straw hat and single large sunflower. The silent tableau speaks of significance and tribute.

When the formal reading ends, I get up and approach one of the two tables toward the back where stacks of the novel are for sale. "How much?" I ask. "Fifteen Cuban pesos." "No, How much in CUC (convertible currency, an effort to

13. Restored glass and ironwork in Old Havana

rein in the black market)." "We're only selling the book in Cuban pesos." "Please," I beg, "all I have are CUC." And a chant goes up: "Sell her the book, sell her the book!" "One CUC," the salesperson finally agrees. Less than a dollar.

After the demise of the socialist bloc, Cubans pulled their belts ever tighter and suffered through the Special Period in Peacetime. There was less of everything. Blackouts were scheduled and daily. Thousands of bicycles took the place of cars that broke down or whose drivers couldn't buy gas. Those were the 1990s. The hardest was 1993. Very gradually production went up, yearly gross national product increased impressively, and life got better. A little bit better.

Today when I ask people if they think the nineties will return, everyone says no. Yet five hundred thousand state workers began being laid off at the beginning of January. People are being forced to accept the fact that work is no longer a given, a right guaranteed by the socialist state. The Cuban workforce was grossly inflated, three or four people doing one job, and no one's salary was

14. Young Cuban dancer, Cienfuegos

really enough to live on. Thus, the mass-scale ingenuity, through which people devised all sorts of creative ways of getting by.

Some people will retire. Many are being encouraged to establish small private businesses. A friend tells me three cafés have sprung up on his block in

15. Man with roosters, Trinidad

just the past month. But these enterprises need capital. I can't see Cuba's banks being able to extend the necessary credit. Investment will have to come from outside the country, and undoubtedly much of it will come from the exile community. These economic transfusions will certainly bring with them complicated quotas of power and influence.

My old friend is a sociologist. He has long been involved with a group whose job it is to analyze the country's problems and suggest policies aimed at solving those problems while preserving some of the revolution's gains: shelter, food, free education and health care, culture, and sports. To what does he ascribe this failure, I ask. "Two things," he says, "trying to go too fast and the paternalism of the state."

Going too fast. Yes, I remember a time early on, when some idealists believed Cuba would be able to create a communist state without going through the socialist phase. The goal was rooted in urgency, the fervent desire for a society based on justice. But the world, with all its corruption, got in the way. And today none of the -isms offer a comprehensive answer. The internationalization of greed makes those long-ago dreams seem utopian.

And then there's the paternalism of the state: a ruling party that makes all the important decisions, allows citizens' input only to a point, tightly controls information, and isolates or punishes those who dissent. The problem isn't that people must conform to a party line but that their innate creativity has been dulled. Every once in a while, a passionate people stand up and demand explanations, answers, apologies. But half a century of authoritarian rule—even while making a genuinely better life for most—has robbed Cubans of initiative. Their sense of real agency has been suppressed.

I link paternalism with patriarchy, a failure to challenge the conventional distribution of power.

While I am in Cuba, someone mentions a news story about the pope urging people not to use "unusual names!" I wonder: unusual by whose standards? Perhaps the Catholic pontiff hopes to encourage the use of names from the Old or New Testaments. I don't know how children are named in Africa or Asia, what rules apply in the Arabic world. In Egypt and Jordan I met a great many Mohammads. And Jesús and María are popular throughout the Spanish-speaking countries.

In Cuba unusual names have proliferated, since the revolutionary victory and before. I remember, early on, hearing about a girl called Usnavy—U.S. Navy. Her parents were intrigued by the large letters they saw on the underside of the wings of a North American military plane.

When I lived here, the president of our block committee was a jovial black man from Camaguey. We always called him by his surname, Masa. His wife was Elena, but their daughter was Krupskaya. One of my poet friends is from a community deep in the countryside at the eastern end of the country. His parents named him Bladimir, after Lenin, spelled just like it sounded in their ears.

Children's names often reflect their parents' heroes; and if an idol falls from favor, the namesake suffers. Lenin remained popular for boys, more so than Vladimir. But I won't forget three young exiled brothers from the Dominican Republic. Their names were Stalin, Lenin, and little Mao. In Cuba the baby especially was in for a tough time—as if exile without their parents wasn't enough of a burden.

As beauty aids and other consumer items disappeared from the shelves of Cuban stores, nostalgia developed for certain brands, and their names came into favor. Miladys and Ivorys are two I remember. Adding the *s* at the end seemed to be the twist that made a product name fit for a human being.

Cuban magic realism is unique to the island. The pope would have a hard time imposing his plea against unusual names here.

After fifty-three years—eleven of which I shared in everyday bus stop waits and lines outside the fried rice restaurant, and after a half-dozen return trips—I find I have a single question: why did some Cubans leave and others stay? I'm not so interested in the stark ideological differences or in those more amorphous reasons such as tedium or exhaustion. I want the answers hiding within the answers, that complex fabric of emotions, decisions, choices that finally tip the balance in one direction or the other.

To leave or not to leave, a painful dilemma. The first waves of emigrants were the superrich, whose expectations and lifestyles went beyond mere class. There was the sugarcane magnate who resettled in Peru, only to find himself facing another nationalization, and the Bacardi family, whose elegant mansion was turned into a clinic, where my youngest daughter awaited her parents'

16. Tiled house, Caimanitas, outskirts of Havana

arrival. All up and down Miramar's lavish Fifth Avenue, homes once belonging to the wealthy were transformed into boarding schools, where, at five o'clock each weekday afternoon, doors opened and thousands of children of all ages and skin shades ran shouting and laughing between dorms and dining halls.

Before the revolution, if you were a black child in those neighborhoods, you could only have been the son or daughter of a maid or gardener.

People kept leaving, at first sure they would be back in weeks or months. Then, that conviction fell apart, and they made their lives outside, complete with organizations dedicated to the destruction of this political process that, in their sense of things, had robbed them of life as they knew it. There was Operation Peter Pan, through which parents, who believed the wild rumors about children being taken from their families, sent their children to the United States in care of Catholic Charities. Many of those children were all but orphaned, not to be reunited with a mother or father for decades.

There was the Camarioca boatlift in 1965, followed by the so-called freedom flights that lasted until about 1972 and brought some of the first waves of Cuban emigration to Miami, New Jersey, and elsewhere. The media has often quoted 260,000 refugees. And the United States granted these refugees special status, guaranteeing them residency and citizenship. One confluence of events after another provoked the major exoduses: 125,000 *Marielitos* in 1980, the *balseros* who sailed from Cojímar in 1994. Until there were more than a million Cubans living off their island. They amounted to 10 percent of the population: not as much emigration as produced by a whole lot of other countries but clothed in a hysteria that inflates the numbers.

The U.S. and Cuban governments engaged in their calculated games of chess. Sometimes one side was caught off guard; sometimes the other. But the chess pieces were human beings, with illusory hopes—a desperation that sometimes outweighed fear, resentments, and, too often, sorrows no one could really decipher. Much of what has been published about these great human migrations has been little more than an attempt to justify one side or the other.

Fought against extraordinary odds, the Cuban Revolution nurtured a bristling pride. One had to place it at the center of one's life, support it against all odds, agree with its tenets, trade silence for argument, let go of or hide religious belief, be willing to embrace a routine in which dissent was not permitted and travel didn't exist. Being forced to defend a single ideology, combined with the daily sacrifices implicit in creating a society that works for everyone, made many feel like outcasts in their own land. As families were torn apart, this too became a factor. How could a mother contemplate never again seeing her son or daughter? How could a child reconcile never again embracing a mother or father?

For years, those who left were called *gusanos* ("worms") and battered by repudiation on their way out. In 1980 I looked out my ninth-floor windows and witnessed mobs gathered in front of the homes of those whose names were on the exit lists: sneers, spittle, rotten eggs. To what did this rage respond?

If a person who made the choice to leave had up until then assumed a revolutionary self-righteousness, one might understand a degree of resentment. Opportunism rarely leaves a pleasant taste. But why the mob scenes aimed at ordinary citizens who simply decided they wanted out? What emotions of their own were the batterers hiding?

I remember the shame I felt and also the unspoken expectation that if you supported the revolution you naturally took part in those demonstrations. When the time came for their cowering targets to be transported to boat or plane, police escorted them courteously, protecting and keeping them safe. It was easy for those of us who supported the revolution to argue the repudiation was spontaneous emotion, not official policy. But the atmosphere was one of hate. Couldn't the revolution just as easily have prevented those scenes in the first place?

For much too long, Cubans on the island were encouraged to break with their relatives who left. Telephone calls were difficult. The Voice of America's blatant propaganda painted a picture of idyllic life in the North. Even letters were frowned upon.

In time, the true spirit of revolution won out, and this crass rigidity was tempered. Cubans on the island, comfortable in themselves, with nothing to prove and nothing to hide or of which to be ashamed, pushed for better relations with Cubans outside the country. More-thoughtful members of the diaspora initiated contact with those who'd stayed. The Cuban Communist Party relaxed some of its more exclusionary rules, such as denying membership to those with religious beliefs. People began traveling back and forth; the audacious color snapshots of full refrigerators and late model cars gave way to a more realistic storyline. And some U.S. administrations were slightly less belligerent than others with regard to the small island nation to the south. No U.S. administration has had the intelligence or courage to dismantle the blockade. But both governments have found ways—some public, some less so—to obtain what they needed from each other.

The word *gusano* is an echo, never far from my ear. How many times, during the years I lived here, did I myself use that ugly epithet? What currency did it offer? Why did I think that if I wasn't out there on the front lines, I was somehow absolved of blame? It's been a while since I've heard anyone who emi-

17. Huge *Tree of Life* by Alfonso Soteno Fernández, Metepec,
Mexico. Gift to Casa de las Américas.

grates labeled a worm. Gusano. But those six letters continue to prick at my consciousness, begging exploration or redemption. In my synesthetic mind they should be a dark silvery blue, but streaks of bilious yellow run through them, rivers of nausea and shame.

Now, thirteen years after my last visit and fifty-three from the revolution's birth, I ask everyone I believe might have something to say. What do you think makes some Cubans leave their country and others remain, faithful beyond expediency? Not the obvious reasons—a worldwide wanderlust, aging relatives abroad, the perception of greater professional success, or an easier middle-class life? No, it's the other reasons I'm looking for, deeper and less easy to decipher.

Several friends tell me they think it's about personal space. If they are committed to the revolution and have a minimal geography of privacy and movement, people aren't so likely to want to go. Those who are forced to share their living quarters with too many others, even perhaps an ex-spouse or aging parents, may be more inclined to give up and emigrate. I ask my question again and again, and one after another refers to the importance of space. An ample map on which to stretch, move, hide, and be who we are called to be.

More profoundly, I suspect it has to do with a deep love of country and culture, an identity that depends on place for full expression. Or, alternatively, on what another beloved figure of the diaspora, Lourdes Casal, once called "a marginality immune to all returns."

Yuca al mojo de ajo. Ron añejo. Platanitos. Even *chícharos,* that staple that has become the stuff of so many jokes. *El son matancero. Changó. Yemeyá. Oyá la Furiosa Patrona.* Waves breaking over the malecón, and ocean as far as you can see. Landscapes both wild and gentle. And always those beaches with their stands of royal palms. Images, smells, sounds, tastes. Bits and pieces of an answer impossible to translate.

Perhaps my question comes too late, or has become irrelevant. Today so many leave and come back to visit without the strictures of years gone by. It is in this coming and going that the fabric of an answer is woven.

Sonia Rivera-Valdés is a writer and professor of Caribbean literature who was born in Cuba and immigrated to New York because she didn't like the revolution. She wasn't a child taken by her parents. She knew her own mind. And then, through the years, her mind changed. Her path and the revolution's crept toward one another until they touched and finally embraced. Earlier she had joined a group of exiles beginning to question their initial assumptions. In time, the necessary opening arrived, and she boarded a plane.

Since then, Sonia has made many trips back to the country of her birth. In the context of this literary event, in which we are both judges, I notice people sometimes refer to her as a Cuban American, sometimes as a Cuban living in the United States. But she always calls herself Cuban. She speaks of her first trip back: "When I left Cuba, I left a house. No one took it from me, but when I returned, it was inhabited by a family with lots of kids . . . and I was happy. I realized there was no room for resentment."

When asked why she, in contrast with so many exiled Cubans, hasn't gone the way of resentment, Sonia says, "Maybe because they haven't lived, like I have, the experience of a little girl in Peru asking me what a book is for, because she didn't know what it was, she'd never seen one. In the context of how complex this process of five decades has been, a process in which I too have lived through many difficult moments, stories like that say it all."

Tunisian Postcards

The Romans called Tunisia their breadbasket. Curtained by the proud shoulders of the Atlas Mountains, the fertile valleys and hillsides of the north are luxuriant with citrus orchards; fig and pomegranate trees; vineyards producing grapes for red, white, and rosé wines; wheat; barley; sugar beets; and almonds that taste like real almonds.

But most of the country is desert, of three distinct types. The first is a salt desert so flat it looks as if it had been planed by a giant trowel, rose beige sand providing a thin cover for the blinding white of salt. Along the lonely highway, a perfectly even ribbon of shallow water glistens. Once this was the bed of an ancient lake.

The second is the Sahara sand desert: vast undulating dunes, naked at times and then again dotted with sparse but tenacious gray-green brush. Its dunes move relentlessly: dramatic hulks of fine sand springing into action at wind's whim. And windstorms come often. Camels roam, heading for the water they can smell; desert foxes and other mammals run wild; and small rodents and insects leave their crisscross tracks.

Near natural springs, great date palm oases shade the horizon. These are holdings of gold. The trees, with their green frond fans, bring millennial riches. More orderly plantations, called *palmeraies*, are planted in straight rows. In whichever configuration, each tree—although wind polinated in the wilderness—is now more advantageously pollinated by hand, and specialized farmers

18. Chebika Oasis, Atlas Mountains

shimmy up the rough trunk to carry out this task. A single male tree can fertilize one hundred fruit-bearing females. The seed clusters are gathered together on the branch until the tiny green pebbles begin to grow into Deglet Noor, Medjool, and a dozen other varieties. Then the fertilized bundles burst and fruit matures.

19. Desert sands, Sahara

The third is the rock desert: gaping wide-open mountains and valleys where wild canyons hide isolated stone or adobe villages. Periodic floods have rendered these villages uninhabitable, devastating abandoned troglodyte berms that have become an extension of the rock itself, melting into its jagged folds. The mouths of their windows and doors cast small dark shadows across such resistant land. Nearby, more-modern yet simple homes are painted a blinding white. There is always a mosque and a school, both carefully tended. A few worn rugs hang over low walls, and a coffee can of rhododendron or oleander registers a culture's yearning for color.

This small cone-shaped country of eleven million inhabitants, wedged between much larger Algeria to the west and Libya to the east, also has an eight hundred–mile–long Mediterranean coastline. What it offers to the world is agriculture, phosphate, textiles, steel, and some manufacturing. A rich mix of ancient cultures and unique contemporary philosophy imbue it with a particular, sometimes contradictory, and often surprising philosophy: the spirit that, in the fifteenth century, embraced Muslims and Jews living together in harmony when expelled from Spain and, in January 2011, produced the first revolution of the twenty-first century.

The tone was set by Habib Bourguiba, Tunisia's first postcolonial president. At mid-twentieth century, when the North African countries began defying colonialist Europe, military men such as Egypt's Nassar, Libya's Gadaffi, and Algeria's Ben Bella shaped their nations' independence. While these larger North African countries vied for power and influence, Bourguiba understood that his small land would always be militarily weak, and he cultivated other priorities. Education was primary; and during the early years of his mandate, 63 percent of the gross national product went to building schools and staffing them with the best teachers that study abroad could buy.

In an era of neighboring generals, Bourguiba, a lawyer, paid more attention to social welfare. This meant important changes for women. Even before the new constitution, the Personal Status Code (PSC) was drawn up in 1957. It illegalized polygamy, required the consent of both parties for marriage and raised the minimum age for girls, instituted divorce, and outlawed the burka and chador—calling them "odious rags." Bourguiba established full legal and labor equality and asked that the title "Emancipator of Women" be inscribed on his tomb.

Today women outnumber men at all educational levels, Tunisians of both genders earn equal salaries, 46 percent of the country's doctors and 58 percent of its teachers and professors are women, maternity leave is impressive (full pay for the first six months, 75 percent for the next three, and none for the final three but with job security upon return to work), and abortion is legal during the first trimester. The Tunisian army builds roads, helps harvest crops, and is involved in other communal projects. A year of military service is obligatory for men but optional for women.

20. Chenini, Berber village

Bourguiba is the beloved father of the nation. He opened the political system to opposition parties. He modernized the country, emphasizing free education and health care for all. And he diverged from most of the other Arab countries by supporting a negotiated settlement between Israel and Palestine. But he also made the mistake so many founding fathers do. He conceived of himself as president for life. When senility overtook him in the mid-1980s, Zine el-Abidine Ben Ali staged a bloodless coup. At first he continued his predecessor's democratic reforms and investment in economic growth. But he became increasingly autocratic and corrupt. Opposition efforts were crushed. The new president and his family bled a poor country dry.

Phosphate miners organized and tried to rebel in 2008, only to be put down brutally. The press and other media were rigorously controlled. It is against this backdrop that, toward the end of 2010, Tunisians lit the spark that would soon enflame Egypt, Libya, Syria, Bahrain, and other countries of the region.

The Western press—and at first many within Tunisia as well—spoke about an incident between a street vendor and a policewoman who confiscated his scales because he lacked the proper license. It was said that the vendor immolated himself in protest, and this, it was reported, set the country ablaze. International news media, always avid for catchy sound bites, called it the Jasmine Revolution.

Tunisians prefer to call it the Dignity Revolution. They say its seeds were planted by those phosphate miners several years earlier. When initial public rage around the incident leading to the street vendor's suicide gained momentum, it was briefly seen as a generating force, and he as a martyr. But when people learned the story behind the vendor and policewoman, they stopped referring to it as the incident that sparked their revolution. It seems that when the woman took the vendor's scales, he made a remark about using her breasts to weigh his goods. Incensed, she slapped him. He doused himself with gasoline, having instructed a few friends to come to his rescue before he could be seriously injured. Somehow, they weren't quick enough.

Most Tunisians today see the famous vendor as a fool, who was also disrespectful to women. Both these versions sound a bit too simplistic; who knows where the truth lies? In any case, desperation and will had ripened to the point of rebellion. Young people—adept at cell phone, Facebook, and Twitter communication—took over. Demonstrations were large and well organized. There was very little loss of life, and on January 14, 2011, Ben Ali fled to Saudi Arabia.

On the short flight from Djerba to Tunis, I flipped through the pages of Tunisair's inflight magazine. The issue's introductory note caught my attention. I read it and begin to cry. The internal tension created by juggling widespread revolutionary fervor with the hard cold facts of what has so far been accomplished gave way to simple delight in the victory won. Despite a less than perfect English translation, the note's sentiment comes through loud and clear:

The historical wind which blew on Tunisia has well revolutionized the spirits. The people are living a new age marked by a vision liberated from all forms of restrictions. Have we ever seen jasmine flowers open in spring? That was the case in our country with elegance and without too much violence. The jasmine revolution was started by young people, ravaged by distress, against an autocratic power; their claim was not only bread: "but bread in dignity" they were shouting very high. Their cries were relayed notably by other youths politically conscious, hungry for freedom and

21. Tozeur, man at Date Palm Oasis

democracy, and hooked to the global means and methods of communication (Internet, Facebook and Twitter). As a result a new world bravery was born out of the new and unprecedented relations established on the political, economic or social levels, between citizens sharing fraternal ties and happily recovering their most cherished value: freedom.

The dark page is definitely turned over, the people awoke, conscious of the damage inherent to any overthrown regime, ready to start the programs of economic revival with loads of work ahead. But it is not to disturb its certainty because the climate is encouraging and youth is carrying its destiny over its shoulder. This upheaval is from now on engraved in the national and even in the international memory. The tourist, the visitor and the Tunisian people have got many things to share among which freedom of speech with its positive effects of the direct contact without the fear of being bothered or disturbed: the wall of silence, which often separated the visitor from the Tunisian people, was broken . . .

These words, offered by an airline hoping to rekindle tourism in a country people are afraid to visit, exude so much more than awkward translation. They speak of the relief and joy people feel when they can suddenly voice long-stifled opinions. Fear is gone, and everything remains to be done.

My partner Barbara and I traveled to Tunisia in May 2011 with twelve other U.S. Americans. We were fortunate to have a wonderful guide—a forty-year-old art historian, husband, and father of two—named Mohamed Mastouri.

Now, four and a half months after the dictator left, with ongoing demonstrations, some curfews enforced in areas where they have been particularly intense, and occasional reports of police brutality, there were few tourists in the country; almost no one from the United States. During our stay we saw a half dozen groups of French and German visitors. Ancient archeological sites were empty. The narrow lanes of villages and medinas and the broad avenues of large cities were clean and orderly: people were going about their business with a sense of security and palpable spirit of expectation.

A hotel where we spent several nights near the Libyan border also housed refugee workers in their tan vests with UN stamped in pale blue on the back. Norwegian relief workers from some sort of Christian aid organization were in the dining room at breakfast. Tunisians themselves, poor as they are, were collecting truckloads of food and medicines. One day we saw a caravan of fifteen thousand tons heading east.

Bearded and turbaned white-robed men from the United Arab Emirates roamed the lobby of that hotel, often accompanied by medical personnel in blue surgical scrubs. We learned the former are financing refugee camps (there were 330,000 Libyan refugees in the country the day we arrived; two weeks later that number had risen to 440,000).

An interesting aside regarding the United Arab Emirates' use of their exuberant oil wealth to support the refugee camps: even as it does so, it has invited the U.S. paramilitary company Blackwater to establish a mercenary army within its own borders. This army seems to be filling with Colombian recruits, and the usual suspects—retired British, French, and U.S. officers—are its advisors. Clearly, the UAE wants to be prepared for any threat to its own system of autocracy. When I voiced surprise at this seeming contradiction, Mohamed said he didn't find it at all contradictory. "One policy has to do with human rights," he explained, "the other is an attempt at preserving a political system."

22. Ruins at Dougga, detail of theater column

At Tunisia's great archeological sites—Carthage, Dougga, Kerkoune, Sbeitla—
we roamed alone, often for hours, without running into another foreigner.
Roman influence dominated, although we also saw the contributions made by
Phoenicians, Greeks, Vandals, Byzantines, and Sicilians. We were grateful for
the rare opportunity to experience these places without crowds, even as we felt
for the country's loss of needed revenue.

Dougga was my favorite, situated as it is among green fields, with olive groves
and a profusion of wildflowers. The vast site includes a well-preserved theater,
baths, communal latrines, a large forum, housing blocks, and a gorgeous temple to Jupiter, Juno, and Minerva (the Roman trinity). On the esplanade near
this temple, I could just make out the immense sundial-like circle called Wind
Roses. Twelve directions of wind are still faintly engraved on its face.

Tunisia is a Muslim country. Of the population, 99 percent identify with Islam,
and an hour a week of religion is included in the public school curriculum
(non-Muslims may opt out of the class). But in some ways, separation of church

and state seems more respected here than it is these days in the United States. For example, sharia law is not observed. Alcohol is sold (Libyans drive across the border to buy it), and many Tunisians drink alcohol and smoke tobacco. At the resorts, discos are hopping throughout the night. Although, if asked, the vast majority will say they believe in the Koran, people seem pragmatic and practical. They live their faith in diverse ways.

As in all Muslim countries, the call to prayer rings out across cities and towns—beginning about an hour before sunrise. One of the five pillars of Muslim religious practice is to pray five times a day. But only on a couple of occasions did I see someone stop what he was doing to fulfill this obligation. The attitude toward another pillar, making the Haj (or traveling to Mecca at least once during one's lifetime), also seemed to be quite casual. When I asked Mohamed if he intended to make the trip, he said "Well . . . maybe someday . . . but there's always something one has to spend one's money on: buying a house, a car, maybe something for the children."

In the holy city of Kairouan, we visited a mosque, where Mohamed had arranged for us to meet with a retired imam. The theologian would answer any questions about Islam we might have. Muslims know there are many misconceptions about them in the West, and this would be a chance to hear the truth from an authorized source. The imam greeted us and said we should go around the circle and not be shy. For every answer, he consulted a copy of the Koran, which he had in bilingual edition so that Mohamed could read us the translation. By the time they came to me, I realized our questions tended toward the political and the Koranic answers were religious—something of a disconnect— so I passed.

Then it was Barbara's turn. She asked if the imam would mind if she stood, and then addressed him very respectfully. I noticed several in our group gasped audibly; they must have thought she was going to ask about homosexuality. But this wasn't what she had in mind. She stated, very simply, that she is an atheist and also a moral person who wants to do good in the world. Her question: What does the Koran have to say about someone like me? Our travel companions breathed a sigh of relief. The imam searched for the appropriate verse and had Mohamed read it. Nonbelievers cannot go to heaven, the Koran says, but Allah himself may decide if such a person may escape hell. Barbara thanked him and sat down.

It was obvious that the imam was intrigued by Barbara's question, and several minutes later he had more to say on the subject. And then, as we were leav-

23. Mosque, Holy City of Kairouan

ing, he called her back for a few final words, looking with kindness into her eyes. He told her she is on a journey, to take her time and persevere.

In the busy medinas and souks, where shops offered beautiful handmade native crafts and also hawked Chinese fakeries, vendors were clearly eager to sell but never insistent. Dignity overcame their need for a sale. Walking through Tozeur's medina, Mohamed said both his parents had grown up there. He told us the stories he heard from them, of a time when the narrow streets were spotless and covered with rugs where children played, women cooked food for an entire neighborhood, and communal life was slower than today. He told us about his grandmother, who was forced into an arranged marriage at the age of eleven—only realizing she was married when, at sixteen, she had to go to live in her husband's home.

One of the two double doors leading to each walled home still stands slightly ajar, an invitation to passersby to enter the shelter of a vestibule always present

24. Bardo Museum stairwell, Tunis

between the street and the house's inner sanctum. In that vestibule, strangers have access to cool water, sometimes even food. Visitors may also spend the night. Customs that speak of a different time and of a culture born of desert harshness, which are still practiced today.

***

Crafts of different sorts are in evidence throughout the country: fabric, ceramics, leather, silver and gold jewelry, and the ever-present mosaic—with its rich presence from the ancient ruins to modern workshops that produce so much of what decorates many Tunisian homes and public buildings. The Bardo Museum in Tunis is breathtaking, both in its building (a stunning renovation of the nineteenth-century harem of the beys of Tunis) and in its contents. There, in the most beautiful natural lighting I have yet to encounter in a museum—walls, floors, and even ceilings are covered in mosaics large and small, many dating back to centuries before our era.

Each tiny tessera of marble, with its unique color, came from a different part of a world long gone; the yellow was local, the green and white were found in what is now Italy and Greece, the red granite was from Egypt, and other colors came from elsewhere in the Mediterranean and North Africa. Considering how long it took, centuries ago, for shiploads of this variety of stones to arrive at an artist's shop, the artistry and craft are nothing short of astonishing. Those visionaries had to conceive of their images with the complexity of sources and ancient trade routes in mind. The smaller the individual chip of stone, the finer the tessellation and overall mosaic.

The art of mosaic continues today, and we visited a small workshop where a dozen young women were engaged in the craft—in this case following prescribed patterns used in tabletops, trivets, wall pieces, and other commercial manifestations. Despite not sharing a language, some of the young women and I joked around. I took pictures. They wanted to see them on the camera's monitor and to select which they felt I should keep and which I should erase.

At one point, Barbara had quite a conversation with two of these women. They asked to see her earrings—also made of mosaic turquoise—and she took them out to show. They examined and then insisted on replacing them themselves, at the same time putting a red carnation behind her ear. When one of them noticed her ring and asked if she was married, Barbara said yes. The woman then looked around the room and asked to whom. Barbara pointed to me. All the young women seemed deeply shocked. One quickly hid her face behind her scarf. Others turned away. I'm not sure if Barbara gave them something useful to think about or ruined their day. We have been holding hands on this trip and generally acting as we do at home, although being careful not to deliberately offend a cultural sensibility very different from ours.

As Lana Asfour writes in *Granta*, "One of the most interesting aspects of the Tunisian Revolution from a feminist perspective is that many of the women who participated in the protests that brought down Ben Ali are now campaigning to defend rights they've already been enjoying for some time, fearing that the post-revolutionary period might bring a surge in popularity for the Islamist party, Al Nahda ('the Renaissance'), and a swing towards traditionalist ideas about women."[1]

Not two weeks after the January 14 victory, on the twenty-ninth of that month, the country's two independent women's organizations joined the women's commission of the national trade unions and the Tunisian League for Human Rights in a demonstration to make sure their rights would be protected during the transition and afterward. I'm told that many women marched proudly down Habib Bourguiba Avenue. They carried placards and chanted slogans in support of the revolution and aimed at safeguarding women's rights. The women had to contend with attacks from ruffians hired by elements of the old ruling party and, at a certain point, were forced to disband. Individual women also must argue with men who don't see the new Tunisia as necessarily including women's rights. Tunisian feminists are working hard to make sure women will be represented in the constitutional assembly—itself already pushed back from July to October.

I'd been in Tunisia for a week before I realized there are no McDonald's restaurants in the country, the ubiquitous golden arches nowhere to be seen. Coca-Cola is sold, though. Tunisia has its own fast foods, most of them liberally saturated with harissa, which is a spicy paste present at every meal. Harissa is made from red chile, garlic, salt, olive oil, coriander, caraway seeds, and cumin.

There's no Tunisian Disneyland, either, although in the seaside resort of Hammamet, we saw a Carthageland, complete with a larger-than-life tableaux of Hannibal mounted on his elephant.

The country does, however, have a strange little personage, seen prominently in almost every town and village through which we passed. It stands upright and is modeled after a caricature of a desert fox, although its ears are longer, it wears a baby-blue suit, and has something resembling a school bag slung over its shoulder. Its chest bears a badge with carrots and other vegetables. Sometimes a second, smaller fox—the main figure's sidekick—stands beside him. Mohamed told us these odd statues symbolize Tunisia's new environmentalism.

Tozeur is a city of yellow brick. Forty percent of every new construction must be faced with these bricks: a way of preserving a style and keeping people working. Here we visited one of the hundred or so men who labor to make this building material, digging local clay, mixing it with water and sand, removing small stones by hand, molding the bricks in wooden forms as people have for

25. Monument to Oranges, entrance to Nabeul

two thousand years, covering them in ash, drying them in the sun—ever hopeful a hard rain won't ruin weeks of production—and finally baking them in crude ovens.

The young man showed us each step of this laborious process. He fires up his kiln with dry palm fronds, also from the area, and the only way he can be sure it has reached the necessary temperature of 900°C is if it is packed with exactly ten thousand bricks. There is no thermostat. The palm fronds are balanced on an interior floor with holes that allow the heat to circulate. A few bricks will come out red, but most will emerge dull yellow like the desert surrounding the town. This is backbreaking work. In the 120- to 130-degree summers, this man may labor twelve to eighteen hours a day. The cold winters, when it rains, can devastate production.

Entering the town of Kairouan, the country's rug-weaving capital, we passed a monument four stories high depicting intricate rugs rendered in mosaics. Entering other towns, equally large monuments advertised their specialties: one with a giant bowl of bright oranges, another with a huge ceramic pot.

Rug weaving is a Berber specialty, an age-old tradition. In contrast with Egypt, there is no child labor here. Adult women do most of the weaving in their homes, and each family has its traditional designs. Centers seem to use a system similar to the one fast fading from the U.S. American Southwest's trading posts, whereby looms and yarns are provided and the rugs, purchased outright. Such support promotes community and encourages the most authentic work. Examples range from the crudest weaves, with ten thousand to forty thousand threads per square meter, to the finest silk, with a million threads in the same space.

In Kairouan we had lunch at the home of a local family. The mother and father have two grown sons and a daughter. An eighty-four-year-old grandmother also lives with them. Our language barrier kept us mostly silent during the hearty meal. Then, over mint tea, we all relaxed and, with the help of Mohamed, began to ask a few questions of each another. Their first question was how we had the courage to come, when so few from the United States are doing so. We said we felt privileged to be here at this particular time. One in our group remembered our country's popular movement against the war in Vietnam and said she was no stranger to demonstrations.

We wanted to know what each of them does and learned that the father worked in copper, until the price of his raw materials became too high. He brought out a few beautiful hand-hammered pots and platters for us to see. Now he and his sons run a coffee shop at street level in this building where they live. The daughter is still studying. The mother stays home and runs the house. Our attention turned to the old woman. She was feeling ill, and one of her grandson's lovingly stood behind her chair massaging her shoulders.

Someone in our group asked what they think about what's going on in Libya. They got excited as they expressed their disdain for Gaddafi, their sorrow that there has been so much bloodshed, and their hope for a rebel victory. "Gaddafi is a fool," one son said, taking out his cell phone on which he had recorded a new rap song mocking the dictator. Then the other son turned to the grandmother, obviously urging her to show us something. Amid laughter and her

26. Grandmother impersonating Gaddafi

quickly vanquished reticence, she retired to a bedroom and soon reappeared dressed as Gaddafi—a turban, dark glasses, and a white towel her props. She waved the towel in true dictator style as she repeated an Arabic phrase we couldn't understand.

We learned she was playing with words from a recent Gaddafi speech, the one in which he vowed to go "street by street, door by door," until every so-called agitator was rooted out. Despite not feeling well, she was obviously enjoying herself tremendously. Mohamed told us that before the Libyan uprising, she liked impersonating Michael Jackson.

At the beginning of this trip, flying from Paris to Tunis I noticed there would be an hour's time difference. But wait. It would be an hour earlier in Tunisia, despite that country being one time zone east of France. Shouldn't it be an hour later? I asked the flight attendant, who explained that France observes daylight savings while Tunisia does not. I sat and thought about that for a while. Wouldn't this then make it two hours earlier? Or the same time? I went around and around with this but couldn't make it work. I went to Air France's inflight magazine and searched for the world map. As I suspected, it included the time zones. Tunisia: to the east of France. No way I could figure it out.

Time itself, the essence of time, seemed to accompany me throughout this trip like a great rubber band, stretching and contracting. With so many out of work, the cafés were filled with men of all ages, sipping tea or drinking beer, gesticulating in a language I don't know (Arabic or French, sometimes a symbiotic blend), playing cards, occasionally smoking from a hookah or water pipe. Women, as everywhere, walked arm in arm, whispered to one another, carried bundles, shopped, took children to and from school. But their pace seemed slower than in other places I have been. The heat of summer was still a couple of months off. We were told it routinely reaches 120°F to 130°F in August and September. In May it hovered around a pleasant 80 degrees.

But the time issue seemed to embrace centuries. The ruins of Carthage, for example, blend almost seamlessly with the present-day busyness of a modern capital. Around the Gulf of Tunis, three thousand years of civilization—Phoenicians, Romans, Vandals, Muslims—lack the continuity of documented history due to the fact that the Romans, after destroying and before rebuilding the city, did away with important sources. The story of Queen Dido told in Virgil's *Aeneid* may be more about attitude than accuracy. Kerkoune, a 2,300-year-old Phoenician ruin with the Mediterranean lapping its low stone walls, is unique in that every house had its own private bath: a time warp if ever there was one.

27. Girl walking in street, Testour

Most of the hotels where we stayed, if they had Wi-Fi at all, had it only in their lobbies. One morning, very early, I sat in the reception area of one, using my laptop. The night watchman rose from a couch where he had spent the night, stretched, and gave me a shy smile. Then he came over to where I was working. "Are you writing to the United States?" he wanted to know. When I told him I was, he asked what time it was there. I explained that mine is a large country, with several different time zones. The concept didn't seem to register. "But what time is it where you're writing?" he asked again. "Eleven thirty last night," I replied, before realizing how absurd that sounded. "I mean it's still yesterday where I live."

The man was incredulous. Clearly, he could not conceptualize it being yesterday somewhere in the world, when here it was already today. The people of Tunisia, who through largely peaceful protest have just changed the course of their history, must play a new game with time. How long is too long to wait for change? How will memory and political expediency deal with past abuses?

Time also has a different history in the small village of Testour, in a lovely valley above the Mejerda River. There, the square minaret of the oldest mosque bears the imprint of a clock whose numbers run backward. As with any modern timepiece, the twelve is at the top. But the one is to the left rather than to the right, and the rest of the numbers continue counterclockwise around the face.

This minaret, which also displays eight Stars of David, dates to 1609, when Muslims and Jews—expelled from Spain together—settled here. They longed for their Andalusian homeland, and this backward-moving clock symbolized that longing. Unfortunately, the clock's hands are missing, so I had to imagine a movement of time that may or may not have been mechanically possible.

We saw the Star of David often, on ornate doors, in the beautiful tile work on so many mosques and other buildings, even on signage. Tunisians seemed proud and at ease with the Jewish presence in their country. Early in our visit, we had lunch at Mamie Lily's, a small family-run establishment in Tunis, which we learned is the only remaining kosher restaurant in the country, possibly in the entire Muslim world. Two women prepared a meal of barley soup, salad, and lamb. Then Mamie's son Jacob, the place's gregarious owner, gave a short talk about the history of Jews in Tunisia: from their seventeenth-century arrival, through most of them leaving for France in the mid-1950s after postcolonialism gave them (and all Tunisians) French citizenship, through various emigrations to Israel, and to today's paltry population of around 1,500 who live in productive harmony with the overwhelming Muslim majority. Jacob had an incisive sense of humor.

Later, on the island of Djerba, we visited a very different sort of Jewish site. Djerba is often referred to as the island of diversity. Among its ninety thousand inhabitants, Christians and Jews mix with Muslims. Even once-defined ghettos have disappeared, and they no longer speak of Christian or Jewish quarters. At Djerba we visited La Ghriba Synagogue, in continual use since 586 BC. The small, richly tiled place of worship is said to contain stones from the Temple of Solomon in its foundation.

In 2002 Tunisia suffered its own Al Qaeda attack, when a suicide bomb detonated near a bus of German tourists near this site, killing seventeen plus their local guide and driver. Today security is rigorous. Next to the synagogue, a large hotel welcomes Jews from around the world. Although they may stay at any hotel on the island, this is where they can meet friends and family members and where a kosher kitchen caters to their needs. In the synagogue itself, several elderly men were reading the Torah, seemingly oblivious to our presence.

In other Muslim countries, such as Egypt, Jordan, and Turkey, I remember

28. Sixteenth-century mosque in Testour, clock with backward face

29. Sixteenth-century mosque in Testour, minaret with eight Stars of David

being shown a synagogue, often in disrepair, as evidence of "different religions coexisting peacefully." Most often these were more museum or monument than place of worship. In Tunisia, despite the very reduced number of Jews still living in the country, I had a sense of mutual respect and fellowship—although

30. Berber village of Chenini, mosque

I'm sure the wellbeing of both the Christian and Jewish minorities has been influenced throughout history by the country's overall political situation.

The Berber village of Chenini is a short drive from Tataouine, originally a prison site—thus the French phrase "Go to Tataouine!" meaning "Go to hell!"—and then a center for nomadic tribes. Now Tataouine is a city, not far from the Libyan border. Along the highway, small stands sell smuggled Libyan gasoline, much cheaper than that found in Tunisia. Headed inland, we saw many elegant cars belonging to the wealthier Libyans, who are not confined to the refugee camps.

The landscape in this region is dotted with hundreds of villages like Chenini, but none are more beautiful. Their old uninhabited dwellings, invisible at distance, are carved into mountainsides the same color as their eroding stone. But Chenini is unique. Partially, perhaps, because it is so large. The old city soars up a mountainside and beyond, creating a skyline reminiscent of some of the

Hopi villages but a hundred times larger and more ornate. Few people still live up there since a flood in 1969 washed important pieces away.

Below is the new Chenini: freshly whitewashed homes with their proverbial blue doors and window frames. About halfway up and already in the older section is a white mosque. The bright blue sky was studded with high cirrus clouds; we call them mare's tales. The entire tableau was a sight to behold.

We hiked up a steep and winding stone pathway as far as the mosque. At one point, Mohamed told us the story of "The Seven Sleepers," a sort of religious Rumplestiltskin. "This is in the Koran," he said, "but . . . well . . . I will tell it as a legend" (his first admission that he regards at least some of Islam's holy scripture as stories rather than the word of God). The tale is about seven Christian men who went to sleep in a cave during Roman times, only to wake up centuries later as Muslims (when Islam had become the official religion). This is supposed to have happened in this village.

On our way down, Mohamed asked if we would like to visit a friend of his, a woman in her eighties named Miriam. She lives alone in her small house in Chenini's ancient heights, although a granddaughter comes to stay with her every night.

Miriam showed us through her tiny rooms, cut cave-like into the rock: one for sleeping, one for weaving, another for cooking. When some of us, conscious of her extreme poverty, offered her half a dinar (roughly thirty-five cents), she seemed grateful. One in our group gave her a silver dollar, apparently believing he was bestowing a special gift. Discretely Miriam asked Mohamed if she would be able to exchange the strange coin "for something useful."

Throughout this vast rock desert, situated for visibility and protection atop mountain ridges, are the seventeenth-century *ksars*, or storage warehouses where nomadic tribes kept foodstuffs and other necessities. The women and children remained wherever the community was camped, while the men divided themselves into groups and rotated, one staying behind to defend the ksar while others traveled in every direction in search of grains, beans, olives and olive oil, dates, even tiny sardines from the coast, which were dried to last through the harsh winters.

These ksars are huge complexes, often four or five stories high, made up of small rooms with low doors, no windows, and a web of winding staircases lead-

31. Miriam

ing to the upper levels. From the very top of each stack of rooms protrudes a sturdy stick—much in the manner of Amsterdam's narrow many-storied houses—to help in hauling goods to the top.

My favorite of the several ksars we visited was Ouled Sultane. It is an architectural wonder. I could have spent hours just photographing its elegant angles.

32. Ksar Ouled Sultane

Barbara could have spent hours sketching them. Two other ksars were used by George Lukas as destinations in his *Star Wars* films, a fact of which Tunisians are proud—although few of them seem to have seen the blockbusters.

From the rugged Atlas Mountains in the north, across great deserts that left me gasping at the force and power of landscape, through cities and villages where we saw vestiges of cultures that have shaped one another for centuries, at archeological ruins where we were the only visitors, on the still-embattled streets of Tunis, in cottage industries, mosques, and a synagogue, I received a taste of what Tunisia is today.

Only four months prior to my visit, the country made a dramatic change, one that must be defined and sharpened for it to truly make a difference in people's lives. Enthusiasm for the revolution is palpable, from big cities to the smallest village. Broken shop windows, graffiti on many walls, and continuing demonstrations all attest to an ongoing process. In many places, the number seven had been ripped from a facade or monument. This was Ben Ali's favorite number—he assumed the presidency on November 7, 1987—and it became a symbol of his regime. Now it symbolizes corruption. I noticed that paper bills in Tunisia also bear a very large seven in the upper right-hand corner. "Will you also be printing new money?" I asked Mohammed. "No," he laughed, "we are not rich enough for that."

In this North African country, time and memory converge in ways that run from the surreal to the deeply pragmatic. If I return in a year or two, I believe I will find progress—whatever that may mean. And I will find, again, a country of rich history and culture, warm hospitality, and enduring dignity.

Goose Quill to Thought-Capture, Stopping at Books

When I was a child, the image was seductive: a graceful hand resting on a surface suffused in darkness, perhaps a large table of polished wood. The fingers of the hand—most likely a right hand—held a goose quill, feathers furling broad at the top then tapering just before the tip, a slender white stem. Nearby, an inkwell. My imagination did the rest. I could see those fingers dipping the tip of the quill in India ink (did all ink come from India, or only the best?) and then carefully inscribing words on a scroll of paper. Yes, always a scroll, its far end also disappearing into the painting's dark shadows.

For this was long before photography, and long before such painting treated us to anything but aristocratic writers, those with the money and prestige to commission a portrait by an artist of note. I dreamed of pale consumptive poets penning love poems to one another. The Brownings were the first couple I knew of where the poems of both were honored.

Later in life, if trying to imagine the first writers, I would have conjured an image of a prehistoric man or woman using a sharp stone to scratch the surface of a softer stone wall. Or someone leaving a careful record on a clay tablet. Perhaps a roll of papyrus, stored in a desert cave, to be discovered, faded and torn, millennia later. But those messages lacked the personal quality of an individual's fingers curved about the goose quill's stem, the proximity of a small square bottle of ink, the sense of a single person writing.

This is about writing and reading, its movement through my body and time.

I stepped onto the writing train and found myself in the Palmer Method car.

For someone like myself—who, from earliest memory, knew I would be a writer—reading and writing went together. It somehow seemed logical that reading would come first, but I can no longer separate the experience of learning each.

I recall Miss Peek, my teacher in first and second grades, walking past my desk, looking down at the careful curves and loops crossing my neatly margined paper from left to right. I still hold the feeling in my hand, wrist, arm, body, slant of back, and snug fit of buttocks in that chair-and-desk combination, as I followed instructions and dreamed about some future when the exercise would surely morph into something more interesting than repetitive pencil scratchings on a piece of classroom notebook paper.

In the 1940s we started with cursive writing, skipping printing altogether. Later that was reversed, but I was of a generation that had to make our mark connecting all the letters. And we were told economy of motion was important. We were supposed to move from one letter to the next at the point of least resistance: precisely where it made most sense. But what did making sense even mean?

One's signature was also of interest. I remember being told that a great deal about my persona could be gleaned from how I wrote my name. I spent hours trying on one signature and then another. Would I be the decisive or elegant me, flamboyant or retiring, energetic or diffident? Initial flourishes eventually gave way to a simpler way of signing.

Ideas also abounded about the ways in which one's handwriting reflects one's character and personality. What kind of person wrote with a backward slant or crowned their *i*'s with circles instead of dots? What could be told from fat rounded letters or long thin ones? What did it mean if one's writing went uphill or down, crowded at the margin or trailed off the page? As with so many popularized versions of scientific disciplines, the handwriting analysis to which I had access was superficial to say the least. I remember consciously trying to cultivate those qualities I thought would show me to be a better person in the opinion of my peers.

From the beginning, I was right-handed. Trying to do anything, particularly something that demanded such fine motor skills as writing, with my left hand always ended in disaster. Yet I envied left-handed people. My father told us he had been born left-handed, then forced to change. My daughter Sarah is left-handed. Barbara also began writing with her left hand and was badgered into changing, but her range of competency makes it easier for her to do some things with one hand, some with the other. I've always secretly wished I were left-handed, because I saw it as a sign of intelligence and creativity.

Early on, though, I found that writing by hand a lot hurt. It would cramp the roof of my palm, causing me to take any shortcut available. I wanted to be a writer but didn't enjoy the physical act of putting words on paper. As an adult, I actually developed small cysts in my hands, which periodically had to be removed.

Perhaps this was what led to my early determination to own a typewriter. Or maybe I simply knew that writers used them and wanted to get a head start. I asked for my first model at age nine. My parents, who often employed this way of approaching their children's desires in order to make sure we weren't asking for something we would soon abandon, told me if I earned half the money, they would contribute the other half. They also wanted me to demonstrate my seriousness by studying touch-typing.

What could a preadolescent girl in suburban Scarsdale, New York, do to make money? No one yet trusted me as a babysitter. I decided to get a newspaper route. I can no longer remember how I secured that job, but soon I was receiving my morning package of papers, rolling and tying them with lengths of sewing thread, and was out on my American Flyer before the sun came up, tossing each to a waiting neighborhood stoop. To be honest, when I began, I had to dismount and walk more papers than I successfully tossed. But after a while, I became more adept at the task, throwing with increasing flair as I wheeled past each house.

My memory jumps from that rolling and tying and tossing to the seventy-five dollars I earned in a few short months. Mother and Dad immediately made good on their promise to provide the other half of what I needed, and I bought my first typewriter: a black Royal Portable in a square case with a handle. The machine sat securely in the bottom part of the box, clamped into some mechanism that held it fast. The hard rubber roller smelled of perfection; the whole model exuded a slight scent of oil. Each glistening metal-rimmed key displayed its letter or symbol, and each was linked to a thin arm ready to imprint its contents on a fresh page I would line up and roll through, adjusting its evenness before I set the clamp and let the bar fall. Throwing the carriage to the left each time I reached the end of a line was a motion that filled me with pride.

Of course I took my prize possession seriously, and I also made good on my vow to learn to touch-type. In fact, I vowed to be the fastest, most accurate typist in the land. I can still remember the scratchy 45 RPM record I set on the turntable and the notes of "The Syncopated Clock," to which I practiced J-U-G JUG, C-A-T CAT, and all the rest of the exercises leading to my proficiency. By the time I was ten, I was typing 60 words a minute. By the time I was twenty, I was doing 150. I had no doubt this would start me on the road toward becoming a professional writer.

I've written about how hard it was for me to learn to read. When, at the end of my first-grade year, everyone but me had mastered the mystery, my father took it on himself to spend that summer making sure I knew before I had to enter second grade in the fall. My school might even have told my parents I wouldn't be able to move up if I didn't know. Social promotion wasn't so automatic back then. Every night after dinner, I would nestle in Dad's warm tweed-smelling lap, and he would open the book with the red paperboard cover embossed with black letters.

I am sad that I cannot remember that book's title. Today we would call it a chapter book: characters to whom I could relate enticing me from one adventure to the next. At first I struggled with each word. Dad's patience never wavered. Almost imperceptibly I soon realized I was pronouncing most of them, with only an occasional nudge from him. I think I learned fast. I'd probably needed the individual attention and to arrive at the time in my own development when my mind was ready.

Meanwhile, what sort of literature was I beginning to know? My two earliest favorite books, read to me by my parents, came from my mother's childhood. They were *The Ballads of the Be-Ba-Boes* by D. K. Stevens (1913) and *The Water Babies* by Charles Kingsley (1916). Mother was born in 1910, so I imagine her parents or their friends gave her those volumes, which were worn and a bit ragged by the time they reached her children's hands. I loved the illustrations: slightly old-fashioned and romantic. Someone named Catharine Maynardier Daland had done those for *The Water Babies*, and even today they seem magical to me.

A few years ago, my brother John, who is a used- and rare-books dealer, gave me a newly reprinted facsimile edition of *The Water Babies*. I thrilled, especially to its exuberant full-color plates, as I remembered entering its world so many years before. He also found an original of *The Ballads of the Be-Ba-Boes*, which I was able to peruse. The great disappointment was discovering both books expressed such traditionalist values. The be-ba-boes seemed downright racist.

Once I mastered the art of reading, I devoured all sorts of titles. My parents had floor-to-ceiling shelves, seductive with their book-of-the-month-club selections and a number of large format art books, whose pages I turned slowly, excited by reproductions of paintings and sculptures I dreamed of seeing one day in the original. The next two books that marked me I found on those shelves. One was Curzio Malaparte's *Kaputt*. I don't know what drew me to it, but I still shiver, repulsed, when I think of the description of bloody finger stumps that I came across on its very first pages.

I think the scene was a World War II concentration camp. The book was published in 1944, and that first edition is probably the one I opened, slammed shut, and then returned to again, each time repelled by its subject matter and then seduced by some macabre need to experience the fear. I had no idea, at the time, that Malaparte was a Communist who wrote against man's degradation of man (as it would have been described at the time). I remember my mother's astonishment when she found me with the book and her asking me why I didn't just close it for good.

Another book I remember from that period excited me from beginning to end. It was *I Married Adventure* (1940) by Osa Johnson, and it related the experiences she and her husband, Martin, had while exploring and photographing the people of Borneo. I, too, wanted to marry adventure—better yet, to have some of my own. It wasn't until many years later, when I came across a copy of that book in a used bookstore in western Massachusetts and reread parts of it, that I understood *I Married Adventure* was at least as racist as *The Ballads of the Be-Ba-Boes*. The Johnsons thoroughly objectified the native people they wrote about and photographed.

Like most of the young girls of my generation, place, and social class, I loved *Lassie* and *Black Beauty*. I read all the *Nancy Drew* and *Hardy Boys* mysteries, easily imagining myself solving their cases along with them. Louisa May Alcott's *Little Women* was a favorite. I alternated between imagining myself as Meg or Jo and thought it auspicious that my given name is Margaret Jo, a combination of the two. Jo won out in the end. She was the nonconformist and hardworking writer I wanted to be.

But when I think of my youth, the book I recall with the greatest gratitude is *The Diary of a Young Girl* by a young Dutch victim of Nazi fascism, Anne Frank. I was in bed with nephritis when my father handed me that book inscribed, "For Margaret. I know your confinement won't be as long as Anne's."

He was right. My confinement wouldn't be as long, and it wouldn't end in death as hers had. He was also right in his choice of that book for me. Just as he had opened me to other cultures with much earlier gifts of children's books about the Amish and the Pueblo Indians of the U.S. American Southwest, Anne's diary allowed me to learn about human yearning, fascist horror, and the immense value of recording life stories. Looking back, this book may have started me on my lifelong custom of journal keeping. It certainly made me understand how important honest memoir is, the importance of getting it all down.

In junior high and high school, poetry was taught by rote. Memorizing Longfellow's "Hiawatha" or "The Raven" by Edgar Allen Poe and having to recite them from memory was a heartless experience. It made me hate poetry. If only our teachers had known how to talk about those poems, link them to our lives, make connections that would have allowed us to enter their rhythms and understand their emotions.

But the 1950s also gave me *Howl and Other Poems* (1955) by Allen Ginsberg. "Howl" was the first poem that changed my life. I heard it read aloud at a party in the canyon east of Albuquerque about six months after its initial publication, and I would never be the same. Here was someone speaking—no, screaming—the social hypocrisy of my time. As a young white middle-class provincial woman, my experiences were not Ginsberg's or Solomon's.[1] But I could relate to the feelings.

Later in that same decade, *I Wanted to Write a Poem* (1958), by William Carlos Williams, felt closer to my own poetic need. I, too, wanted to write a poem, one that transformed the thoughts and feelings I alone knew into something others would read or listen to, nodding their heads because my words resonated with them. I wanted to stand at the mike in one of those Village coffee shops, my hair full and wild, not a tremor in my voice.

By this time, I lived in New York City. I sent a sheaf of my first poetic attempts to Dr. Williams, who lived across the river in Rutherford, New Jersey. He invited me to visit. When I got off the interstate bus, I bought a few sprigs of pussy willow, which I offered shyly to Williams's wife, Flossie, when she opened the door.

That afternoon was pivotal in my sense of myself as a poet. Williams, who had suffered a stroke, could no longer read his own work; so he asked me to read one of his recent poems out loud so he could hear its sound, and also one of my own. Mine was called "Eating the Snow." His critique was careful and encouraging, modeling what I have wanted to be for the newer poets who have come to me seeking help throughout these many years.

In New York, as the 1950s waned and we entered the turbulent '60s, I walked the city streets—almost always below Fourteenth—noticing things like the cornices of old buildings, the eggshell skeletons of those being torn down, the way the light moved through the branches of brave cement-imprisoned trees. I noticed people and listened to the particularities of their speech. I noticed everything. And I began to write seriously. Soon I was reading my first tentative poems on coffeehouse stages and publishing them in the pages of a few of what we called little magazines back then. Little, perhaps, because of their institutional independence or because of their small readership.

Sometimes I wandered the used bookstores along Fourth Avenue, looking for bargains, whatever caught my eye. In those days, I was intrigued by Wilhelm Reich and Gertrude Stein. I read the former's *Function of the Orgasm* in the New York Public Library's banned-books room, sitting alone at a table, occasionally looking around to see if anyone watched. At one of the city's used bookstalls, I found a decent copy of Stein's *Making of Americans*. In pencil and in his unmistakable hand, there was the name of Robert Creeley, a previous owner of the book. Later Creeley and I would become friends.

Thus began a life of finding those books that would move me again and again. And it is the force that pulls me back to the pages of a book I've already read that sets the book apart, producing an experience of unequalled power. Such a book, through my early twenties or thirties, was Agnes Smedley's *Daughter of Earth*. How I loved every page. The Women's Press edition, which is the one I own, is dated 1973, yet that seems late. It is copyrighted 1943, but that would have been much too early for me. I guess I did read it for the first time in '73, but this would have put me in my mid to late thirties, which seems wrong. Perhaps the fact that I read it over and over has blurred the moment we first connected.

Although our origins couldn't have been more different, I identified powerfully with Smedley. She was the daughter of poor sharecroppers in the U.S. South, who came of age during World War II. Her life was always a struggle, yet she managed to take part in the movement for the independence of India as well as accompany the Chinese Communists' Eighth Route Army. She wrote passionately about all that and more, but *Daughter of Earth* was an autobiography of her early years. It has many scenes I won't forget. One in particular is when the writer describes her father asking her mother how she voted, her mother refusing to tell him, and him threatening to leave her if she didn't. Smedley's mother would not back down, and he did leave, for good. The mother's determination not to divulge one of the few secrets she could call her own moves me to this day.

In the 1970s, I discovered the poetry of Peruvian César Vallejo. Once again, a poet changed my life. I have only read Vallejo in Spanish (existing English translations just don't work for me). *Poemas Humanos* and *España, aparta de mí ésta cáliz* are my favorites among his books, but all his poems combine words in ways that go beyond the power of any language. That decade brought me Roque Dalton, as well, a revolutionary poet from El Salvador who helped me attempt my own renditions of Vallejo and gave us his own irreverent and magnificent work.

I can point to dozens of books from the 1980s that marked me profoundly. Among them is Alexandra Kollontai's *A Great Love* (I read the first English edition in 1981). Nawal Al Saadawi's *Woman at Point Zero* (1983) also left a lasting impression. I've read both books many times. The first tells the story of a brilliant revolutionary woman whose talents are ultimately betrayed by the great male revolutionary she loves. The second is the life story of an Egyptian prostitute, recorded by Saadawi the night before she would be executed for murdering a man who abused her. Both helped me move toward the woman I want to be.

Memory of Fire is Uruguayan Eduardo Galeano's three-volume history of the world as told by the ordinary men and women who are its protagonists. I had previously read other books by Galeano, beginning with *The Open Veins of Latin America*, a copy of which Hugo Chávez handed to Barack Obama at a conference early in Obama's presidency, hoping he might read it and gain some understanding of the endlessly shameful relationship between the United States and its southern neighbors. But *Memory of Fire* is Galeano's masterwork, at least to date.

The Fact of a Doorframe (1984), the anthology that gathers together Adrienne Rich's poetry from 1950 to 1984, was important to me for several reasons. First, just because the poetry is so extraordinarily powerful. So many poems from that volume will be remembered as among the best from a generation, at least in English. The book's brief title poem has guided me since the day I read it. And the last poem, "North American Time," felt like it was written for me. During the ordeal of my immigration case, I went back to this poem again and again, reciting stanzas as a mantra helping me maintain my own sense of perspective.

But one of the book's later poems affected me in a way that may be difficult to explain. It is "Paula Becker to Clara Westhoff," from Rich's 1978 *The Dream of a Common Language*. I had just returned to the United States after a quarter century in Latin America. I felt broken by having left my comrades behind in war-torn Nicaragua, and breathless at reclaiming my landscape and language. And I had just realized my lesbian identity. I was close to fifty. I remember wandering the halls of the University of New Mexico, where I was teaching a couple of adjunct courses at the time, reading that poem out loud to whomever I could get to sit down and listen. I'm not a religious person, but the lines of that poem felt to me like what I imagined prayer to be.

June Jordan's *On Call* was almost as important in my experience of that decade and those that have followed. Jordan's 1985 collection of political essays includes "Many Rivers to Cross," which I have read out loud on the first day of almost every university class I have taught. Alice Walker's *In Search of Our Mothers' Gardens* also made an impact.

I have returned again and again to one novel written at the beginning of the 1990s and one written at the end, always astonished at how right their authors got the complex subjects they tackled. The first was *He, She and It* (1991) by Marge Piercy. It predicts a world we now recognize is coming on fast, more than twenty years after it was written. Piercy's genius resides, among much else, in telling part of her story in the mid-twenty-first century and the other in 1600, thus demonstrating the continuity in how we struggle with the meaning of human identity.

Barbara Kingsolver published *The Poisonwood Bible* in 1998. For me, it is one of the all-time great novels, ranking with Proust, Victor Hugo, Gabriel García Márquez, and Russia's iconic examples. Kingsolver takes on fundamentalist religion, missionary fervor, and postcolonialist Africa on the threshold of liberation. She does so in brilliant prose and mostly through the voices of women.

In the same decade, two gay men produced books that have drawn me repeatedly to their pages. One is Paul Monette's *Last Watch of the Night* (1993), a collection of essays about the devastation of AIDS. The pandemic, which by that point had already been taking tens of thousands of beloved lives for more than ten years, had gained a distance from which some writers were beginning to be able to approach it in poetry, fiction, and nonfiction. I had long loved Monette's work, and this book made me cry and then go back for more. There's nothing maudlin about his accounting. He himself succumbed to the disease just before the book appeared.

The other book is *Then We Take Berlin* (1995) by Canadian Stan Persky.

Again, Persky is a writer I always find interesting, but this is the book of his to which I keep going back. *Then We Take Berlin* explores the fall of European Communism through a travelogue depiction of the author's journey through a number of countries that had recently clawed their way out from under Soviet control. As Stan hustles for casual lovers, he gets to know each situation through their eyes. The book taught me more about social change than any political treatise.

Toward the end of the 1980s and into the '90s, I found myself grappling with my own experience of childhood incest. Working with an astute psychotherapist, I was able to unearth a history long hidden by disassociation and denial. This was a difficult time, and there weren't yet many books that could help me shed light on my past. Then I found Judith Lewis Herman's *Trauma and Recovery* (1992).

As Herman researched the "commonalities of symptoms and residual trauma between rape victims and combat veterans, battered women and political prisoners, the survivors of vast concentration camps created by tyrants who rule nations, and the survivors of small, hidden concentration camps created by tyrants who rule their homes,"[2] she began to see the parallels between private and public, individuals and communities, men and women. Her book not only helped me personally, it allowed me to begin to explore the connection between the invasion of a woman's or child's body by someone who controls her and the invasion of a small country by a larger, more powerful one.

The new century continues to bring extraordinary books, some of which I find myself revisiting as I have their predecessors. *The Secret Knowledge of Water* (2000), by Craig Childs, is only one of several books about the U.S. desert Southwest that feed my ravenous appetite. I love reading about the Ancestral Puebloans who inhabited this landscape, but Childs's book goes to the basics: the life of water on parched land, desert water's ability to drown as easily as kill by thirst, and the thousands of unseen creatures who accompany human beings on that terrain.

The year 2001 brought another novel, comparable to *The Poisonwood Bible* in ambition and scope but with a very different theme. *Embrace* by South African Mark Behr tells the story of the end of apartheid from the viewpoint of a young white Afrikaner at a school for boys with exceptional singing voices. The protagonist is not of the same wealthy stock from which most of his classmates come, so class is also rendered in striking tones. And this is a gay coming-out story as well. The first time I approached *Embrace*'s more than seven hundred pages, I had trouble finding my way in. Once it grabbed me, though, I have invited myself back many times.

Another South African book, this one a first-person narrative of the author's ongoing account of her country's Truth and Reconciliation Commission experience, is Antjie Krog's *Country of My Skull* (2002). Rarely have I read a more in-depth examination of (self-) guilt, sorrow, and forgiveness. Krog doesn't make it easy, on herself or her readers. I have assigned this book to students of mine but have found it's too much for the limits imposed by most class calendars.

A memoir that meant a great deal to me when it appeared in 2002, and still does, is Nicaraguan Gioconda Belli's *The Country under My Skin*. I read it first in Spanish and then in English and return to it in both languages in order to keep reminding myself of what strong women endure at the hands of patriarchal men, even when their talents and courage are needed to win a war. Belli writes what she lived, doing so with a critical eye for her own choices as well as for the era. Several of my friends whose lives intersected with the author's couldn't accept the raw truth of this book. I resist the temptation to argue with them, because I know that assimilating this memoir would necessitate a look at the self, which they are perhaps not ready to endure.

Another recent memoir that has beckoned me back and back to its pages is Susan Sherman's *America's Child: A Woman's Journey through the Radical Sixties* (2007). This is one of those books that should be required reading for anyone interested in the era. It got a rave review in the *New York Times* then disappeared in the void into which so many small presses launch their books. Sherman's story brings the U.S. American 1960s alive as only someone can by living it, writing exquisitely, and being honest enough to tell it like it was.

Equally gripping is Diane di Prima's *Recollections of My Life as a Woman* (2001). A fine poet of my generation, di Prima traces her life from a childhood lived among Italian immigrants to breaking onto New York's 1950s and '60s poetry scene. She skillfully deconstructs the woman artist's painful lot as she re-creates the talent and energy that carried her through. Sexuality, motherhood, the acquisition of belief systems, relentless double standards, and the development of her own poetic voice are explored with wisdom and in beautiful prose. As I read this book, I relived so many of my own experiences.

Poetry that has lured me to read and reread it through the beginning of this new century can be found in consecrated poet Joy Harjo's *How We Became Human* (2002) and new-on-the-scene Mary Oishi's *Spirit Birds They Told Me*

(2011). Yes, the poems are magnificent, but what draw me back to both of these books are their introductions. Harjo's is a journey through her life in poetry to that point. Oishi's tells a heartbreaking story of war, abandonment, and racism in the voice of a woman with a mother who was a Japanese war bride, a father who was a U.S. soldier in World War II's Pacific theater, and a history, mixed heritage, and sexual identity that made her a scorned outsider in the Christian fundamentalist Appalachia where she grew up. Both are stunningly revealing and vital to understanding ourselves.

One more novel has knocked me out of late. It is Minrose Gwin's *The Queen of Palmyra* (2010). Gwin revisits the U.S. American South in the year 1963, just as the civil rights movement was moving into high gear. As with most life-changing movements, most of the characters in the novel are unaware of the profundity of what's going on around them, while a few are deeply conscious. Blacks and whites, revolutionaries and Klansmen, preadolescent girls and knowing adults meet in these pages. Gwin captures the era and its multilayered meanings in a way I have had to return to often, in order to remember our history.

I myself have written a lot of books—poetry, essay, oral history, memoir, and first-person narrative. When someone asks me how many, I cringe. Unlike birthdays, it's not about numbers. And I want to think of my literary output in terms of quality, not quantity. Almost every time I finish writing a book, I experience a strong desire that it be my last. "I'm going to stop writing," I make the mistake of saying out loud. Then, after a day or two, a week at most, I find myself beginning again. It is as if I cannot stop. Lately I've been waking up at one or two in the morning, forced to stumble from a warm bed to get an idea down on paper, which, these days, means into my computer.

This brings me to the life of books. How much longer will our younger generations be willing to read them? With the direction in which cyberspace and ever smaller and quicker electronic devices are taking us, old-fashioned books—with their awkward heft, ungainly format, and need for miles of shelves—are pretty much doomed. I can easily foresee a time when they will be collector's items, relegated to museums where we will go to view our past. Yet I continue to cherish them. To me, there is nothing like curling up in a quiet place with a real book in my hands. I want the feel of the paper, beauty of design, faint scent of print, texture of binding, relationship between form and content: the object itself.

No sooner did the Kindle come on the market, making it possible to store hundreds of books and take them anywhere, than iPads appeared, with similar storage space that allows for full-color viewing and pages that are turned to better simulate the experience of reading the original. These devices allow the prospective buyer to try a sample before purchasing the whole book, and they also make it possible to travel carrying dozens or even hundreds of books. The claim "but I prefer to read a real book" echoes fainter and fainter.

But digital reading devices alter the reading experience in important ways. Because the person reading can change the typeface to his or her taste, one is not "on page 44" but rather "16 percent through the book." Particularly where poetry is concerned, the placement of words on a page is important, and on a Kindle or iPad or Nook the white space is distorted. Friend and editor Bryce Milligan, of Wings Press, is currently exploring algorithms aimed at dealing with this disjuncture.

The technology of writing has changed as radically as that of reading. From the pencil or pen that cramped my hand, when I first learned to write; to my old Royal Portable; to an IBM Selectric, when that was once the nonplus ultra of writing machines; and into the age of personal computers—progress comes faster and faster. It has often been hard for me to keep up.

Returning to the United States from Latin America in the mid-1980s, I came late to computers. They existed in Cuba and Nicaragua back then, but only in offices or institutions. No writer I knew had one. Suddenly, here everyone had his or her personal model. I remember the old Kapro, a dull-green metal box that folded into itself. A friend recommended it, and I made the leap, only to find myself stuck with a dinosaur. Then a succession of newer models came into my life: first PCs and eventually Macs. Floppy discs gave way to flash drives. Models became lighter and faster and did more.

But this hasn't only been about streamlining the object. Not for me. The technological journey has changed the way I write, bringing the speed of my fingers into line with the speed of my mind, enabling me to cut and paste, reorganize and reemphasize, according to the demands of the work itself. My manuscripts once went through four or five messy drafts. Now they go through twenty or thirty. There's no doubt about it—I've become a better writer since using a computer, and not only because I'm older or wiser or more experienced.

I remember the days of onion skin and messy carbon paper, the advent of ballpoint pens, the replacement of snail mail with e-mail, the careful preparation of a manuscript that would make its slow journey to a perspective publisher giving way to sending that manuscript in seconds as an e-mail attachment. At poetry readings these days, I occasionally see a poet reading not from the page but from the tiny monitor of his or her cell phone.

Remembering and writing this text has allowed me to recognize each struggle to master initial reading or writing skills and to linger with many of the books that have added immeasurably to my life. Somewhere between the goose quill pen and an electronic chip implanted in my body—for I am sure that is in our future—my life as a reader and writer unfolds.

Coyote Grin

I have no objection to imagining Dom DeLuise hocking a fat globule of spit on Albert Einstein's thick, white mane or delivering a devastating karate kick to the groin of Pope Benedict XVI. Even Michael Jackson defecating on a salmon burger wouldn't be too extreme an image if visualizing it did something ongoing and profound for my memory.

By linking such images of bizarre acts to playing cards and then committing those acts to memory and practicing running through the images in his mind—faster, faster, faster until the stopwatch registered less and less time needed to repeat the cards in random order—the 2006 champion U.S. memorizer walked away with first prize. In a *New York Times Magazine* feature, Joshua Foer described the study sessions as grueling but definitively his pathway to success.[1]

Foer's success and mine are light-years apart. My problem is I have no interest in memorizing a deck of playing cards in any order, or number groups from here to infinity. Games leave me cold, and contests can be won by others as far as I'm concerned. It is life I want at my fingertips, my life, ready and waiting to be remembered, experienced in every season. By "remembered," I mean reexperienced. Life enhanced by the ability to reconnect to earlier experience, despite the popular "live in the moment" adage, is the only sort of life worth living.

I want to remember the perfect word and, more than that single word, the meaning running through a landscape of words like a train running along an unbroken track, propelled by its own power, accompanied by its own rhythm of hisses and clangs and intensifying then slowly fading whistle. I want to retain the shifting seam between river's edge and ancient rock, recognize the canyon wren's pure note, and hold until death the curve of your breast, knowing it is *yours*. I want those life-changing poems by Vallejo and Rich, not a rereading of their lines as they swept me into their arms the first time around, but how I receive them the hundredth time, layered with the electrifying memory of each of the first ninety-nine. How this poem made me feel and where. How that poem changed me.

Or my name. Your name. Their names, and what the owners of all these names mean to one another. *Los vasos comunicantes*, the connective tissue: a necklace where every hanging gem basks in unique light as it settles against a canvass on which the whole illuminates with grace and brilliance.

This is definitely not about a particular number, word, or group of symbols waiting in repetitive boredom to take its place in rote recitation. It is about delicate pieces of life and what happened seconds before each one unfolded, or minutes after, parallel or in chorus, retreating to take their places among the great body of voices, then each stepping forward to inhabit its own spectacular moment once again.

Fabric is everything—context part of what gives all memory depth.

Here is an example. When I began to write about sitting at that small round table at a Lower East Side café, 1959, I knew I must retrieve the feel of the table-top against my sweaty palms, my posture in the ironwork chair, the slant of my body toward or away from the person sitting across that table from me. I needed to conjure the longing in my eyes and set of my mouth, the person who faced me and why, the tiny catch of breath in my throat, the temperature of outside air, the drink that stood half consumed in the small cup I fingered with nervous hands and the amount of liquid that ran down its sides to pool in the saucer beneath. Did I return that spill to the cup? Drink it from the saucer? Or was I too nervous to indulge myself in this way?

And on my way to the café, what did I feel as I approached, what visions battled with the little superstitious tics sparring between my temples? And when I got up to leave an hour later, what forced rearrangement of emotions turned the contents of shop windows smaller, more distant, less accessible? Could I still remember how it had felt to imagine owning that expensive leather bag, the rainbow chiffon of a party dress I'd passed on my daily rounds without so much as stopping to contemplate its fragrant enticement!

The foregoing is my memory of the first time an editor extended an invitation to coffee, only to tell me the novel I'd sent him was bad, that I might as well go back to my hometown, marry, have children, and give up my dream of becoming a writer. His recipe word for word. Note the either/or that pits pursuing writing against being a mother. I can pull our conversation up and toss it lifeless across the page. Or I can evoke the tremors, shortness of breath, chemical body changes that complete the story. It all depends on how organic my memory remains and how hard I work to bring it up.

The first version is information, a laundry list of facts that may or may not reflect what really happened so long ago. The second pulls me back to that time, and the reader into my living memory bank, to this day—even after a hundred published books—pulsing with embarrassed disappointment.

Just as there is no single truth, individual memory strands are ragged imposters in the complex weave of history's cloth. And participants remember events differently. Since my early twenties, I have thought of that little round café table a thousand times. The editor may have remembered it once or twice, if at all. Doubtless he'd rejected a hundred books before dispensing with mine and would do away with thousands more throughout his long career. Most rejections would be carried out by mail: the preprinted form letter with the would-be author's name inserted. At best a brief handwritten note at the end, suggesting another destination or meaning to encourage those with talent to keep trying.

For me, it was my first novel and first major rebuff. He called and asked me to meet him for coffee because we were from the same southwestern city and he knew my parents. We'd met a few times. I had mistaken simple courtesy for a glittering promise of acceptance.

A good deal older than I, that editor may be long gone, dealing with another sort of memory or none at all. Until that moment comes for me, I revisit this scene that meant nothing to my writing career but insists on periodically shouldering its way to the surface, each time dragging with it an additional layer of detailed defeat.

Now I ask my memory to tell me which details belong to the original tableaux and which I have invented along the way.

My memory laughs, a broad coyote grin.

Like disparate truths, each person's memory re-creates an event in its own way, shaped by a lifetime of prisms. Lenses are age-, race-, class-, and gender-specific, as well as influenced by other variables. Optics are cut and polished from the myriad crystals of time, light, weather, season, temperature, loyalty, belief system, cultural history, and emotional connection. How important was the event in the grand scheme of the person's life? How trivial? And what other events unfolded or never happened because of the one now taking center stage?

I've kept a journal since 1969. Tens of thousands of single-spaced pages. I started the practice when I was hit with political repression in Mexico and was forced into hiding until I could find a way out of the country. I didn't know how long the difficult situation would last or what its outcome would be. I'm sure I started writing because I wanted to leave some proof of my existence. Just in case.

The habit extended itself, through that underground period, to years lived in Cuba, in Nicaragua, and then back here in the United States. It has become my constant. I may write everyday or a couple of times a week. I may stop writing for a while, only to experience a rekindling of the need some weeks later. The nature of the journal has grown and changed, but not its practice.

At first I wrote about what happened, what I did, and what others did (as I understood what it was that they did). What began as a quasi-personal diary soon morphed into something I shared with small groups of family and friends. When I found myself in the midst of history-making moments, I shared what I wrote further afield, coming to see myself as a bridge between what was going on in parts of the world about which little news reached the United States and the people in my country, who I believed wanted, indeed needed, that information.

Years of overused typewriter ribbons and grubby sheets of carbon paper. Then years of electric typewriters, their even pressure embossing the page in steady determination. With the advent of personal computers some degree of mass production was possible. I could even include images. The Internet and cut and paste do wonders for memory. In my experience, at least, while certain technological advances seem to dull or subsume memory, others aid its preservation.

Back in my early days of journaling, when I wrote about what was happening, I wrote from a particular point of view. I analyzed events according to the convictions I held at the time. Feelings were little explored and always took a back seat to "facts." Back then I believed that facts were self-evident, easy to decipher and just as easy to judge.

I kept writing through my return to the United States, with all the complexities of that transition. For the first time, I was living without any of my children, who had gone on to build their own lives, most of them far from me. I came out as a lesbian and remembered—after a lifetime of disassociation and denial—that I had been sexually abused by my maternal grandparents. And I had to wade through those years when the government was attempting to deport me, deny my desire to live close to my parents as they aged, and disrupt my choice to reconnect with the landscape and language of my creative life.

Each of these was a profound event composed of multiple prisms through which a display of smaller events and reactions sparkled in perpetual movement. The man walking toward me on an evening street, his face unreadable. Would he attack or pass without stopping? The handwritten notes I never wanted to remove from their menacing envelopes. The boys staring back at me from a car waiting just ahead of mine at a long stoplight, their hands holding a sign with the hastily scrawled word "pinko" in large letters. The woman on the courthouse steps screaming *Go back where you came from, bitch! Why? Because I say so, and I'm a* REAL *American!*

And yes, I discovered that I had been hiding beneath a quilt of often-competing feelings and sometimes only wanted to look out at the world sporadically. Transcribing those feelings, as well as the easier to express events—those happenings I still thought everyone perceived in the same way—proved a much more challenging endeavor.

Slowly, I learned that facts are shape-shifters. They change form and import, depending on all sorts of variables, from the position of the scribe to the impact a truth assumed to be inalienable has on the person telling its story. Relationship is everything. And only by making room for feelings, juxtapositions, angles, and a mix of simultaneous views can we approximate anything remotely resembling reality. That's when memory acquires its most subtle gradations and most interesting contradictions.

Around this time, I also discovered I have a condition called synesthesia, a breakdown of the customary frontier between one sense and another. In my case it is between image and sound, manifest as words and parts of words producing particular colors. *M* and most words beginning with *M* are a deep, pulsing red. "Sun" isn't yellow but brownish cream. And so on. My synesthesia is automatic, nothing at all like the bizarre invented scenes Dom DeLuise has developed to help him remember number sets or playing cards.

I began writing *To Change the World: My Years in Cuba* from memory. The book is a recounting of my eleven years participating in the Cuban Revolution. Even now, as I write "from memory," Coyote grins over my left shoulder. I was so sure I accurately remembered those dramatic times. After a year, writing every day, I had what I thought was a pretty advanced draft.

Then I decided to put my manuscript aside and take a few months to reread my journal from that era, pages I hadn't revisited for decades. Each day brought a startling revelation. An incident central to my story hadn't unfolded how I remembered it, but differently in a number of important ways. I had told another story with the presence of only a few of those I thought had been involved. Or placed people in locations or times they'd never inhabited. Years also expanded and contracted. This event actually happened before that other one, or vice versa.

Having those thousands of journal pages, each in neat chronological order, changed my book considerably. It made it stronger. Still, in retrospect I realize I was only able to close some of the gaps in my own fading memory. Had I had access to the memories of others with whom I lived and worked throughout those years, my book would have been a great deal richer. Even perhaps, in a few details, more accurate. Despite my own considerable research and the publisher's careful copyeditor, a few misspelled names and erroneous addresses remain.

But I'm not concerned with that type of small factual error, not in that book or in my memory overall. What concerns and compels me are the places where memory for fact and memory for feeling overlap, interact, and produce an individual's truest recall. Even the best-intentioned, presumably most honest, rendering often dissolves in a swamp of impossibility. And how we perceive ourselves and wish to be perceived by others often makes a courageous exploration of feeling seem like self-betrayal. These may be dual battlefronts in an unwinnable war.

Toni Morrison created the hyphenated word *re-member* to describe those reconnections we need to make between the supposedly separate "members" of ourselves: mind and body; thought and feeling; past, present, and future— a thousand memories shattered by shame and betrayal in our patriarchal world.

I continue to ask my questions. Memory keeps on displaying its coyote grin. But as I age, rather than let go of memory, I sense we are dancing closer, dissolving in a fiery embrace.

"Star Built Memory," Last Words of Meridel LeSueur

This is like adolescence—all your body is
changing . . . the glands . . . the center glandular
shift . . . fast changes . . .
substance tempo another kind of sleep . . .
my reality seems different . . . I am a stranger to
myself . . . where are these alien feelings coming
from?
O come to me . . . I am entertaining
some other person and nothing is familiar to me.
It's not sleep . . . I am simply gone . . .
entirely gone from memory of the body and also
as if some dramatic character has
fallen from you and left you amazed alone
without your personality. Yes
you have died . . . that traditional person
and all her memories and took on alien
memories.
It is strange you are taking
on a new personality . . .
a stranger . . . alienated . . . unfamiliar.
I write differently . . .
Then I seem to be gone[1]

These lines are a gift from beyond that frontier we will all cross eventually but from the far side of which we rarely receive trustworthy news. It is not a gift from just anyone, but from one of our great scribes, a woman who lived the palpitations of her time and transmitted them in commanding voice: filled with all the pain and satisfaction of fighting the good fight. And despite or perhaps because of the fact that they were written on pages found on and around her body when she died, they are a climactic culmination of her unique voice and work.

Meridel LeSueur was a troubadour, a midwestern socialist who knew the breadlines and hobo trains of the 1930s, suffered the McCarthy silencing of the 1950s, and blossomed anew with the second wave of feminist consciousness in the 1970s. Her life spanned almost a century.

And she was a friend.

Meridel and I only coincided for any length of time in the same geographical space for a few months in the late 1980s, when I did a one-semester teaching stint at Macalester College in St. Paul, Minnesota. By then we knew of, and had sporadically corresponded with, one another for more than two decades. It was logical we should meet. Each from her own experience had traveled similar paths and had similar concerns. It's not surprising that our separate journeys merged in the great fabric of struggle and creativity woven by women like ourselves. When we met, it was instant recognition for us both.

When I came home in 1984, after almost a quarter century in Latin America, I was faced with an Immigration and Naturalization Service deportation order because the government judged my writing to be "against the good order and happiness of the United States." Most of my friends sent messages of outrage or condolence; they were sorry to hear about the harassment. Meridel was glad. She wrote that she was proud, was sure I would never have been able to live it down if the government had "let me back in just like that." After my first shock at the unexpected response, her take on the situation pushed me to find my own pride in what was happening. I gained enormous strength from that.

During those years, I spent some time with Meridel when she came to Albuquerque on one of her last reading tours. She put notable energy into a powerful presentation at Salt of the Earth, the wonderful independent bookstore my brother owned at the time. That was the night she first spoke to me about age and what it was doing to her body. She hated no longer being able to drive, not being able to get into her old Volkswagen van and simply head off somewhere. In frustration laced with a bit of humor, she mentioned the time a well-meaning young man who had offered to drive her somewhere started the car while she was still struggling to get in, leaving her injured at the curb.

When Meridel talked about the physical decay of age, she said her body was effervescing, that the cellular breakdown actually produced a sort of luminosity, an energy that could be harnessed in short intense bursts. She explained that she had to alter her work rhythm to include fifteen-minute naps at odd intervals but that the energy sparked by that effervescence could be channeled in new and interesting ways. I remember this whenever I need to find a positive side to one or another of the many physical changes that come with age.

During the time I lived in the Twin Cities, Meridel and I did two public readings together. Both were benefits for younger women. One was to raise money for young women college students so they could rent busses and travel to Washington DC to take part in a great reproductive rights march. I remember that night moving a small flashlight across the page so that she, in her wheel chair, could pronounce her poetry. Her eyes faltered, but her sonorous voice remained magnificent.

My partner and I attended Meridel's ninetieth birthday party—a gala two-day affair to which hundreds traveled from all over the country. Pete Seeger and Ronnie Gilbert were among those who came to pay tribute to their old friend. Perhaps the most impressive contingent was the chorus made up of dozens of Meridel's grandchildren and great-grandchildren. As they sang a cantata specially composed for the occasion, they reminded us all of how a single woman's influence can fan out, carrying her spirit and talent into new configurations of resistance and creativity. Meridel's generosity with younger generations was legion.

After Meridel's death, I took part in a collective reading of one of her last books, *The Dread Road*. John Crawford, West End Press publisher who had brought her work from near-oblivion to a newly grateful public, had just produced the ambitious volume with its three concurrently running columns of text. Now he, Pat Smith, Joy Harjo, and I participated in one of many memorial readings, giving voice to that book's multiple voices. Pat baked a sheet cake, I remember, with the image of a small suitcase embossed on the icing. It referred to a scene in the book where a poor woman riding a Greyhound bus carries the lifeless body of her baby in such a suitcase.

In *The Dread Road*, Meridel took the 1914 Ludlow massacre and wrote about it in the voice of a woman who many years later was living its greater meaning. That narrative ran alongside a series of news clippings describing the historic event, and a third column with fragments of Edgar Allen Poe's poem "The Raven." Great stories of oppression and resistance were often Meridel's subjects, but she always energized them with her unique signature. Although she excelled at giving voice to poor working people—especially women—she was not a social realist writer. Her work sang with passion and innovation.

And her work spanned a number of genres: poetry, novel, short story, essay, article, experimental prose, and 133 volumes of journals (1918–1991) that now reside at the Minnesota Historical Society. Just thinking about that span of time gives a sense of the life lived: from World War I through the Great Depression, other wars and social upheavals, single motherhood, civil rights, the women's movement, to five years before her death, almost at the end of the twentieth century.

All of this is to say that Meridel and her observations touched my life deeply. I considered her a mentor. We didn't see one another often. But for me our meetings were pivotal, and each produced some kernel I would find useful into the future. As with so many people whose lives she influenced, our times together were undoubtedly more meaningful to my life than to hers. When one of her characteristic letters arrived—written on a conventional typewriter long after most of us were using computers, and with an unevenness of pressure that often faded parts of words and made them illegible—it always carried some germ of wisdom that came at just the right moment.

Now I reread the lines that appear at the beginning of this essay. Barbara Tilsen, one of Meridel's family members engaged in the delicate balancing act between protecting and distributing the writer's work, sent them to me almost a year ago. They have been on my desk ever since. When more-recent letters and manuscripts threatened to bury them, they invariably made their way back up to the top of the pile. It is as if Meridel's last written words—do I dare imagine they were her last thoughts?—insisted and reinsisted themselves into my field of vision, my eager and grateful consciousness.

For who among us doesn't long for a glimpse, a message, anything at all of what it feels like to begin that final exit? Who among us—perhaps especially those who are closer to death than birth—would not trade hours or days of our own life for a sense of what someone with Meridel's wisdom and experience saw, heard, and, most importantly, felt as death approached? Or perhaps more to the point, who among us wouldn't wish for our personal version of this experience in our final hours?

As if fearful she would not be able to get it all down, the lines quoted at the beginning of this essay make frequent use of ellipses. She rushes from one sensation or idea to the next. Meridel's daughter Rachel, most familiar with her mother's writing, transcribed those lines, wherever possible respecting margins and breaks. I have a sense of reaching, reaching for the next phrase and hurrying to put it to paper. An exercise in transmitting what is all but impossible to transmit.

"This is like adolescence," Meridel writes, remembering the momentous upheaval of those earlier changes. But those shifts that take place as one moves into adulthood had long since flowed and congealed for her into references destined to be part of a memory that could be told. References to which one might return, with ever-greater powers of discernment and analysis. This new change would simply end. I am almost completely sure Meridel did not believe in eternal consciousness, á la any sort of religious dogma, although her body of work clearly reveals the conviction that all matter is energy and our bodies, like all matter, go on living in other forms.

"It's not sleep," she writes, "I am simply gone . . . / entirely gone from memory of the body [. . .] / as if some dramatic character has / fallen from you and left you amazed alone / without your personality." Lack of punctuation seems to indicate an urgency to keep writing while she is able, not to be stopped by such superfluous additions as commas or periods. And the shift from "I" to "you" in these lines does not denote a change in person; I read this as a figurative you, perhaps an effort to draw the reader more fully into her description.

This reference to the nakedness of pure being is stunning. And the precision of what is happening is spelled out in Meridel's insistence that what she is experiencing is different from ordinary sleep. She knows there will be no awakening, or at least not an awakening to anything she can predict. I am intrigued by her reference to self as a dramatic character, falling away and leaving her without her personality. In other words, without the identity to which she had grown accustomed through almost a century of life, the body of experience and response she knew so well.

The conventional or traditional person is already dead in these lines. I am reminded of the farewell note a young Nicaraguan revolutionary left to his mother before embarking on an action he correctly imagined would result in his death. It was 1956 and Rigoberto López Pérez planned to try to shoot the dictator Anastasio Somoza at a large private party. He signed his letter in the past tense, "from the son who loved you very much." There is something deeply poignant about such a farewell: the still living person speaking from beyond the grave.

But while Rigoberto's words are those of a young man whose single-minded drive was to rescue his country from dictatorship, Meridel's are those of a wise scribe and are much more complex: "I am entertaining some other person," she writes, "and nothing is familiar to me." Her words carry the promise of a forward motion splitting into alternate personalities. They move implacably toward the future, even if it is a future she will no longer inhabit.

The woman writing these words is doing so from some vividly witnessed other side. A place beginning to be imagined in the very last moments of earthly experience. The first faltering but willing steps on an unfamiliar bridge. Her memories have become alien, yet they are still her memories. Perhaps they are beginning to be memories of the future. Much of Meridel's previous work carries this powerful mix of bridge and memory, a reconnection to history that is also prophesy: the essence of epic literature. The fact that these last lines were written on her deathbed invests them with a singular gravity.

So the traditional person is already dead. But in the very next line, she writes, "you are taking / on a new personality . . . / a stranger . . . alienated . . . unfamiliar." Alienated because strange, as yet unknown. Unfamiliar but recognized, seen. In these moments preceding her death, Meridel lets go of her familiar self and greets someone new, who is also and at the same time the person she has known all her life. She retains that deep consciousness she has honed throughout her ninety-six years, but recognizes that it is assuming a different form.

This recognition seems innate, almost automatic. The indented last lines of this first fragment bring form and content together in a way that is new to literature: "I write differently . . . / Then I seem to be gone." She is conscious that she inhabits a qualitatively different experience and, at the same time, understands these will be her last words. Every scholarly treatise ever written about form and content pale before the evidence of these two lines.

Later in these pages, Meridel writes of wind blowing into her valves, caves, habitat.[2] Valves as in mechanisms that carry out continuous function. Caves as in primordial refuge. Habitat as in an entire milieu, social as well as intimate. As she has so often in her work, she gives place to body, acknowledging it as home to a unique combination of knowledge and experience, thought and feeling. Strong metaphors for the mind/body construct.

She writes of wind and of a tide sweeping the identity of a powerful woman, using natural forces as metaphors. Intense self-knowledge, and one that evolves, is constantly moving. A movement of forces greater than herself, circulating, flowing. There are references to removing the persona as if it were a dress, to making "a study of bones." She speaks of shedding and molting. And of a "return to depth," completing the life cycle: spiral and ever more profound.

Throughout, there is the power of memory looming large, carefully tended as it is confronted by all the complex ways in which those who would manipulate and control us try to erase our knowledge of the past, personal as well as collective and historic. Meridel suffered the multipronged attempts of erasure aimed at her poverty, her femaleness in an era when men ruled almost without challenge, her single-motherhood, her defense of all who are disadvantaged or trivialized; and she repeatedly raised her voice to speak against such travesty. She spoke in defense of workers, farmers, women, and also the land: "the great cotton woods . . . trees of opulence." Her poems and stories often include vivid snapshots of this country's heartland.

The many-faceted drumbeat of memory filters through the highly sharpened yet wide-ranging consciousness of this great poet dying. There is memory of times and places essential to her history and to her personal story within that history. It is all here in cryptic but evocative shorthand: observed, relived, retold, and gratefully acknowledged. "What is real," she reiterates just before her hand falls from the paper.

We write for many reasons, often more than one at a time. We write because we must, because expression through language is necessary to our survival. We write to communicate, publish, teach, polemicize, and leave something behind. I am sure that most of these reasons for writing were no longer relevant during Meridel's last transcription. There is no evidence of them on the pages found scattered over her body and in her bed. She would not have been thinking of publication, not then. Teaching or leaving something behind may have still been on her mind, although it is not likely that either was a conscious priority during those final moments. Rather, the style and content of these pages seems a natural extension of what she had written up to that point, only sharpened by the urgency bestowed by a closing in of time.

Reading Meridel's last written words makes me wonder how she looked lying beside them in death. Did she still grasp pencil or pen? Was her hand still touching that precious piece of paper? Was her mouth open or closed? What about her eyes? Were people with her, or was she, finally, alone? I'd heard that Meridel organized the nursing home staff during her years there, teaching and encouraging people to defend their interests well into her final years.

The physical image of Meridel I most clearly retain is the one of her visit to Salt of the Earth Books in the mid to late 1980s. Her white hair is parted in the

33. Meridel LeSueur

middle above large horn-rimmed glasses. Her lips are slightly separated in speech. She is looking neither directly at the camera lens nor intentionally away from it, but she seems to be gazing inward and outward simultaneously. She is wearing a couple of strings of beads, from one of which the small figure of an animal hangs, emblematic of her lifelong connection with fetishes and native arts. One hand is outstretched, the other rests on a book.

This was not the last time I saw Meridel. I think that may have been at Minneapolis's exuberant May Day parade the year I taught at Macalester. She was in a wheelchair by then, being pushed by someone at the head of the parade. As they passed, a great roar of appreciation rose from both sidewalks. Minneapolis loved Meridel, and its love was more than evident that day. Or I might have seen Meridel for the last time when I visited her at her home just over the Wisconsin state line. But I have no clear recollection of what she was wearing on either of those occasions. Nor even what we talked about.

Among her last lines, there is a phrase that makes a particular impact on me: "Star built memory." This may be because I recently saw a Chilean film set on the Atacama Desert, where the memory of disappeared revolutionaries and the memory of stars are intertwined, present in a series of enormous telescopes and in the almost futile wanderings of mothers still walking the desert searching for their murdered children's bones. The film makes a connection between the calcium that is a major element in stars and in bone.[3]

This sense of history's vast expanse is present throughout Meridel's large body of work. Living so long and witnessing so many social changes enhanced that perspective. At one of the many moments of collective despair throughout the late 1980s and early 1990s, I remember once confiding to her that I felt depressed by the state of the world and our inability to turn things around. She said her experience had taught her that struggle was like a pendulum, swinging in long arcs from hope to desperation and back again, and that I shouldn't let the low points on that arc get me down. Her last written words seem to corroborate her sense of the rhythmic repetitions that characterize human struggle throughout time.

Rarely is a poet, an expert weaver of words, able to bequeath such a multilayered gift: the intensity of her last feelings and thoughts written in her own hand as she surrenders to whatever is next—or to the void. It is not a passive surrender or one in which she entrusts herself to a "higher power." She is fully conscious that *she* is the power: what she has seen and heard and what she has done with the time that was hers to live. Even when set among the questions natural to such a momentous transition, this consciousness of her power is palpable.

Everything Meridel LeSueur learned and nurtured throughout her long life came into play in those final hours or moments. The discipline that enabled her to write every day (she had paper and a writing instrument at the ready, even on her deathbed, and didn't hesitate to use them both). The reverence for ordinary people that kept her style accessible while never trite or mundane. A language that was uniquely hers. The music, so long and finely tuned, that made it possible—even at a time when everything was happening at once—for her to choose just the right words for this final message. And the courage to keep speaking to the end.

Not for Myself

It's Wednesday, so I'm in Flagstaff: the catchall joke when you're on a book tour or otherwise moving from one city to another too fast to easily keep track of where you are. From the inside, university auditoriums or local bookstore venues begin to look disarmingly alike. Actually, if you can keep grounded, you know each place has its personality, and Flagstaff is appealing. The feel of the town, the people here, the enthusiasm, recollections of friends in common, and shared dreams all shape the experience.

My host had asked for a reading of border poems. Appealing to the most comprehensive definition of *border*, I found I had quite a few: the cruelly contested border between Mexico and the United States, directly south of where we are; the border between Israel and the occupied territories, where Palestinians struggle to survive in conditions of containment and ongoing repression; the Berlin Wall, redeemed years now but displaying historic scars; the ever-receding borders of migration; the still crumbling borders of queer identity; the obstinate border between those who have and those who always end up being had; border holograms dividing humans from animals, weaponry from flesh, rational thought from the most egregious traps of contrived belief.

As I read, borders of all sizes, shapes, and imports swirl about me. I look at each face in the audience: young students, professors decades younger than I, a few community people. After the last poem, I invite questions, comments. A deep silence settles throughout the room. People seem immersed in thought, feeling. Then, tentatively, a young woman toward the front raises her hand. She says her parents favor Arizona's draconian immigration law and that she had never questioned its rationale—until hearing my poems. *They've changed me*, she says. I feel a burning behind my eyes and fight to hold back my tears.

From the rear of the room, a man speaks about my early work, says mine has been a household name in his family for three generations and that he has read some of my work to his own children. I am both grateful for and slightly embarrassed by his admission. Later, signing books for him and his parents, I ask him how old he is. He tells me fifty-one. My son's age, I realize.

A woman remembers seeing me on a city bus in Managua, Nicaragua, in 1983. A *city* bus? I ask, trying to imagine why someone would remember another person sharing space on a city bus almost thirty years before. She had read a book of mine, she says, and recognized my face. *Someone offered you a seat, but you refused*, she adds hopefully, trying to shatter the armature of time and evoke a connection I might recall. *Do you remember that? No,* I have to admit, *I don't.*

The day advances: so much time for public events, so much for food, so much down time (not very much), so much for meeting new people I try hard to store in my mental database by linking them to blazing colors, my synesthetic advantage.

Right now my host, others from among his Northern Arizona University colleagues, my partner, and I are gathered round a welcoming table at a restaurant that turns out to serve delicious food. I'm not always so lucky. There is a bit of time before my evening reading. Conversation is fluid and warm. Someone is talking about why one writes. *Well, first of all, for oneself*, she says. As if this is an unquestioned assumption. And we move on to other topics.

I try to be fully engaged in conversations, even when mentally preparing to speak. I've never been one to simply nod and smile. My opinions, asked for or not, are generally close to the surface, eager to be articulated. This time, though, I retreat into the easier option of nodding and smiling. But inside my head the idea begins its complex meandering, dodging the neurons firing in my brain, hiding behind synapses only to reemerge at odd moments over the next few days, demanding exploration, agreement, or rejection.

No, I realize, I do not write primarily for myself, although for many years I, too, accepted the platitude. I write for others. If I wrote for myself, I wouldn't really need to *write*, itself an act of communication. It would be much easier and less exacting simply to think the thoughts, feel the feelings, explore the emotions and connections, without concern for that perfect turn of phrase, attention-getting opener, surprise leap or sudden change of direction, clear follow-through, smooth or arresting presentation, and above all closure—closure that hopes to leave readers satisfied while urging them to pick up where I left off and move wherever their own imaginations may take them.

I write for others. I write to plumb the state of the world as I perceive it, to polemicize, and to provoke a response from my readers. I want dialogue. When other writers build on what I put out there, it makes me happy. When they disagree, it is exciting as well; for I have as much to learn as to offer.

I write to bring some small measure of beauty to our lives, create a balance of sorts in the midst of so much paternalism, violence, stereotype, cliché, and disrespect for language. I write to push the malleable edges of expression. And I write to make new or previously ignored connections at a time when keeping us separate from one another is one of the many subtle ways the system makes sure we continue to fight against our own best interests.

This urge to make connections is one of my greatest goals. For many years, I thought of myself as a bridge: between places off-limits to my countrymen and countrywomen and their impoverished or fabricated sources, between memory and current reality, the realms of the spirit and everyday routine, socialism and feminism, mind and body, age and youth, one in-vogue philosophy and another that may have fallen from popular favor.

Memory is a precious commodity, sold to the highest bidder in our crude marketplace of distortions, the criminal theft that passes for polite society. My writing is engaged with searching out and digging up memory, retrieving and reassembling its broken pieces, resituating it at the center of our lives. Fighting for memory has become a lifelong struggle for me; and writing, the tool with which I try to reestablish memory's place and balance, encourage others to give it its due.

I have long thought of myself as a bridge, but no longer one that presumes that I am the only way from here to there or that my particular journey is useful to everyone. To say that I want to make connections—in all sorts of directions—acknowledges my position as one among millions doing this work of weaving the whole cloth in so many different tongues and at a time when fragmentation is one of the most dangerous and effective weapons we confront.

So no, I don't write for myself, although I get great satisfaction from the act. I write for others. And it is hard work—a job without security, cost of living raises, even much in the way of honor. There is that painful filling up and then enduring enormous pressure as the body turns itself inside out: raw flesh, muscle, and bone all shivering in icy cold as they are exposed to the vitiated air of twisted values and polluted oxygen. Writing can hurt, and I am no masochist.

I wonder why it has become such an accepted assumption that writers do creative work primarily for themselves. Perhaps it is a way of acknowledging that if you are a writer you *have* to write; if a painter, to paint; if a musician or any other sort of creative being, the art form is necessary to your life. The assertion that *writing is like breathing or eating* is meant to convey the deep need an artist has to practice his or her craft. This is certainly true; so in this sense, I might agree that I write for myself—although I am not my target audience.

Maybe claiming that you are making your art primarily for yourself is also a way of saying *I don't care if the work gets published (or heard or shown), because I make it, because it is a necessity, a part of who I am.* Perhaps that claim is a way of protecting oneself against loneliness and failure.

Maybe, too, in today's commodity-oriented world, there is a fear of appearing too involved with the marketing end of artistic production. Artists are supposed to have a sort of "purity" that situates us above the commercial fray. Most are untrained in the marketing side of artistic promotion, embarrassed or uncomfortable asking to be paid for what we make, since our society places such a low value on art and we ourselves have been educated to devalue it.

We are shamed into claiming we make art for ourselves and thus avoid admitting the difficulty many of us have promoting our own work and/or the embarrassment we feel if we cannot do that successfully. If we say we're just doing it for ourselves, or primarily doing it for ourselves, we avoid uncomfortable questions and expectations. We avoid thinking of ourselves as losers.

I am as privy to all these awkward emotions as the next artist or writer, perhaps more so because I am a woman old enough to have grown up with my generation's load of social shame. Our gendered values continue to make it easier for male artists to demand the space, time, and support they need to prioritize their work. Women who write or paint or make music or practice some other creative genre are still often forced to choose between art and family, rage and acceptability, sickness and health.

Like so many other women compelled to creativity, I struggled for years trying to juggle my artistic expression with the roles of wife and mother, almost always feeling I was shortchanging both. Experiencing shame. Making excuses. Sneaking late-night hours for my most important work. Hiding. Lying. And then finally—aided by the second wave of feminism and by my own deep need—building block by battered block the room of my own I so desperately sought.

I can only speak for myself.

I write to communicate with a sea of people out there, of all cultures, races, ages, genders, and belief systems. Increasingly, I try not to make assumptions in my work, to use language in ways that assume my readers have the same point of departure or references I do. When I reread my earlier output, I find this to be one aspect that annoys me. The use of rhetorical expressions is another. Today I try hard to avoid those words and phrases that are so overused they have become meaningless. At the same time, I want to restore language twisted by our sociopolitical system to its original power.

I write because I must. For me, too, it is like breathing or eating. But it is also, and powerfully, communication.

So no, not for myself. For you.

Notes

Shaping My Words

1. Fidel Castro and others believed that by attacking Moncada Military Barracks in Santiago de Cuba, they would give rise to a movement that could wage a successful guerrilla war against dictator Fulgencio Batista. They chose July 26 because it was during the city's yearly carnival with its attendant partying and confusion. The action ended in military defeat but led to others and eventually to the victory of the Cuban Revolution on January 1, 1959.

2. See Margaret Randall, *Cuban Women Now* (Toronto: Women's Press, 1974). *La mujer cubana ahora* (Havana: Editorial Ciencias Sociales, Instituto Cubano del Libro, 1972) was the Cuban edition. Other editions were published in Brazil, Holland, Venezuela, and the Dominican Republic.

3. Norway suffered a tragic terrorist attack on July 22, 2011, and made the immediate decision not to react by limiting personal freedom or in any other way changing the nature of a society that has always prided itself on its openness.

Roque Dalton

1. Roger Atwood, "Gringo Iracundo: Roque Dalton and His Father," *Latin American Research Review* 46, no. 1 (2011): 126–49.

2. *El Corno Emplumado / The Plumed Horn*, 1962–69, was a bilingual literary journal cofounded and coedited out of Mexico City by the author and Sergio Mondragón.

3. See the inside cover of Roque Dalton, *Taberna y otros lugares* (Havana: Premio Casa de las Américas, 1969). Translation mine.

4. Dalton, *Taberna y otros lugares*, 7. Translation mine.

5. Roque Dalton, *El intellectual y la sociedad* (Mexico City: Siglo XXI Editores, 1969).

6. Roque Dalton, *Pobrecito poeta que era yo* (San José, Costa Rica: EDUCA, 1982).

7. Roque Dalton, *No pronuncies mi nombre: Poesía completa*, ed. Luis Alvarenga, 3 vols. (San Salvador, El Salvador: Consejo nacional para la cultura y el arte [CONCULTURA], 2005–9).

8. Zepeda's reference to this quotation is from the prologue to a Mexican edition of Roque Dalton, *Taberna y otros lugares* (Mexico City: La Letra Editores, 1988), 11. Translation mine.

9. The ERP, with four other guerrilla organizations, joined forces in 1980 as the Farabundo Martí Liberation Front (FMLN). This represented a victory for Dalton's political positions. The FMLN battled U.S.-backed forces in a brutal twelve-year civil war in which approximately seventy-five thousand people were killed. After the war ended in 1992, the FMLN became a political party. A 1993 amnesty law that protects those accused of war crimes would not apply to Dalton because his case originated before the official start of that war.

10. Juan José Dalton, "Si Carter usa blúmer," *Contrapunto*, March 31, 2011, online at Juan José Dalton's blog, sent to the author via e-mail from Jorge Dalton. Translation mine.

11. Dalton, "Si Carter usa blúmer." Translation mine.

12. This is true, to the best of my knowledge, of "Nevertheless, My Love," "The Crazy Ones," and "The Cynic."

13. Roger Atwood, e-mail message to the author, 2011.

Closing the Gap

1. William Carlos Williams (Rutherford, New Jersey, 1883–1963). He was a family doctor as well as one of the United States' most important poets. He broke away from the European poetry aesthetic, proclaiming "no ideas but in things" (the point of departure for the second piece in this book).

2. Cesar Vallejo (Peru 1892–Paris 1938) published only three books of poetry during his lifetime but is one of the great poetic innovators of the twentieth century. His work radically changed Spanish-language poetry.

3. Nancy Morejón (Cuba 1944) is one of the most important living Cuban poets.

4. Violeta Parra (Chile 1917–67) was a great folklorist, singer-songwriter, and visual artist, considered by many the mother of Latin American folk music. She had a popular *peña* in Santiago de Chile but took her own life shortly before the Popular Unity took power in her country.

5. Miguel Hernandez (Spain 1910–42) was an important poet of the Spanish generation of 1927. He died in prison during the Spanish Civil War. One of his prison poems is called "The Onion."

New Map of Wonder to Explore

1. Synesthesia is a neurological condition that affects the boundaries between the senses. A person with the condition may hear objects, smell ideas, or experience some other neurological breakdown. In my case, I see and hear words and sounds as colors.

Horizon

1. Ollantaytambo is a town and an Inca archaeological site some thirty-five miles north-west of Cuzco. During the Inca empire, what is now the ruin was the royal estate of Emperor Pachacuti. At the time of the Spanish conquest, it served as a stronghold for Manco Inca Yupanqui, one of the leaders of the Inca resistance.

Sex

1. Monica Lewinsky (born 1973) is an American woman with whom the then U.S. president Bill Clinton admitted to having had an "improper relationship" while she worked at the White House in 1995 and 1996. The affair and its repercussions, especially the attempted impeachment of Clinton, became known as the Lewinsky scandal. It showcased powerful men's belief that they can get away with anything and was also used by Clinton's conservative enemies to try to destroy his presidency.

2. Although practiced throughout history, in recent decades torture has been publically defended by several governments that would previously have denied its existence or considered it off-limits. Even some prestigious academics have declared it necessary in the "war against terror." Violence has also become more widespread, and many consider it natural. This legitimization of torture and other types of violence, by governments claiming to be democratic and humane, is a dangerous and troubling phenomenon. I believe it should make us revisit and rethink all practices in which power is misused.

3. Leonardo di Vinci, Walt Whitman, Marcel Proust, Arthur Rimbaud, Gertrude Stein, Federico García Lorca, Emily Dickinson, Virginia Woolf, Willa Cather, Peter Ilyich Tchaikovsky, and HD, among many others.

4. The second wave of feminism exploded in the United States and western Europe at the end of the 1960s. In 1969 the impact of the movement could be felt in Mexico, where we began receiving publications and news of actions and initiatives. The impact on me was such that I collected some of the more interesting pieces, from several different points of view, wrote an introduction to situate the movement for Latin American readers, and offered the anthology for publication. The book was simply titled *Las mujeres* (The Women), insuring it would be able to pass the censors of those years and be sold in most Latin American countries (Mexico, Siglo XXI, Editores SA, 1970). For many women, *Las mujeres* was their introduction to feminism. The book has gone into numerous editions and is still in print.

5. More about my immigration case in the essay "Passports and Me."

Wheels

1. Sergio Mondragón and I founded and edited *El corno emplumado / The Plumed Horn*, a bilingual quarterly that ran for thirty-one issues between January 1962 and midsummer 1969.

2. Efraín Huerta (1914–82) was an important Mexican poet, good friend, and also someone with useful connections in a variety of circles.

3. Monika Ertl (1937–73) was the daughter of the German cameraman Hans Ertl. She joined the armed political underground movement in Bolivia and was a central figure in several of its best-known operations.

4. Emma Goldman (1869–1940) was an anarchist known for her political activism, writing, and speeches. She is famously rumored to have said, "If I can't dance, I don't want your revolution."

5. Bantu Stephen Bikko (1946–77) was a law student who became one of South Africa's most influential and radical leaders of the Black Consciousness Movement (BCM) in the 1970s. That movement, along with others, lead to the end of apartheid.

Our Table

1. Copán is a Mayan archaeological site, located in western Honduras not far from the border with Guatemala. It was the capital city of a major Classic Period kingdom from the fifth to ninth centuries AD.

2. Mary Elizabeth Jane Colter (1869–1958) was an American architect and interior designer who worked for the Fred Harvey Company, which built railroad hotels and a number of important buildings at Grand Canyon, Arizona.

3. Georgia O'Keefe (1887–1986) was a great American artist who lived much of her adult life in Abiquiu, New Mexico, in the midst of a landscape that figured prominently in her paintings.

4. Margaret Randall, *Hunger's Table: Women, Food, and Politics* (Watsonville CA: Papier-Mache Press, 1997).

Do You Really Believe All That?

1. My maternal grandfather, DeWitt A. Davidson, was an imposing and self-indulgent man. Because he was a minister, in our family he was sometimes called "the saint." I never felt comfortable with him and, as an adult long after his death, retrieved memories of his having sexually abused me when I was very young. So what I write about him necessarily carries highly charged emotions. See my book *This Is about Incest* (Ithaca NY: Firebrand Books, 1987).

2. Ammon Hennacy (1893–1970) was an Irish American militant pacifist, Christian anarchist, vegetarian, and social activist who was a central figure in New York's Catholic Worker movement in the 1950s and '60s. He frequently spent time in prison for his ideas. Later he went out to Salt Lake City, where he founded a Catholic Worker house. He remained there until his death.

3. The Second Vatican Council, convened by Pope John XXIII in 1962, prescribed a gospel-oriented content for Christianity and a more socially conscious doctrine than that of previous papal encyclicals. A general ecumenical opening allowed for dialogue with other denominations and with non-Christians. Lay people were given more responsibility in the church's pastoral work. Liturgical reforms included the introduction of language, songs, and instruments native to different cultures and an end to masses in which priests kept their backs to the people. This new way of looking at faith and these new practices became known as liberation theology. In 1968 Vatican II found its Latin American application in the meeting of bishops in Medellin, Colombia. There the documents of the council were interpreted in light of the continent's impoverished and war-torn reality. The bishops declared that the people were oppressed by the "institutional violence" of internal and external colonial structures, which "seeking unbounded profits, ferment an economic dictatorship and the international imperialism of money." These shifts in church philosophy had an enormous impact on the era's movements for social change.

4. The English edition of this book is Margaret Randall, *Christians in the Nicaraguan Revolution* (Vancouver BC: New Star Books, 1983).

5. California's Proposition 8, in 2008, which would have granted civil marriage rights to same-sex couples, was defeated with the help of millions of dollars put up by the Mormon Church.

6. In early 2012, Church of Beethoven was forced to change its name due to a legal dispute with a member of its late founder's family. It is now called Sunday Chatter.

The Courage It Takes

1. My immigration case is documented in my essay *Coming Home: Peace without Complacency*, first published as a small book by West End Press in 1990, which was reprinted in augmented form in my collection *Walking to the Edge: Essays of Resistance* (Boston: South End Press, 1991). It is also referred to in more detail in this book in the essay called "Passports and Me."

2. More information about die-offs can be found, among other sources, in Peter Fimrite, "Earth on Track for Epic Die-Off, Scientists Say," *San Francisco Chronicle*, December 19, 2009.

3. See Gay Block and Malka Drucker, *Rescuers: Portraits of Moral Courage in the Holcaust* by (New York: Holmes and Meier, 1992).

4. For a detailed account of Oñate's assault on the Indians of the U.S. American Southwest and of the debate surrounding the erection of several statues in his honor, see Margaret Randall, "Oñate's Right Foot," in *First Laugh* (Lincoln: University of Nebraska Press, 2011), 109–21.

5. Edmund DeMarche and Associated Press, "Tucson School Board Votes to Do away with Mexican American Studies Program," FoxNews.com, January 12, 2012, http://www.foxnews.com/us/2012/01/12/tucson-school-board-votes-to-do-away-with-mexican-american-studies-program/#ixzz1jjUpkror.

6. For a detailed account of the Arizona situation, see Brenda Norrell, "Tucson Schools Bans Books by Chicano and Native American Authors: Native Authors Include Leslie Marmon Silko, Buffy Sainte Marie and Winona LaDuke," *Narcosphere*, January 14, 2012, http://narcosphere.narconews.com/notebook/brenda-norrell/2012/01/tucson-schools-bans-books-chicano-and-native-american-authors.

Mirror, Mirror on the Wall

1. Many versions of this tale exist, in slightly differing variations from Albania and other countries as well as the German original. The definitive English translation was made from Jacob and Wilhelm Grimm, "Sneewittchen," in *Kinder-und Hausmärchen* (Berlin, 1857).

Lord Power

From the French *droit de seigneur* or Spanish *derecho de pernada*, used in both cases to describe a man's sense of entitlement to initiate his sex life by forcing himself on a woman or girl of lower social status. Among the wealthy in Latin America, *derecho de pernada* refers to an upper-class young man's presumed right to have his first sexual experience with a prostitute or the family maid. Families often fear contagion with the former and so prefer the latter. *Seigneur* and *pernada* mean "lord" or "master." For the purpose of this essay, I have rendered the English as "lord power."

There's Plenty of Time for That Later

1. "Leading Egyptian Feminist, Nawal El Saadawi: 'Women and Girls Are beside Boys in the Streets," interview by Amy Goodman, *Democracy Now!*, January 31, 2011, http://www.democracynow.org/2011/1/31/women_protest_alongside_men_in_egyptian.

2. Nawal El Saadawi, *Woman at Point Zero* (London: Zed Books, 2002).

3. On February 11, 2011, CNN's Lara Logan was covering Mubarak's resignation, when she

was separated from her security detail and brutally gang-raped. The attack required hospitalization.

4. Glen Johnson, "Tahrir Square, 8th March: Not a Good Day for Women," *Le Monde diplomatique*, March 2011, English edition, blog posts, http://mondediplo.com/blogs/tahrir-square-8th-march-not-a-good-day-for-women.

5. Margaret Randall, *Sandino's Daughters: Testimonies of Nicaraguan Women in Struggle* (Vancouver BC: New Star Books, 1981).

6. Margaret Randall, *Sandino's Daughters Revisited: Feminism in Nicaragua* (New Brunswick NJ: Rutgers University Press, 1994).

7. Margaret Randall, *Gathering Rage: The Failure of 20th Century Revolutions to Develop a Feminist Agenda* (New York: Monthly Review Books, 1992).

8. Judith McDaniel, *Sanctuary: A Journey* (Ithaca NY: Firebrand Books, 1987).

9. Randall, *This Is about Incest* (Ithaca NY: Firebrand Books, 1987).

What Are They Afraid Of?

1. I'm speaking here about white citizens. People of color, and particularly interracial couples, had to fight for years for this right.

2. In 2009 David Boies and Theodore Olson—erstwhile antagonists from the *Bush v. Gore* litigation—filed a same-sex marriage lawsuit in a California federal district court. Their aim is to take their case to the Supreme Court, and they hope to overturn the federal Defense of Marriage Act (DOMA). The gay rights community has been divided on the strategy.

3. Nathanial Brooks, "Behind N.Y. Gay Marriage, an Unlikely Mix of Forces," *New York Times*, June 25, 2011.

Keeping Us Safe

1. Judith McDaniel, "Making It Safe for Charles," in *Sanctuary* (Ithaca NY: Firebrand Books, 1987), 59–61.

Passports and Me

1. David Edwards, "State Department Wants Passport Applicants to Reveal Lifetime Employment History," *Raw Story*, Monday, April 25, 2011, http://www.rawstory.com/rs/2011/04/25/state-department-wants-passport-applicants-to-reveal-lifetime-employment-history/.

2. Draft comments prepared by the Consumer Travel Alliance.

3. The official Mexican government figure for the number of dead was twenty-six, sometime later adjusted to around three hundred. It is generally acknowledge, though, that

more than one thousand mostly young people lost their lives at Tlatelolco, the plaza where the massacre took place.

4. For eight years, from 1962 through 1969, Sergio and I and later Robert and I edited a bilingual literary journal called *El Corno Emplumado / The Plumed Horn*. On two occasions, we published small anthologies of new Cuban poetry, at the time unknown in the United States. This contact with Cuban poets led to my visiting Cuba twice: in January of 1967 and again in January of 1968. Thus the relationship that facilitated sending our children to that country and following when we were able.

5. See "The Courage It Takes," in this book. I have also written most extensively about my immigration case in Randall, *Coming Home*.

6. Margaret J. Randall et al. v. Edwin Meese III et al., 854 F.2d 472 272 U.S. App. D.C. 63, No. 87–5230 (District of Columbia Cir. Feb. 4, 1988, decided Aug. 16, 1988). This document states that "Randall seeks an adjustment of her immigration status to that of a permanent resident so that she may again become a United States citizen. She has so far been denied that relief by the Immigration and Naturalization Service . . . We hold that her resort to court is premature, and we therefore affirm the district court's judgment dismissing renewal of Randall's claims, in a proper circuit, including her contention that her status should be adjusted as of October 2, 1985, the date the district director denied her application." As I have noted, my status was finally adjusted by the Court of Immigration Appeals in August 1989.

Forgiver's Dilemma

1. Paul M. Hughes, "Forgiveness," *The Stanford Encyclopedia of Philosophy*, ed. Edward N. Zalta, Winter 2011 ed. (Stanford: Center for the Study of Language Information, Stanford University), http://plato.stanford.edu/archives/win2011/entries/forgiveness/.

2. All biblical quotations reference the Jerusalem Bible Reader's Edition.

3. Marina Cantacuzino, "Forgiveness: A Way out of the Darkness," The Forgiveness Project, http://theforgivenessproject.com/about-us/founder/.

4. See Marina Cantacuzino, "The Dangers of Forgiving Too Easily," *Huffington Post*, April 17, 2011, http://www.huffingtonpost.com/marina-cantacuzino/forgiveness-project_b_850156.html.

Going Places

1. The Terracotta Army was discovered in 1974 in the eastern suburbs of Xi'am in China's Shaanxi Province, when a group of farmers were digging for water. The 8,000 larger-than-life-sized soldiers, 130 chariots with 520 horses and 150 additional cavalry horses,

many of which are still hidden in two large pits, are funerary art buried with the first emperor of Qin in 210–209 BC. Every figure has unique facial features, leading some to believe they were modeled on individuals.

2. Kiet Seel is one of three ruins at Navajo National Monument, a U.S. national monument managed jointly by the Park Service and the Navajo Nation. The other two are Betatakin (daily ranger-led hikes take visitors close to the ruin) and Inscription House, which has been closed for years. Between May and September, twenty people a day are allowed to make the hike to Kiet Seel. Attendance at an orientation session the day before is required. Once there, a ranger accompanies you inside the ruin, which preserves a number of items of everyday use, such as ceramic vessels and tools.

3. My first husband was Sam Jacobs, a young boy from a wealthy Cincinnati family. We ran off to Ciudad Juárez, Mexico, although we didn't really elope, because we told my parents where we were going and why. We were married almost four years, and it was an unhappy marriage. Many years later Sam died in his forties of a heart attack.

4. The details of my deportation order and immigration case are explored in a previous essay, "Passports and Me."

Cuban Postcards

1. Haydée Santamaría is more fully described in this book's initial essay, "Shaping My Words."

2. What Cubans call the U.S.-orchestrated invasion at the Bay of Pigs, when counterrevolutionary forces tried to defeat the new government in April 1961.

Tunisian Postcards

1. Lana Asfour, "A Revolution of Equals," in "The F Word," *Granta*, 115 (June 2011), http://www.granta.com/New-Writing/A-Revolution-of-Equals.

Goose Quill to Thought-Capture

1. Ginsberg dedicated "Howl" to his friend Carl Solomon, a brilliant contemporary who was institutionalized at Rockland Psychiatric Center in Orangeburg, Rockland County, New York.

2. Judith Lewis Herman, *Trauma and Recovery* (New York: Basic Books, 1992), 2–3.

Coyote Grin

1. "Secrets of a Mind-Gamer," *New York Times Magazine*, February 20, 2011.

"Star Built Memory"

1. *Meridel LeSueur* (1900–1996) was a great midwestern poet and writer. This is a fragment of the writing found in her bed when she died, later deciphered and transcribed by her daughter Rachel. These lines were written November 13–14, 1996. Meridel's estate titled this poem "This with My Last Breath" and brought it out with *Rites of Ancient Ripening*, reissued as *This with My Last Breath*, a private edition by the Meridel LeSueur Family Circle (Minneapolis, 2012). This and other excerpts in this piece are used with permission from the Estate of Meridel LeSueur. All rights reserved.

2. All fragments quoted in this essay are from the poem Meridel's family has titled "This with My Last Breath," found with her body when she died sometime during the night of November 13–14, 1996. Out of respect for the fact that this poem is included in its entirety in the book the family published in 2012 (*This with My Last Breath*), I have not reproduced it in full in my essay.

3. *Nostalgia por la luz* ("Nostalgia for the Light"), by Patricio Guzmán, Atacama Films, 2010.

Previous collections of essays by Margaret Randall

Walking to the Edge: Essays of Resistance (1988)

Gathering Rage: The Failure of Twentieth-Century Revolutions to Develop a Feminist Agenda (1992)

When I Look into the Mirror and See You: Women, Terror, and Resistance (2003)

Narrative of Power: Essays for an Endangered Century (2004)

To Change the World: My Years in Cuba (2009)

First Laugh: Essays, 2000–2009 (2011)